Doing Philosophy
at the Movies

Doing Philosophy
at the Movies

Richard A. Gilmore

STATE UNIVERSITY OF NEW YORK PRESS

Published by
State University of New York Press, Albany

© 2005 State University of New York

Printed in the United States of America

For information, address State University of New York Press,
90 State Street, Suite 700, Albany, NY 12207

Production by Marilyn P. Semerad
Marketing by Susan M. Petrie

Library of Congress Cataloging in Publication Data

Gilmore, Richard A.
  Doing philosophy at the movies / Richard A. Gilmore
      p. cm.
  Includes bibliographical references and index.
  ISBN 0–7914–6391–5 (hardcover : alk. paper)—ISBN 0–7914–6392–3
    (pbk : alk. paper)
  1. Motion pictures—Philosophy. I. Title.
PN1995.G495 2005
791.43'01—dc22

                                                                2004008050

                    1 2 3 4 5 6 7 8 9 10

Contents

Preface

Less than two months before he died of cancer, Wittgenstein wrote the following, which was included in the collection of his writings entitled *On Certainty*: "I am sitting with a philosopher in the garden; he says again and again 'I know that that's a tree', pointing to a tree that is near us. Someone else arrives and hears this, and I tell him: 'This fellow isn't insane. We are only doing philosophy.'"[1] I read this as a sort of philosophical joke. It is a joke that says a lot about what Wittgenstein wants to criticize with respect to philosophy, but also about what he wants to celebrate and pursue in philosophy. He wants to criticize a kind of empty arguing about concepts that are being considered outside their ordinary contexts in our everyday language practices. He wants to celebrate and pursue philosophy's ability to determine when concepts are being misused in this way, as well as its ability to help us get some perspective on our ordinary ways of using language so that we can avoid slipping into bad, philosophical-type practices there as well.

For my purposes, I would like to focus on his expression "We are only doing philosophy." I like this formulation because it signals how philosophy is an activity like any other, like doing work or doing sports or doing one's taxes. It has rules, primary concerns, secondary concerns, goals, successes and failures, and, most important of all, when it is done properly, it should be useful, it should serve some purpose, it should *do* something. Right up to the time of his death Wittgenstein continued to do philosophy. His close friend Normal Malcolm reports that on his deathbed, Wittgenstein said, "Tell them I've had a wonderful life!"[2] His life was, in fact, filled with many hardships, but the central activity of his life was doing philosophy, and, in the end, that seems to have been more than enough for him.

When Wittgenstein speaks in this passage of "doing philosophy," as though philosophy were a particular kind of activity you can choose to do or choose not to do, he implies that, like other activities you might choose to do, as you do more of it you will get better at it. Like any such activity, it may be difficult at first, but it gets easier as you practice doing it. I do

not know whether it is important that everyone should do philosophy—
my sense is that it is—but it can certainly be a source of pleasure and
empowerment for those who do learn to do it.

In the chapters that follow I will be considering some very popular
movies from a philosophical perspective. Perhaps *the* philosophical intuition is that there is more going on than mere appearances suggest. It is
the sense that a more complicated dynamic may be at work in a situation
than at first appears. You may have the sense that there is more going on,
but not be at all clear what that more is; philosophy is all about tracking
down what that more might be. There is a point in watching movies at
which this idea inevitably begins to dawn on you. You begin to register
signs, clues, that there may be a larger narrative at work simultaneous to
the explicit narrative of the primary plot of the movie. This might be
called the meta-narrative of a movie. I will be considering meta-narratives
in movies that derive from philosophical ideas from the great philosophers
in the Western tradition.

I will be doing "readings" of the films that I consider. I will be looking
at these movies not just as entertainment, but as texts, just as Descartes'
Meditations or the Bible are texts. The assumptions here are, first, that
there is something important in these texts, something worth learning
about, and, second, that what it is that is important may not be immediately obvious, may need to be searched for in the text. This search for
meaning is generally referred to as an interpretation, and that is what I
will be doing with the movies I will be discussing. I will be interpreting
them to try to understand some of the lessons that they may have to teach.

As with these movies, I see life, and the world in general, as like texts.
There is a literal level to what happens, the simple facts of the case, but
then there is also a higher, more abstract level, the level of relationships
between things, the trajectory of a situation, a narrative of what is really
going on. At the literal level you may see two people talking, but there are
also all sorts of clues that you interpret and you see that these two people
are not just talking, they are also in love. The love part is literally invisible, but can be plain as day if you know how to read the signs, if you
know how to interpret the situation. And, of course, to be able to see
when two people are in love you have to know a lot about people, about
how people act when they are doing business and how they act when they
are just being sociable, and how they act when they are in love. That is a
lot to learn. A lot of what growing up is about is learning to interpret the
world at this level. Knowledge of this level is very empowering. And, of
course, there is always more to learn because the relations between things,
between people, or in any situation, are infinite. There is always a larger
story that can be told. There is always more to understand. So that is
what I will be looking for in these movies; not symbols so much as clues

to the relationships between things, to the relationships between people and things, to the relationships between people and people, and to the potential trajectories of a given situation.

By referring to "the potential trajectories of a given situation" I just mean recognizing the signs in a situation that suggest where the situation might be going. This idea is sort of like Aristotle's notion of an entelechy (literally, the end contained in something). For Aristotle this is the energy in a thing to become what it is supposed to be, the thing in an acorn that drives it to become a mighty oak. There is something similar to this in every situation, a kind of directional energy which, if you know how to read it, will help you to anticipate what is going to happen. We are doing this kind of reading of situations all of the time. We do this in conversations, anticipating what a person will say next. We do it while driving; if a car ahead of us has put on its left blinker three times in a row without turning it tells us that this driver is not sure where he or she is and may stop or turn erratically. Again, to be able to read this kind of beyond-the-literal narrative in a situation will take study and practice to learn—which is why teenagers have so many car accidents (which I know from my own personal experience).

Since the primary activity that I will be doing, the primary lens through which I will be reading film, is philosophy, I would like to make a couple of final introductory remarks about philosophy and movies. Stanley Cavell says that "the creation of film was as if meant for philosophy."[3] I would like to add that the inverse of that also seems true to me, that the creation of philosophy was as if meant for film. What I mean by that is that what I take to be the best part of a film is the part of the film that is about the higher, nonliteral realm of relationships and the trajectories of things. From this perspective, as entertaining as the literal story of the film may be, the real measure of how good a movie is is determined by the conversation after the movie. An exciting conversation will be inspired by a movie in which the relations suggested larger and larger ramifications, or a more and more complex network of interrelations. Philosophy is, in some sense, just about trying to understand as much as possible of what is going on in a situation, on all levels. Philosophy is all about trying to figure out what is really going on. To talk about a movie, to try to understand what went on in it, to try to interpret it, is to do philosophy. Over the centuries philosophers have developed some very sophisticated tools for interpreting things. I will be using some of those tools for interpreting popular movies.

I have mentioned two levels of reality (which is itself a very philosophical idea); a literal level and a more abstract level of relationships between things and trajectories of situations. There is another level that I want to suggest also exists, and exists as real-ly, as those two levels, but is even *more* abstract and more difficult to learn to see and read. That is the level of the mythic or the spiritual. At this level there is a sense that what we are seeing is true not just for these particular people or this particular situation, but that these scenes say something about all people, say something that is true of experiences everyone has. At this level there is a sense that this narrative we see unfolding in this situation is really part of a much larger narrative that has to do with issues much larger than those with which any one person in a particular situation is dealing. We get this sense frequently when reading great literature. There is something strange and haunting, for example, about Ahab's relentless, possessed pursuit of a white whale in Melville's *Moby Dick*, a great and mythic American text. We get the sense that this is about more than a man and a whale, that the man is not just a man but stands for everyone, and the whale is not just a particular whale but also represents some vague specter that haunts the life of everyone. This level, too, may exist in every situation, literal as well as fictional. In every situation there will be the outlines of a much larger narrative. There will be the suggestion of mythic themes in very ordinary situations—themes of desire and loss, striving and overcoming and the failure to overcome, the thrill of victory and the agony of defeat; themes that, if we can see them will speak directly to our own lives in deeply meaningful and spiritual ways. In the work that follows I will be arguing that such deep, mythic themes can be seen to operate in even the most popular, often apparently unexceptional, Hollywood movies.

Acknowledgments

There are several people who have played pivotal roles at turning points in my history of thinking about movies. Kurt Mosser first taught me how to think and talk seriously about movies. My colleague Gregg Muilenburg challenged me to defend my claims that there were some philosophical themes that one could identify in *The Terminator*, which set me off on a search to try to identify some. Tony McRae very generously allowed me to participate in a film course that he had been teaching for twenty-five years, which was in many ways a formative experience. I would also like to express my appreciation to my other colleagues in the philosophy department at Concordia College for their continuing support of my interest in film, George Connell and Susan O'Shaughnessy. I have gained some, what have been for me, extremely valuable insights about some particular films from teaching a film course with Edward Schmoll in the classics department.

The Society for the Philosophic Study of the Contemporary Visual Arts has been a source of considerable sustenance for me. Every chapter in this book was first read in its initial form as a paper at a meeting of the SPSCVA. I especially want to thank Dan Flory, Thomas Wartenberg, and Kendall D'Andrade for their support and advice over the last few years. Earlier versions of chapters 1, 4, 5, 6, and 7 appeared in the publication of the SPSCVA, *Film and Philosophy*. I would like to thank Daniel Shaw, the present editor of *Film and Philosophy*, for permission to reprint the parts of those essays that remain.

Finally, I would like to thank my wife Ellen Aho, with whom I love to go to the movies because the conversations afterwards are so good and teach me so much.

Introduction

What It Means to Do Philosophy

Wittgenstein at the Movies and the Uses of Philosophy

In his memoir of his experiences with Ludwig Wittgenstein (1889–1951), Norman Malcolm tells how Wittgenstein, after teaching an especially demanding philosophy class at Cambridge University, would rush to a movie theater. He preferred Hollywood movies, musicals, westerns, and detective movies. He always sat in the very first row.[1] I find this behavior especially striking because much of Wittgenstein's later philosophy, what appears in *Philosophical Investigations*, is somewhat ironically devoted to the problem of finding a way to stop doing philosophy. As Wittgenstein says in one of the central sections of *Investigations*, "The real discovery is the one that makes me capable of stopping doing philosophy when I want to.—The one that gives philosophy peace, so that it is no longer tormented by questions which bring itself into question."[2]

In the *Investigations*, Wittgenstein treats philosophy as a kind of sickness that a person needs to be cured of, and his later antiphilosophy philosophy is meant to be just such a cure. The sickness feels like a kind of anxious preoccupation with something that seems to desperately need resolving. Wittgenstein's diagnosis is that we are sick with worry about non-real problems. Wittgenstein's philosophical cure is to show us how what seems to be a philosophical problem, when looked at rightly, when looked at from the proper perspective, is not really the problem we thought it was. What he means to offer us is a kind of peace. What is ironic here is that Wittgenstein himself seems to have found a cure for his own philosophical illness that he never mentions in his book, namely, to go to popular Hollywood movies.

Why would one of the twentieth century's great philosophical geniuses be so attracted to what is commonly regarded as a kitschy non-art, such as, Hollywood movies? It was certainly not because of a lack of

1

sophistication in the arts. Wittgenstein was raised in one of the wealthiest and most artistically sophisticated households in all of Europe. Brahms was a frequent houseguest. Gustav Klimt painted a portrait of one of Wittgenstein's sisters. There were as many as five grand pianos in their house. One of Wittgenstein's brothers was a concert pianist.[3] It was not a lack of exposure to sophisticated art that drew Wittgenstein to Hollywood movies.

It is likely that it was partly just to escape from such sophisticated levels of aesthetics appreciation, and the intellectual rigors of philosophical work, that Wittgenstein went to the movies. There are many accounts of the great toll doing philosophical work and teaching philosophy took on him. But the case that I want to make here is that there was more in Wittgenstein's going to the movies than just escape, and that, indeed, there always is, or can be, if we go to the movies in a particular way. I hope to lay out what that particular way of going to the movies is, but the short answer to the question is to say that one can go philosophically.

There is a long philosophical tradition of considering the relation of the individual to popular culture, and what it is about popular culture that makes it popular. For Plato and Aristotle popular culture meant primarily poetry and theater. I will be primarily concerned with movies.

There is an irony that runs through Plato's discussions of popular culture. In the *Republic* he is very critical of popular art forms like poetry and theater, and yet he presents his ideas on these topics in the form of dialogues between various Athenian and Greek people. Plato writes his philosophical criticism of art in an extremely artistic form, a form that is both poetic and dramatic. There is in this ironic tension the seeds of a solution to the problem of how to regard popular culture. Plato's objection to popular art forms is that they appeal primarily to peoples' emotions instead of to peoples' intellect, the consequence of which is that their understanding of the world is formed by their emotions instead of their emotions being trained by their reason. Plato's problem with this is that emotions tend to be highly reactive and context specific. They also tend to preempt choice. In the moment of experiencing an emotion we do not have much choice about what emotion we are experiencing. Plato's fear is that the ideas people will form while in the grip of a momentary, involuntary emotion will be reactive rather than considered, context specific rather than universal, and, in general, lacking in thoughtfulness.

For Plato, the result of the intellect being subservient to the emotions is a degenerative ethical culture. Plato acknowledges the great power of popular art forms to influence people, and for that very reason endorses a strict form of government censorship on all popular art forms. The idea is that since people will not be able to choose rightly for themselves (since they will make their choices based on the dictates of their emotions instead of on those of their reason), someone, or some people (who *are* able to make rational choices), should choose for the rest of the people the themes and stories that will get expressed in popular cultural forms. Plato's call for governmental censorship of certain forms of potentially dangerous ideas, visual images, musical forms, or other popular cultural content is being echoed by many people today. There does seem to be some evidence to suggest that a high degree of exposure to, say, violent content on television or in movies can lead to negative more violent (i.e.,) behavior. Is the call for governmental censorship the solution here? Well, let's reconsider the case of Plato and see if a more complicated response may not be suggested.

Constance Penley in *The Future of an Illusion: Film, Feminism, and Psychoanalysis* says, "the shackled prisoners fascinated by the shadows on the wall of Plato's cave are the first 'cinema' spectators; the only historical changes in the apparatus since then have been little more than technical modifications."[4] This description seems strikingly true enough and uncannily highlights Plato's genius; it identifies him as a potential source for philosophical insights about the nature of going to the movies, as well. Penley goes on to describe what Plato has done as having created a "simulacrum of the psyche." Plato's allegorical goal in the *Republic* as a whole is to free people (probably not all people, but some who might be rulers) from the cave. Interestingly, one of his primary techniques for effecting this freedom seems to be through his dialogues, which are both poetic and dramatic, which is to say, very cavelike. A way out of the cave would seem to be through the cave. Another way to say this might be to say that a way out of the cave is to use cavelike things, but to use them in the proper way. What is the proper way? Well, it would seem to be to use them thoughtfully. The initial appeal might be the emotional attraction that such cave-like works may have for us, but, ultimately, escape from the cave can only come through a kind of transcendence of this emotional appeal. One must learn to regard them with some intellectual detachment and thoughtfulness.

It is not that the emotions themselves are bad. The philosopher who escapes from the cave may experience great joy. It is more that some emotional responses are less informed than others because some emotional responses are more purely reactive, making us as individuals more passive and less in control. In the *Symposium*, for example, Plato talks about erotic love. Erotic passion in its most initial form, when we are most slavishly in its grip, is when we feel an erotic passion for another person's body. We must *learn* to be attracted to a person's mind or soul. But, and this is the important part, an attraction to another person's mind or soul will be a deeper and longer-lasting pleasure, and so anyone who could choose would make that choice. For Plato, theater and music hit us so emotionally fast and hard that they can inhibit our developing the deeper understanding, the deeper appreciation which gives us a choice. They will have a tendency, therefore, to keep us at the level of emotional development of teenagers, gaga for bodies and for the surface of things. Plato's allegory about escaping from the cave is really about transcending these initial (reactive) emotional responses to the surface of things.

This notion of transcendence is central to Plato's whole conception. We have to be freed from the shackles of this-worldliness in order to be able to transcend this-worldliness and make our way out into the light of the REAL world, which, in the language of Plato's later metaphysics, means the realm of the Forms. A similar trajectory of experience is described in Aristotle's otherwise very different philosophy in the *Poetics*. In the *Poetics*, Aristotle describes, somewhat indirectly, a condition of shackledness, of retention and constraint, the remedy for which is a kind of purging, a catharsis. The notion of transcendence is a bit less explicit in Aristotle, but I think it can be usefully engaged. There is in Aristotle a similar notion of inhibited functioning, and a way of gaining freedom from that condition. That freedom can be achieved, for Aristotle, through, again, the cavelike forms of drama, especially a tragic play.

What I am trying to suggest here is that in both Plato and Aristotle, from the earliest forms of Western philosophy, there is a notion of a needed escape from our quotidian ways of being, a way of being which is characterized by a kind of thralldom, and a thralldom that is characterized by an emotional investment that is somehow superficial and unhealthy. There are suggestions in both that this escape can be achieved by means of an encounter with a dramatic art form. For both Plato and Aristotle, the escape is an escape from a condition that is intimately connected to our own emotional responses to things, hence the escape is an escape from some condition of our self. It is an escape not just from, but also to, to a better condition of our self. This better condition I will call being in a state of philosophical health. To remain healthy in this philosophical way will require a constant exercise of those parts of us that can contribute to our freedom from certain kinds of restraints, and one of the most effective modes of exercise for those parts of us can be engaging with dramatic works of art that have a kind of narrative structure, like movies.

In the George Stevens movie *Shane*, Shane tells Marion (in response to Marion's concern about Shane's teaching her son Joey about shooting a pistol), "Marion, a gun is just a tool, no better and no worse than any other tool. It is as good or as bad as the man [*sic*] who holds it."[5] A similar idea underlies my way of coming to the movies. Movies are not "safe" or "dangerous" in themselves, but rather are more like tools, tools that can be used well or poorly, for good or for ill. This comparison of movies to tools invokes Wittgenstein's idea in the *Investigations* that language is a tool, and that various language games are like different tools in a toolbox (§11). Each one is useful in its appropriate context and misused if used in an inappropriate context (as it would be misuse of a screwdriver handle to hammer a nail with it).

Most of Wittgenstein's later philosophy is devoted to methods of ascertaining the appropriate contexts for different language games—which amounts to trying to figure out how to think in ways that are appropriate to the situations we are in. Our immense daily anxiety suggests that this is a real need. Wittgenstein thought of this as a philosophical sickness, one he attributed to a misunderstanding of what contexts are appropriate for a specific language game, and so as a kind of misuse of our tools. To speak of movies as tools implies the requirement of a certain amount of training in their appropriate uses, as well as correctives (*à la* Wittgenstein) for those situations in which we may be tempted to misuse them. Against Plato, I advocate less censorship and more training in how to use the tools of popular culture to attain greater philosophical health.

Philosophy is also a tool. If it is used properly it can be used to great benefit, especially in bringing us peace from the anxieties that plague us; if it is misused, it can do considerable harm, i.e., increase those anxieties. Wittgenstein argues in the *Investigations* that there are many different purposes that philosophy can serve. Different contexts will require different kinds of philosophical methods to fix the philosophical errors we may be subject to in those contexts. I, however, want to identify a more singular underlying philosophical goal. If philosophy and movies can be usefully thought of as tools, then their appropriate uses will be determined by what we need to get done with them. We have many needs that both philosophy and movies can satisfy for us, but one need in particular, a need that is both essential and pressing, and which movies seem particularly well-suited to address, is the need for (for lack of a better word), transport.

By *transport* I mean the need for a medium and a mechanism by which we may escape from our given condition, whatever that may be, and enter into a new condition. This new condition may be described as a new state of mind or a new perspective or a new mood. Wittgenstein needed to escape from the philosophical tangles that teaching his philosophy got him into. Other people may need to escape from anxieties and preoccupations about their own identities or about their jobs or their families or their economic concerns. A sense of this need for escape from one's present condition is nicely captured in a phrase by Stanley Cavell. Cavell is trying to account for why new artworks are continually being produced, why people keep trying to achieve some new understanding through art. They do this, Cavell says, "because what is known is known to be insufficient, or worse."[6] We all live, at least at some times in our lives, with a sense that there must be more to life than what we have. We often live with a persistent sense of disquiet, with the hope of some future possibility of an appeasement, of attaining some peace. To get that peace requires a kind of escape from where we are, since where we are often is not peaceful.

Ideally, however, the escape is not just an escape from but also an escape to. It is an escape from one state of mind, one state of being, to another. This transport from one state to another offers the possibility of growth. It is the possibility of an increase in the intensity in one's life as well as an increase in one's understanding of the possibilities one's life contains. I say "the possibility of growth" because actual growth will require more than just the experience of transport. Certainly people can go to movies, be transported by or into the story of the movie, and leave with no more than a vague desire to do some violence, look fetishistically at women, or escape from work to go on some vague adventure. More is required to get the most from movies. It requires some kind of reflective acknowledgment of the experience of the transport as well as just the experience of the transport itself. Movies are extremely good places, are extremely good tools, for achieving this kind of transport. Philosophy is an extremely good tool for achieving the "reflective acknowledgment" that will yield the increase in understanding, intensity, and growth that make our lives more satisfying to us.

In the preface to *Contesting Tears: The Hollywood Melodrama of the Unknown Woman*, Stanley Cavell says, "the creation of film was as if meant for philosophy—meant to reorient everything philosophy has said about reality and its representation, about art and imitation, about greatness and conventionality, about judgment and pleasure, about skepticism and transcendence, about language and expression."[7] What I understand Cavell to mean by this is that, just as Plato conceived of a way of analogizing our interior mental space as external projection so that we could mentally visualize it and so come to a new understanding of it, movies have made this possibility a literal reality. This, in turn, has opened up new possibilities for philosophy. The fact of movies correlates with the fact of our vision of the world as we move through it. To examine our relation to movies works as an analogue to our relation to our own minds. In movies we find an objective correlative for all of our inner dramas of identity, of confidence (in ourselves and in others), in the reliability of the world. In this way we can say that not only was film as if meant for philosophy, but that philosophy is also as if meant for film.

What movies do to a concatenation of experiences, philosophy can do to movies. What movies do is weave a series of experiences into a story with a beginning, a middle, and an end, the very stuff of good drama according to Aristotle. What philosophy can do with a movie is to weave it into the fabric of our lives, which can also be described as the story of our lives. To have an experience itself involves, according to the great American philosopher John Dewey, just this kind of weaving. It involves something like the construction of a narrative.

In *Art as Experience*, Dewey attempts to describe the trajectory, the basic pattern, of all significant human experience. The central feature of our having an experience, according to Dewey, is that what we do, what happens to us, gets framed in or woven into a narrative account. In order to have an "experience" a sequence of events in our life will have to acquire a kind of narrative form, with a beginning, a middle, and an end. As Dewey says, "For life is no uniform uninterrupted march or flow. It is a thing of histories, each with its own plot, its own inception and movement toward its close, each having its own particular rhythmic movement; each with its own unrepeated quality pervading it throughout." That is, "an experience has a unity."[8] What is most important for having an experience for Dewey is the notion of a "consummation," a period of reflection after an experience in which the experience gets recognized as (is made into) an experience.[9] This, for Dewey, is a creative process, an aesthetic process. Things "are composed into an experience."[10] Dewey refers to this process as "reconstructive doing,"[11] and as "recognition" as opposed to passive perception. The result is a kind of "felt harmony,"[12] a sense of "integration." Dewey says "the experience itself has a satisfying emotional quality because it possesses internal integration and fulfillment reached through ordered and organized movement."[13] This sense of a felt harmony, of a satisfying sense of integration, correlates, it seems to me, with Wittgenstein's idea of giving "philosophy peace." The goal is just a sense of satisfaction, of a felt harmony, and this is achieved when we can achieve, can recognize, can construct a narrative pattern around the events of our lives.

I think this whole idea is best captured in an extended passage from Dewey's *Art as Experience*. Dewey says,

> Life itself consists of phases in which the organism falls out of step with the march of surrounding things and then recovers unison with it either through effort or by some happy chance. And, in a growing life, the recovery is never mere return to a prior state, for it is enriched by the state of disparity and resistance through which it has successfully passed. If the gap between organism and environment is too wide, the creature dies. If its activity is not enhanced by the temporary alienation, it merely subsists. Life grows when a temporary falling out is a transition to a more extensive balance of the energies of the organism with those of the conditions under which it lives.[14]

I see Wittgenstein's idea of giving philosophy peace, as well as Dewey's idea of an experience as aiming at the same thing: the personal, individual growth that results in a sense of "a more extensive balance of the energies of the organism." This "balance of energies" is what I mean by philosophical health. When we feel this "balance of energies" the sense of insecurity is eased and is replaced by a sense of confidence in our own purpose, in our ability to act, and in the sense of having a place from which to act. For Dewey, the recovery of this "balance of energies" comes from our being able to effectively recognize the narrative structure of our lives. Art, for Dewey, is just a specialized version of this general activity of giving meaning to our lives. My idea is that there is perhaps no better place for practicing this activity of recognizing narrative patterns than at the movies.

Noël Carroll, in his very interesting essay "The Power of Movies," identifies a particular model of narrative form that is especially characteristic of movies. He calls it the "erotetic model of narrative."[15] He describes this as a question/answer model in which later scenes of a movie answer questions raised by events that occured earlier in the movie. This erotetic model makes of movies a kind of game, a game of finding the answers to the earlier-asked questions. Another way to describe this game would be to say that it is a game of connecting the pieces of the film into a unified whole, which is just the activity that makes an experience an experience for Dewey, and which yields the sense of a "felt harmony" and the sense of peace that we have been looking for.

The primary enemies of experience, for Dewey, are those things which interfere with our abilities to see the relations between events that happen to us; they obscure the connecting pattern that unifies an experience for us. He says, for example, "Zeal for doing, lust for action, leaves many a person, especially in this hurried and impatient human environment in which we live, with experience of an almost incredible paucity, all on the surface. No one experience has a chance to complete itself because something else is entered upon so speedily."[16] The frenetic drive to be active, so characteristic of us as Americans, inhibits our ability to have meaningful experiences because it interferes with the consummatory period of reflection in which our experience becomes unified, in which we weave the narrative of events into a meaningful, unified whole. If the essence of philosophy is reflection, philosophy can contribute to the completion of the experience of certain movies as we engage in philosophical reflection on them. Thinking philosophically, reflectively, about movies can contribute to the sense of depth and importance of the movies that people see, which would help to contribute to the sense of depth and importance, to the sense of *meaning*, in our lives as a whole.

When we think about movies philosophically, the best part of going to the movies becomes the time after the movie when you get a chance to talk about the movie, over a cup of coffee or a beer or a glass of wine. If movies are seen as tools, tools to be used in reconfiguring our lives to make our lives more intense and more satisfying, then the ways in which a movie can be used, what is good or bad or interesting or dangerous in the movie, is exactly the conversation to have. If we can talk about the sexism, the violence, the gratuitous vs. the meaningful sexual encounters, the nobility of some character or the ethical choices faced by another character, then we are no longer in a position of passively having the values represented in the movie shape our character, but rather we are in the position of recognizing and acknowledging those forces and adjudicating for ourselves how we should regard them within the contexts of our own lives. This process is not just empowering but also pleasurable. The conversation can be as easily about James Cameron's *The Terminator* as about Renoir's *The Rules of the Game*, and as usefully too.

Doing this, we narrativize the themes of the film into the context of our own lives rather than having our lives narrativized by what we see in the movies. The movies then become tools for improving, empowering, and liberating our lives rather than oppressive or manipulating forces that corrupt our lives by making us more violent, solipsistic, or fetishistic in our relationships with other people. Richard Rorty calls this idea of narrativizing "redescription." Working from a Nietzschean perspective, Rorty sees such redescriptions as essential to being fully oneself, to being fully *a* self. To fail to narrativize one's own life, to fail to redescribe oneself, Rorty suggests, is to fail to be fully human. As Rorty says, "To fail as a poet—and thus, for Nietzsche, to fail as a human being—is to accept somebody else's description of oneself, to execute a previously prepared program, to write, at most, elegant variations on previously written poems. So the only way to trace home the causes of one's being as one is would be to tell a story about one's causes in a new language."[17] I read this to be saying something like, either you redescribe your own life, or someone will redescribe it for you.

I want to say: go to movies and redescribe them in terms of the contexts of your own life, or else they will redescribe your life in their terms. To be prepared to redescribe movies in terms of one's own life, one's own truths, is to go to the movies philosophically. I agree with many of the cultural critics and politicians today who say that movies can be a terrible influence on people, but I disagree that that is the fault of the movies. What is called for is a re-education in how to go to the movies. The way to go to the movies is to go philosophically.

The Trajectory of Philosophy

There is a specific pattern of philosophical thought with which I am primarily concerned. It is the pattern that is followed in the process of discovery.

It is the pattern that is followed in creativity. It is the pattern that underlies the experience of meaningfulness. It is the pattern that is experienced in growth. There are various philosophical concepts that identify this pattern. In aesthetics, the experiences of the beautiful and of the sublime are about the experience of this pattern. Hegel's notion of the logic of thesis-antithesis-synthesis is about this pattern. The description of God's creation of the universe in the Kabbalah, the *zimzum*, is about this pattern. Simone de Beauvoir's description of "allowing disclosure" is about this pattern. Wittgenstein's notion of "seeing-as" involves this pattern. The proto-philosophers escaping from Plato's cave follow this pattern. Descartes' discovery of the *cogito* follows this pattern. John Rawls's invention of the "veil of ignorance" as a means for arriving at a just political system follows this pattern.

In the chapters that follow I offer philosophical readings of popular films. Each of these readings is concerned with different philosophical topics and makes appeals to the works of different philosophers. However, there is really a single overarching trajectory with which I am concerned, and I take this to be *the* trajectory of philosophy. I take it that it is controversial to say that there is *a* trajectory of philosophy, but that it is less controversial to say that philosophy is about reasoning. The great and underappreciated American philosopher Charles Sanders Peirce describes reasoning in his essay "The Fixation of Belief" in the following way: "The object of reasoning is to find out, from the consideration of what we already know, something else we do not know."[18] Already, in this brief description of reasoning, is suggested a larger, universal trajectory for thought in general. Thought will be initiated by the sense of a need to know something that we do not know. There will be a process, starting with what we already know, of trying to figure out what we do not know. The conclusion of this process, if we are successful, is an insight, a seeing of a connection that we had not seen before, that will be experienced as a discovery. We will know something new. Peirce describes this trajectory in the following way: "The irritation of doubt causes a struggle to attain a state of belief. I shall call this struggle *Inquiry*. . . ."[19]

Thinking is about trying to understand things. It is the attempt to move from a place of confusion and doubt to a place of understanding and of knowing what to do. This is the narrative of virtually every film that has ever been made. A protagonist moves from a condition of relative peace and contentment into a condition of doubt and conflict. The movie is about how the protagonist goes about trying to remove the doubt and conflict and to figure out what to do. The action of a movie is, one might say, externalized thought.

To see the action of a movie as an externalized performance of an inner drama, of an interior exploration of ideas and possibilities, brings out not just the philosophical aspects of movies, but their aesthetic aspects as well. To see Tom Cruise as Ethan Hunt, in John Woo's *Mission Impossible II*, kick into the air a pistol buried in the sand, and simultaneously, or at least in an instant (and in slow motion), spin, grab the gun, dive, and fire in midair, is to watch a kind of visual jazz. It is like McGyver on speed.

When I was working in construction people used to say, "We'll have to McGyver it." "To McGyver it" just meant to figure out a solution to an unanticipated problem using whatever materials happened to be on the job site at the time. Of course, that is what all of our thinking is like. We are McGyvering it every day, every time we encounter some new unanticipated difficulty that we need to solve to get on with our lives. We McGyver it at work, we McGyver it in our relationships with our family and friends, we McGyver it when we get lost driving. Love is all about McGyvering it. The thing about McGyver was that he was *really* good at seeing the possibilities in a situation, and the same can be said for the character of Ethan Hunt in *Mission Impossible II*. That kind of skill takes practice. It takes training and work. One has to be an excellent musician to be a competent jazz player.

What I want to say is that to McGyver it is just to think, but thinking itself takes some work, takes some will, takes some practice. To think is what it means to reason and to do inquiry. To do inquiry is to do philosophy. There is a kind of philosophy that is done in the towers of academia and there is a type of philosophy that is done in the streets everyday. My contention is that, while some of the subjects of these inquiries may be different, the basic trajectory, the basic pattern of thought, in both cases is the same. And a good place to learn about this trajectory, to learn about the fruits of discovery that this trajectory can yield, and to practice getting better at it, is at the movies.

To go to the movies philosophically is to become a protagonist oneself. It is to be sensitive to and to acknowledge certain mysteries, certain difficulties raised by a movie that cause an irritation of doubt. One must work with what one already knows, but also search for additional clues, be alert to the suggestion of as yet unperceived relationships. It involves seeing new connections between the characters in the movie, between the different parts of the plot of the movie, and between what happens in the movie and what happens in the world and in our own lives. Sometimes this will require a certain amount of attentive patience to see where things are heading. It will take some educated guesswork to anticipate where things are going, like when Leonard Shelby (Guy Pearce) in *Memento* is running along and wondering why he might be chasing this other man only to discover, no, whoops, that this other man is chasing him. A whole new set of imperatives suddenly get engaged. Movies explore this trajectory narratively while philosophy has approached the same trajectory more abstractly and conceptually. My goal is to combine these two ways of doing the same thing in order to have each augment the possibilities for discovery in the other.

What is generated by this process, by undergoing this trajectory (at least when it is successful), is what I call '*meaning.*' An experience is meaningful when it comes to a kind of conclusion and we have learned something from it that we can use, something that will help us get on in the world. This experience is, I believe, one of the most deeply human and most deeply satisfying that we can have. It is the experience of growth. There is always more to learn in the process of our ongoing lives, in this evolving world, which is to say that there is always more meaning that can be incorporated into our lives. This is the core idea of American pragmatism. It is a hopeful and optimistic philosophy, and this hope and optimism is empirically verified again and again. Every time that we successfully negotiate a new situation or successfully deal with an unexpected encounter testifies to our powers of recovery, to our power to discover new solutions and to gain new understanding. The theme of discovering our untapped, unsuspected powers is also recurrent in Hollywood movies, from *The Wizard of Oz* to *Unbreakable* or *The Matrix*.

This philosophy, however, is not without its tragic side. The very fact that more meaning can always be discovered implies that at any given moment we live surrounded by a darkness of which we are only dimly aware, that our understanding is always only partial, that there is always more to know, that there is always a mystery that has not been solved. This is the abyss of the American sublime. It is the vaguely horrifying (vague because so dimly perceived) underside that haunts our American optimism. It is the undercurrent of anxiety that nags even our greatest successes. This is also a theme of some of the best Hollywood movies, such as *Citizen Kane* or *Vertigo* or *Taxi Driver* or *Fargo*. It is also a theme that underlies, or at least contributes to, the fascination with horror movies, which play on the vague dread that there is something lurking beyond the realm of our understanding. This is as true of Romero's *Night of the Living Dead* as of David Lynch's *Lost Highway*.

Finally, I just want to make a few initial remarks about interpretation, a question I will return to in the conclusion. In an essay called "Against Interpretation," Susan Sontag attacks a kind of interpretation that is static and deadening to art. It is the kind of interpretation that works from a kind of template, whether a Freudian or a Jungian or an evolutionary biology template, for example, and, by a process of reduction, by the elimination of all details irrelevant to that template, or lens, comes up with a kind of replacement narrative. X stands for Y, Z for A, so that the resultant interpretation will conclude that some particular movie, say a heist movie, is really about sons wanting to kill their fathers and marry their mothers, or about the oppression of the people by capitalist forces.

I believe that all seeing is interpretive, that there is no non-interpretive seeing. I also believe that there are better interpretations and worse ones. Reductive interpretations may have a function, but it is a narrow one. As Peirce says, we always have to approach what we do not know, do not understand, with what we do know and do understand. This is just to interpret. For me, a good interpretation does not mean that one has divined what the director or writer was really thinking, although I think what the creators of art were really thinking is relevant. For me there really is something like wisdom and so something like progress toward wisdom. The evidence for this for me is my sense of my own lack of wisdom in my earlier selves. I feel like I really do understand more now than I did, so I see more now than I did. A good interpretation for me is one that leads in the direction of wisdom, that leads a person to see more.

Sontag, in her opposition to the reductive, all-too-knowing kind of interpretation, calls for an "erotics of art."[20] I take her to mean that she wants to see a way of reading artworks, say, movies, that does not reduce art but which makes it more complex, more subtle, more ambiguously rich. I understand her to mean that she is not opposed to all forms of interpretation, but just to interpretations of a certain sort. The kind of interpretation of which I take it that she would approve is an interpretation that works the way a healthy love relationship works.

A healthy love relationship works to embrace the other in their otherness, to allow the other to be as they are and to grow into what they will grow into. It involves the attitude of respect and appreciation rather than the attempt to dominate, control, define, and oppress. A healthy relationship also demands a clear vision of the other, not just a projection of what one would like the other to be. There are all sort of tools one can use to help one to see more clearly. There are glasses, for example, and books, books of psychology and philosophy that can be powerful aides to sight. Like any tool, as Shane says, they can be misused, but they can also be well used. A tool is best used when used, as it were, with love. It is to this that I aspire in my own interpretations of movies that I love; I aspire to an erotics of interpretation.

1

John Ford's The Searchers as an Allegory of the Philosophical Search

> The philosophical remarks in this book are, as it were, a number of sketches of landscapes. . . .
> —Wittgenstein, *Philosophical Investigations*

> . . . ain't got no eyes, can't enter the spirit land. He has to wander for ever between the winds. . . .
> —John Wayne as Ethen Edwards in *The Searchers*

The landscapes that Wittgenstein is concerned to sketch in *Philosophical Investigations* are, I will say with irony, something like the landscapes of our interior world of mind. Without the irony, and so without the idea of an interior world, the metaphor refers to something like the associative patterns of our concepts, or, more accurately, the mechanisms and conditions by which we learn and use our concepts. We have a need for such sketches because we are often unaware of the patterns or, say, the landscape, of our own thoughts. We are especially unaware of the conflicts and inconsistencies that exist between our various thoughts. Insofar as we are unaware of the conflicts between our various thoughts, there are things about ourselves that we do not know. A consequence of such lack of self-knowledge is that we can do things in one moment, in light of one belief, that in another moment, in light of a very different belief, will appear to us quite awful or inconsistent with who we think we are. What we require is a kind of self-knowledge. What can help us to understand ourselves better, what can help us to gain this self-knowledge, will be something like philosophy. Doing philosophy can be like going on a journey.

Wittgenstein says of the philosophical sketches in *Philosophical Investigations* that the sketches "were made in the course of . . . long and involved journeyings."[1] *Philosophical Investigations*, which I am taking to be a representative, even paradigmatic, philosophical text, can be described as a text that tells the story of the landscapes seen during "long

15

and involved journeyings." I will argue that John Ford's *The Searchers* can be seen as telling basically the same story, of a landscape and how to pass through it, and that this story is the story of philosophy, broadly speaking. I will further argue that the goal of both stories is to move from a greater amount of confusion, anxiety, and unhappiness to a lesser amount; to progress from self-deception, despair, and a kind of madness to something like a condition of mental health and a sense of knowing how to go on. The problem begins as an epistemological one, of a landscape that is unknown or insufficiently known, and of how one might come to know it, have the eyes, to see it. It ends with the ethical consequence of providing some information that may be helpful to oneself and to others about how to get through that landscape effectively. Wittgenstein says, "A philosophical problem has the form: 'I don't know my way about.'" (§123). A philosopical solution shows me a way to go.

To start more directly with the film, the first shot of *The Searchers* is a tracking shot that starts in a darkness that is broken by the opening of a door. The door is opened by a woman, and the camera follows her shadow-outline in a movement from the darkened interior of a cabin through a doorway to the bright and vast landscape outside. The camera moves slowly forward to go through the doorway itself, still following the woman, to pick up in the distance the tiny figure of a man on horseback making his way through the huge landscape of Monument Valley (which is on the Arizona-Utah border, but, for purposes of the film, is Texas) toward the cabin from which we are watching him.

This opening is significant both cinematographically and philosophically. It is significant cinematographically as a framing device for the movie as a whole, and in its use of motion—a dynamic of space and time—on the screen that is peculiar to the medium of film. It is significant philosophically because of the philosophical issues it raises, issues that will be explored throughout the rest of the film, and which I will connect in this chapter with the work of Wittgenstein and Nietzsche, and more remotely, with Socrates and Aristotle. I am following Stanley Cavell's idea of reading movies as "spiritual parables."[2] Cavell's point seems to be to see in certain movies suggestions on how to distinguish the truly needful from the wrongly assumed to be necessary. In Wittgenstein's terms, it is to determine "the fixed point of our real need" (§108).

The Searchers begins in darkness. Against Jean-Louis Comolli, who in his 1966 "Notes on the New Spectator,"[3] disparages the darkness and the dreamlike character of cinema theaters and (especially) Hollywood movies, Ford seems to intentionally invoke exactly a dreamlike condition. The whole opening structure of the film, in darkness with a door opening onto a whole other world—a structure that will be mirrored at the end of the film—parallels and invokes the structure of dreams. The movie itself is in many ways dreamlike and seems to demand interpretation that follows the logic of dreams—with its repetitions, compulsions, multiplications of a specific character, and its sublime horrors. Where Comolli sees the darkness and dreamlike character of movie theaters and Hollywood movies as escapist and antilife,[4] Ford seems to invoke just those characteristics in order to clarify and expose certain aspects of life.

The opening movement from darkness to light, from inside to outside, is a kind of metaphysical inversion, representing a movement from the daylight world of clarity and consciousness into the darkened, murkier world of mythic dream-life. The issues that will be dealt with in *The Searchers* will be issues that are associated with dreams, primal issues of sexual desire, desire for power and control, fear, terror, and the need for revenge as a way to balance these various, often conflicting forces in us. Our reactions to these forces, like our reactions to the events of the movie, will also be conflicted.

In *Philosophical Investigations*, Wittgenstein describes the problems he is addressing as having "the character of depth" (§111) and adds that they arise from "deep disquietudes." He says that philosophical problems have the form, "'I don't know my way about'" (§123), and he once wrote, "When you are philosophizing you have to descend into a primeval chaos and feel at home there."[5] Doing philosophy for Wittgenstein, is like a kind of sickness (§255, §593) and can look like a kind of madness.[6] Wittgenstein himself often seems to be conflicted about the role and nature of philosophy in his insistence both on the need to put an end to philosophy and on the fact that what he is doing *is* philosophy and is needed. What in fact he is pointing to, however, is our own conflicts with philosophy. Philosophy begins for us with the desire to know and make sense of things, but can move quickly to an avoidance of knowledge, to an avoidance of understanding (Wittgenstein describes this phenomenon in terms of "an urge to misunderstand" [§109]) that takes the form for Wittgenstein of metaphysics, which, for Wittgenstein, is a sure sign of philosophy going wrong.

Nietzsche sees dreams as the origins of metaphysics, but his analysis is ultimately quite similar to Wittgenstein's. Dreams provide the excuse, but the motivations to derive metaphysics from dreams are, says Nietzsche, "passion, error, and self-deception."[7] The problem is to undo the internal conflicts that we have by recognizing our self-deceptions, to see clearly "something that is in plain view." One solution is to map out the landscapes in which we got lost in the first place. This, I propose, is the work that both Wittgenstein (as a representative philosopher) and Ford in *The Searchers* are doing.

The Searchers begins with movement, the movement of the camera, the movement of the woman, and the movement of the rider across the landscape. There are no words spoken throughout the opening sequence of shots. All of the movements are human, and against the still background of the awe-inspiring landscape of Monument Valley. The immediacy of our engagement in the scene has to do with the medium of film, the motion that it can command. In a real sense we in the audience are engaged in this scene in ways that are similar to the ways that the woman is. We are similarly curious, edgy, and threatened in this immediacy. We are not threatened physically, but emotionally. Whether this man who appears to be moving toward us is coming with death or love in mind, we are committed by our presence in front of this drama to some emotional response, and we must prepare ourselves emotionally for how this situation will resolve itself. Given the genre, the sudden outburst of violence is as much to be expected as some touching reunion. We are not passively watching, but actively engaged in the situation, much in the way the woman herself is, with a kind of anxious anticipation we scrutinize the scene, the manner of the approaching rider, for clues about how to respond to this approach. By virtue of this motion across the screen the boundaries between film world and viewer world break down. Because of our own emotional commitments, we are in some real sense as much out on that porch as the woman is, and similarly anxious to learn what bodings this traveler across the land brings.

The fact that this movement is against the background of Monument Valley is surely significant. There is something decidedly uncanny about the place, especially in the panoramic vistas that Ford gets on film. These vistas effectively maximize the possibilities of film that Panofsky defines as "dynamization of space" and "spatialization of time."[8] The mesas and buttes of Monument Valley are both anachronistic and proleptic, speaking simultaneously of time past and of time to come, and hence, of the transformations that occur in space across time. In their simultaneous invocation of time as past and as future, they seem outside of time altogether, commenting on the nature of time *sub specie aeternitatas*. The monuments of Monument Valley are things out of the past, things that attest to an altogether different landscape that was there in the past. The surrounding red desert landscape attests to the future; the monuments are crumbling as we see them, each one surrounded by a ring of its own detritus. It will not be long, in geological time, before they will all be gone, leveled as just more pulverized dirt in a vast and flat landscape. These buttes and mesas invoke the central problem of our lives, the problem of how to occupy space in time—how to maximize the time that we have, what we must do to make the time of our lives worth living.

Ethan Edwards, the protagonist of *The Searchers*, is clearly identified with these monuments in the opening shot. He is first seen as a barely identifiable figure moving between the flat scrub-covered land and the towering monuments in the distance. The monuments of Monument

Valley are things out of the past. He is similarly atavistic. Ethan speaks in phrases that invoke his atavistic, almost atemporal condition—he denies being Methuselah, suggesting by that denial that he might be mistaken for Methuselah; his habitual refrain is "That'll be the day," a phrase which suggests that that said day will never come. He compares his own relentless search to "the turnin' of the earth" which suggests time taken on a fairly broad scale. Ethan Edwards, played by John Wayne, is a figure caught in time, between an old order and a new order, and it will be this conflict between the old and the new order that will contribute to the tragedy of Ethan's life. This is a great theme of Ford's work, the figure that is caught between the old and the new order of the world, and one that will be readdressed even more darkly, and again with John Wayne as the protagonist, in *The Man Who Shot Liberty Valance*. As a figure in this nexus of time, and of course we are all such figures, it will be something out of the past that will haunt Ethan to distraction and will determine his future. What haunts Ethan, I will argue, is not just his love for Martha and the violence that was done to her by the renegade Comanches, but it is also the violence of the world, that the world is a violent place, and that we are too passionate and violent in it, that distresses Ethan. The world is as indifferent to this human violence as those monolithic monuments. It is to this condition, to stand outside the human and be indifferent to it, that Ethan himself, uselessly, aspires. This is an apiration because his actual condition is one of longing and vulnerability with respect to some very specific people, most notably Martha, the woman in the opening scene and his brother's wife. The primary conflict in him that the movie explores is his despair and helplessness with respect to this violence in the world, and his own need and desire to participate in it.

The role the monuments of Monument Valley play in *The Searchers* may most usefully be described as diachronic, metonymically standing for the changes that occur across time, the changes that, in fact, constitute time. It will be the changes that occur in Ethan across time that the movie will track. The changes in Ethan that the film will record will also involve a kind of breaking down. Ethan's ferocious isolation and independence will crumble a bit in favor of something like, but will not exactly be, assimilation. He will still stand alone at the end of the movie, but some of his independence as well as some of his antagonism toward the world will have been surrendered, and surrendered voluntarily, in favor of a quieter and longer-lasting good—the good of the community. His future and the future of those like him are prefigured in Ethan's capitulation, like an allegory of a Nietzschean genealogy. The strength of the strong becomes a weakness and is no longer sustainable. Only through a certain kind of capitulation, only through a reliance on community, can we survive in so hostile a world.

This ethical move, within the context of the movie, to affirm some community association over absolute and solitary individualism is made, ironically, by means of a revolt against the movie's own genre (which itself signals the philosophical). *The Searchers* is commonly regarded as a 'revisionist' western.[9] To say that it is "revisionist" is to say that the film reflects a reevaluation of, or a reflection on, the old version, the old vision of western life. From this reexamination, this reflection, we get a new vision, a new version of how, in this case, the West was. Clearly this new version is as fictional as the old version—it is just a film after all, a story; but also, presumably, the term *revisionist* suggests some kind of progress, some kind of direction, so that the new vision is not just a different vision but somehow a more accurate, truer vision of how the West was.

The old vision of the West was a vision of the world divided into good and bad men. The good men were either all good, or else so basically good that any shortcomings could be attributed to some pressing and obvious constraint. What makes *The Searchers* revisionist is that its protagonist, I will say its hero, is, at best, a morally ambiguous character. He is hyperaggressive, violent, criminal, angry, insensitive, and a blatant racist. For all that, however, there is something attractive about him and we certainly identify with him. We identify with him from the beginning, in part, because we do not know those things about him yet; we identify with him in part because all we do see of him at the beginning is that he is (mostly) warmly received by his brother's family; and we identify with him in part because the character of Ethan is played by John Wayne. We are able to sustain our identification with him because of his obvious strength, which circumstances clearly require, and because the bad things in his character seem to be in response to even more horrifying contexts. But he is a hard man with a hard heart, and he does not seem to be motivated, at least throughout most of the film, by any code of kindness or goodness. He is not like Roy Rogers or the Lone Ranger; he is not even like Shane. This is a different story from those and it is a story that seems to have progressed beyond those, in terms of its complexity, and because of its complexity, in terms of its verisimilitude. Certainly the hardness of the old West must have produced more hardhearted angry men like Ethan than golden-hearted masked men. To be revisionist involves a reexamination of an old picture, an old myth, and then a re-creation of it into a new form that is, in some sense yet to be determined, truer.

This process of revision itself parallels the philosophical process. Philosophy begins with a revision, call it reflection. To begin to do philosophy is to begin to see things in a new way, to begin to reflect. To begin to reflect is to begin to see what is ordinary as something extraordinary, and to move from that sense of wonder at the presence of the extraordinary to giving some kind of account of it. It is from this process that philosophy gets associated with depth. The philosophical move from the ordinary to the extraordinary, and then the further move to give some kind of (ordinary) account of the extraordinary, is a move to get to the bottom of a thing, to move from its appearances to what it truly is. The philosophical discovery, perhaps the philosophical supposition, is that there is more going on than there appears.

I see the story that John Ford tells in *The Searchers* as an allegory for the story I am telling here about philosophy. I want to argue that not only is *The Searchers* structurally and allegorically like a text of philosophy, but that it is structurally and allegorically like the very best philosophical texts. Structurally, *The Searchers* is complex. It is and is not about what it appears to be about. It appears to be a story about revenge, and it is and is not about revenge in just about the same proportion that *Hamlet* is and is not about revenge. It is a story, I am saying, that has depth.

What is deep in *The Searchers* is not just what it has to say about the human condition, but also the way in which the movie is structurally composed to elicit a very specific kind of understanding from us, an understanding that is nothing if not philosophical. The plot of *The Searchers* is actually quite difficult to recount with any detailed accuracy because much is suggested and little is confirmed. There is a suggestion that Ethan is, or was, in love with his brother's wife; that he is a deserter, has stolen money, was, himself, perhaps, married to or loved an Indian woman; is, perhaps, tied by some blood-tie to his fellow searcher, the young Marty (a possibility Ethan repeatedly denies).[10] The very broadest outlines of the story are not much clearer. It is not entirely clear what Ethan and Marty are searching for—whether it is Debbie, Ethan's youngest niece, or Scar, the Comanche chief who abducted her. And if it is primarily Debbie they are looking for, it is not clear what they propose to do with her. It is suggested at one point that Ethan proposes to kill her to keep her from becoming (or being) a Comanche's wife, in which case Marty proposes to keep him from doing that. The result of these uncertainties is that we, as viewers, become hypersensitive to signs, to indications that might fill in the mysteries presented by this story. We are compelled to be on the lookout for subtle forms of additional information. We are forced to accompany the searchers *as* searchers. We are compelled to become philosophers.

Part of this philosophical work will be to recognize and acknowledge some of the odd and dreamlike associations in the movie. The movie is constructed in haunting parallels that conform to a kind of dream logic, and many commentators have interpreted the events of the film along such lines. Ethan's enemy, the renegade Comanche chief, Scar, seems to be Ethan's own symbolic wounded savage other; Marty and Debbie versions of his good and more innocent self; old Mose, his tipped into genuine, but gentle, madness self. The romance between Marty and Laurie seems to be a symbolic playing out of the possible histories (good and bad, possible and actual) of the romance between Ethan and Martha (who will become his brother's wife). Scar will steal and kill the settler's cattle, Ethan will kill the Indians' cattle (buffalo). Scar will kill Ethan's brother and have sex with his brother's wife, Martha (an enactment, apparently, of Ethan's own secret desires), Ethan will steal and try to kill Scar's wife (Debbie), soldiers will kill Marty's Indian (accidental) wife, Look. The relations are too complex, and too complexly rendered, to yield any simple account. They seem to demand a more interpretive response from the viewer in order for the viewer to even begin to make sense of all that goes on in the movie. This defiance of easy assimilation, this insistence on interpretation, has the character of the outrageous that Cavell attributes to philosophy, in general,[11] and signals the promise of something more than mere entertainment from the movie.

One can say almost axiomatically of the character of Ethan that he lives in the presence of absence, hence his need for the eponymous search. What is absent, however, is considerably more difficult to specify. Minimally, one might say that what is absent for Ethan is satisfaction. Whether he wants to kill Debbie or save her, whether he needs most to find her or to find Scar or to find both, at the very least we can say that he is not happy the way he is, and that he is determined to find some kind of satisfaction that is currently lost to him, but which he clearly believes he can at least minimally achieve. The way the ethical is related to the epistemological here is that Ethan does not know what he does not know, and this blindness leads him to want to do what, when he has more insight, he will not want to do, what he will recognize as wrong. To say it most simply, he thinks he knows what he is doing but he does not, and he sees that by the end of the movie.

This is progress, epistemological as well as ethical. What was absent for Ethan is ultimately a kind of knowledge. Just what kind of knowledge was absent, and what it might look like to acquire some of this knowledge is the point that the movie has to make. The failure of Ethan's life, the tragic flaw that makes him such a sad, solitary hero in the movie, is this lack of knowledge.[12] The great irony of the movie *The Searchers* is that the great searcher, Ethan, the man who says, "I'll find 'em, as sure as the turnin' of the earth," is really a flawed searcher, a sometimes poor reader of signs. It is his failure to recognize the original Indian trick to lure the men away from the farmhouses, and then the peculiar trail left by the led-away cows (a peculiarity noticed by the neophyte Marty), that leads to the horrible disaster of his slaughtered family and abducted niece. The search itself takes him five years, and it is not even Ethan who ultimately finds Scar, but crazy old Mose.

The irony of his failure as a searcher is compounded by the fact that in many ways he is a very good searcher. He is better at reading signs, at assessing situations, and generally knows more about what is going on in every situation that occurs than any other character in the movie. We are constantly surprised by how much Ethan knows, by how little seems to escape his notice. Most surprising of all is how much he knows about Indians, the Other for whom he proclaims his greatest hatred and contempt. He knows not just about their intimate customs, such as how they marry, but also speaks their languages, even that of the most hated of all Indians, the Comanche. What he misses, however, end up being the most important things. Perhaps the ultimate irony of his failure as a searcher is his failure to identify the true object of his search. Ethan does not really know what he is looking for. We know this because what he finds in the end has nothing to do with the thing he was searching for all of those years, and yet it is the only thing that can really put some kind of end to his searching.

All of this suggests some ambivalence, some conflict in the character of Ethan. The fact that Ethan is at odds with himself correlates with the very first image of the film, the contrast between inside and outside.[13] The opening sequence, again, begins in darkness, a darkness that we will discover is inside, and moves to the bright, vast, open space of sky and land of Monument Valley that is outside. The association of Ethan not only with the monuments but also with outside in general is further emphasized by the shots of Ethan inside the cabin. Inside the cabin it is cramped, the ceiling is too low, the space too confined for the presence of Ethan along with the rest of the family in the little living room. The camera angle is from below shoulder height, which emphasizes the closeness of ceiling and walls of the room. There is an inescapable feeling that Ethan does not belong in there, that he literally does not fit in there. What we desire for him, and for ourselves, is that he should return to the outside, that he should go out once again among the buttes, the wide-open spaces, and that we should be able to accompany him there to see what adventures he will encounter. Knowing the logic of westerns, we expect something like that, indeed, we will it. The only question is, what will it take to get him back out there now that he has apparently returned to what there is of his family, of his home. Well, we will see soon enough what will get him back outside, back to the outdoors.

We want him out of the cabin, we will it, and what it will take to get him out will be the destruction of his family and this home—which suggests that we willed that, too. The subtlety with which Ford sets up the complexities of the opening sequence of *The Searchers*, it seems to me, rivals the subtlety and the complexities of a Socratic dialogue. Ford compels us to respond in a specific way, just as Socrates compels his interlocutors to a specific response, by means of an appeal to our own considered and unconsidered commitments. Ford asks us, in the language of film, "Do you want Ethan to leave?" just as Socrates asks Euthyphro, "Is it pious because the gods love it or do the gods love it because it is pious?" They ask in order to show us what our own beliefs and desires commit us to. In addition, Ford compels us to identify with Ethan—not just with his sense of loss, but also with his overwhelming sense of guilt, which will compound his horror of the events that occur and fuel his maniacal determination for vengeance. Just as we, in willing Ethan out of the confines of that house, will the destruction of his family, so does Ethan, in his obvious desire for Martha, (his erotic desire for Martha), subconsciously will to do exactly the things that Scar in fact does do, i.e., destroy Ethan's brother and his brother's children so that he can have Martha, sexually, for himself.[14] He does not really want his brother and his brother's children killed, Martha raped and murdered; and yet, the lineaments of his secret desires are no doubt present. And so must ours be; our wanting Ethan's escape from the confines of that house, from family and community, to some wide-open adventure, make what happens to Ethan's family the lineaments of our desires as well. It is because of this that the scene in which the family is becoming aware of the approaching Comanches, which culminates in Lucy's scream, is so terrifyingly horrible. There is no explicit violence shown, and yet we supply all the violence that the scene could hold, and our complicity in the impending violence, along with our ready, if not eager, reconstruction of it, is the source of the extreme horror that the scene evokes.

When there is a decision to be made about whether to side with the resigned wisdom of Mrs. Jorgensen, who asks Ethan to spare the boys and not seek vengeance, or to side with the vengeful fury of Ethan, we do not hesitate, or if we do, we do not for long. Ethan's emotions at this point are our emotions: guilt, resentment, the desire for revenge. The fact that Ethan will, throughout the course of the movie, repeatedly take these emotions more seriously and base his actions on them more completely than we feel comfortable with will in a sense be the lesson that the movie has to teach us—how to find the place where we will feel comfortable with our own commitments, where we will be at peace with ourselves. The themes of guilt, resentment, and revenge fall clearly within the demesne of Nietzsche, and it is to him that I would now like to turn.

The origins of guilt, resentment, and revenge are quite complicated in the genealogy offered by Nietzsche, but in one relatively clear and brief passage from *On the Genealogy of Morals* Nietzsche ties their origin to suffering:

> For every sufferer instinctively seeks a cause for his suffering; more exactly, an agent; still more specifically, a guilty agent

who is susceptible to suffering—in short, some living thing
upon which he can, on some pretext or other, vent his affects,
actually or in effigy: for the venting of his affects represents the
greatest attempt on the part of suffering to win relief, *anesthesia*—the narcotic he cannot help desiring to deaden pain of any
kind. This alone, I surmise, constitutes the actual physiological
cause of ressentiment, vengefulness, and the like: a desire to
deaden pain by means of affects.[15]

For Nietzsche, resentment and vengefulness are a response to pain. The
most resentful and the most vengeful are those who have experienced the
most pain.

By a Nietzschean analysis, Ethan's real motivation is less viciousness
than sensitivity. His resentment, hence his vengefulness, is an attempt at a
kind of anesthesia because he is too sensitive. He cannot, like most of the
settlers, finally accept and accommodate this violence, this loss, this cruelty in the world. In his pain, he finds one to call guilty, namely Scar, his
own secret Other, and sets out to exact revenge on him. Ethan stands outside of society, in part, because he will not be placated, and to be placated,
to be accepting, is precisely what society demands of us.

Nietzsche speaks explicitly to this inside-outside dichotomy: "One
lives in a community, one enjoys the advantages of a communality..., one
dwells protected, cared for, in peace and trustfulness, without fear of certain injuries and hostile acts to which the man outside, the 'man without
peace,' is exposed... since one has bound and pledged oneself to the community precisely with a view to hostile acts."[16] This description of community is considerably more idyllic than that found in *The Searchers*, but the
basic dichotomy remains. Ethan is "the man without peace." He cannot
live within society because he cannot accept the diminishment of self that
that would require, he will not be placated, and so he cannot live among
those who will be. But he cannot exist completely outside society either in
the very Aristotelian sense that he is a human being. Human beings naturally have a need for human contact and society. We need communal associations for some basic level of satisfaction, hence Ethan's original return
to his brother's homestead. Ethan's guilt derives from his attempt to return
to society, to join his brother and his brother's family as a kind of capitulation to his own need for community, without the recognition or the
acknowledgment of the responsibilities the satisfaction of that need will
require. He attempts to return to society with his whole independent and
violent self intact, and violence immediately follows upon his arrival. The
violence is certainly associated with his arrival, even if only as an expression of his own unconscious desires. Nietzsche's analysis of guilt is that it
is tied to the mnemonics of the punishment that a society will inflict on

those who do violence to it. One way or another there was going to be some violence that came along with Ethan, and, in some sense, he must have known it.

The tension between being a member of society or standing outside of society; of being true to oneself or being true to one's community; between solitude, alienation, and restlessness or conformity and the repression of one's desires and hostilities is a tension that characterizes not only Ethan, but also Nietzsche's conception of the philosopher. It is a tension, clearly, that we must all negotiate, but it is the special job of the philosopher to delineate the landscape of this territory.

For Nietzsche, as well as for Wittgenstein, the philosopher is one who necessarily stands outside of society, but he or she does so for the sake of society.[17] The philosopher must stand outside of society in order to understand the forces that impinge upon us as members of a society, of a community. From inside we do not see; we conform and abide. It is only by going outside that one gets a perspective on what those forces are that demand conformity and abiding. By exempting oneself from those forces in order to examine them, one also exempts oneself from all the advantages of society, of being a member of a community. Philosophy is done for the sake of the community because without someone observing and tracking the unseen forces operating in a society, the society is blind. Without philosophy society moves forward through new situations, new crises, new economic as well as new ethical conditions without any sense of where it is going. The philosopher martyrs his or her communal self upon the altar of the community. The philosopher looks at the unlookable, sees the unseeable, and suffers a terrible suffering in isolation for what he or she has seen in order, in some sense, to spare the community those sights, but also to offer alternative visions to help guide the community.

In many ways, Ethan parallels this Nietzschean (and Wittgensteinian) vision of the philosopher. He repeatedly, within the context of the movie, sees unbearable sights, and protects others from seeing them. His life as a whole is a kind of martyrdom to the full expression of the feeling of outrage toward the violence that is endemic in the lives of all of those members of the community of settlers in the movie. Early in the movie Aaron tells Ethan of all those who have given up. The movie itself is the story of the price those who have chosen to stay must pay to stay—the price not just of sons and families, but also of passive acceptance of violence and repression of their own impulse to respond to violence with violence. Ethan's martyrdom serves to spare the remaining settlers having to give active vent to their outrage, and the resolution of his outrage will offer a kind of paradigm for constructive healing that can serve as an example to the community as a whole. The remaining settlers enact a quieter martyrdom for the sake of those who will come after them, as Mrs. Jorgensen describes in her "Texacans" speech. Those, in turn, enacted a martyrdom for our sakes, we who are here now.

Ethan in a very Nietzschean mode, is a kind of warrior/philosopher spirit. He is the outsider who confronts the even further outsider who is, ultimately, a kind of projection of our own worst self—the guilty Other on to whom we press our own worst outrages. What Ethan (hence we) will have to recognize is that this guilty Other is just like himself (ourselves), is a version of himself. This is the knowledge that he has gone in search of, but it is not knowledge that he particularly wants to own. It is a painful knowledge, and I take it that it is, in part, Ethan's ambivalence about its acquisition that extends his search over such a long period of time. It is knowledge that will muddy the pure, clarified world of vengeance with complexity. This knowledge will have to be forced upon Ethan, he must be compelled to confront it—as will we. This knowledge is really an acknowledgment. It is an acknowledgment of something that has always been right there before us, "in plain view." It is something of which we must be reminded.

The method by which Ford enacts this function of reminding, of compelling this acknowledgment, both within the context of the movie (with respect to Ethan) and outside the movie (with respect to us), one could equally well describe as Wittgensteinian or Nietzschean or Socratic. What is compelling about it ultimately comes from something that is already in us. Ford engages it by making an appeal to those parts of us that he sees but we do not. What Ford sees in us that we do not see is our temptation to over-simplify, our fantasies of pure good and evil, our willingness to identify with the strong over the weak in order to deny our own weakness. He sees those things as well as other parts of us that are in conflict with those, for example, our sense of justice, our sense of honesty, our sympathy for the disenfranchised, our awareness of complex motivations, of other points of view, of our own need to be understood in all of our own contrariness. Ford simultaneously appeals to both sides of these conflicting dispositional attitudes of, say, oversimplifying versus acknowledging complexity, at various moments within the film. These appeals work to prick us like the sting of conscience.

I have already discussed one such situation; our conflicting desires with respect to Ethan upon his return to his brother Aaron's homestead. We desire for Ethan to leave, to continue in the heroic loner mode and not to capitulate to the demands of family, routine farm life, and community. We are immediately confronted, however, with the price of our wishing— the destruction of Ethan's family, the homestead, and all that Ethan returned for—and so we are forced to confront our real complicity and the cost behind what we wish for. Our response is horror, but just as

Ethan does, we pass on the blame. We are not yet ethically educated enough to acknowledge our own complicity, and so we identify even more with Ethan in the hopes of having our own guilt expiated through his search for expiation through vengeance.

This pattern is repeated throughout *The Searchers*. The pattern is that of our being led to identify with Ethan, or another character, then our being confronted with what that identification really entails, what it really commits us to. That is the landscape in which we often lose our way. The predominant theme that this pattern draws attention to in *The Searchers* is the theme of racism. These moments are often fairly subtle. When Charlie McCorry comes courting Laurie he seems so inept at this that we feel a certain compassion and sympathy for him, or at least pity. When he laughs out loud and says, "So he married a squaw! Ha ha ha!," there is some recoil from our growing sympathy for him. We withdraw at this surprisingly racist attitude (which actually seems to be shared by all present except Mrs. Jorgenson), especially as a claim is simultaneously being made on our sympathy and understanding by Look, the "squaw" to whom Charlie is referring.

The scenes with Look appeal to similarly conflicting dispositions in us. We are tempted to be and are amused by Marty's inadvertent marriage to Look, but we are then confronted with the gross mistreatment of Look by both Marty and Ethan. Look is presented as entirely innocent in all of the transactions and as acting in good faith. There is something that is at once amusing and shocking in Marty's kicking her out of bed when she has lain down next him in wifely dutifulness. In case any have missed the poignancy here, perhaps by reading Ford's response into Ethan's response, in the very next scene we find Look inexplicably slaughtered by cavalrymen along with a group of other Indians, mostly women and children. Ford's point about the pervasiveness and the perversity of violence, especially against innocents, cannot be denied.

There is the sting of Laurie's racism when she tells Marty, after her own wedding to Charlie McCorry has been disrupted and Marty is again determined to leave her in pursuit of Debbie, that Martha, Debbie's mother, would have wanted her dead rather than married to an Indian (a remark rendered additionally incoherent by Laurie's own desire to marry Marty, who is part Cherokee). It is a startling insight that we suddenly get into Laurie's character and quite unwelcome. The scene is complicated because we like and identify with Laurie, especially with her frustration with Marty, and would feel sympathetic to nearly any subterfuge she might try to employ to get him to stay, but when the virulence of her racism is suddenly revealed (that Debbie is better dead than with an Indian), it is shocking.

The most striking scene of all of Ford's stinging our conscience occurs between the two situations described earlier. In spite of setbacks, our affection, trust, and identification with Ethan grows throughout the movie until a scene in which his absolute Otherness to us is most forcibly pressed upon us, and our own confusion is echoed by Marty. The scene takes place as part of the story within a story that is retold in Marty's letter to Laurie. After an apparently peaceful trading encounter with some Indians, and Ethan's indulging and amused response to Look, there occurs a scene that, as Marty says, "I ain't got straight yet." There is no getting it straight. Ethan and Marty come upon a herd of buffalo. Our sympathy and identification with Ethan are at their highest. The search seems to have been more clearly focused on Scar and less on killing Debbie, and Ethan has proven himself both knowledgeable and accepting of Indians.

He seems now more than ever before sympathetically heroic—more skilled, knowledgeable, and in control than anyone else in the film. It is at just this point that Ethan seems to go completely crazy, randomly shooting as many buffalo as he possibly can, killing them, as he says, for the sole purpose of depriving any Indians from ever getting them, so that they might starve instead. It is an extremely disturbing scene, and the point is to shock us into acknowledging our own complicity with what we really know to be a madman's vicious quest for vengeance. Our response is, "Don't do that! Don't kill the innocent buffalo!," but of course, that is just what he, and we along with him, have been symbolically doing all along, attempting to make life impossible for, i.e., to kill, the Indians. A reassessment is suddenly called for. After that scene we are much more careful about Ethan, as, indeed, we ought to be. Our care will continue right up to the end of the movie and the ultimate confrontation between Ethan and Debbie. In that confrontation we cannot be sure what Ethan will do. We know what we want him to do, what he needs to do, what he ought to do; but he's crazy with hate for Indians, and he could do anything. It is for this reason that the relief is so palpable when he reaches down and lifts Debbie up into his arms and says, "Let's go home, Debbie."

In *The Searchers*, Ford is confronting us with our own conflicting impulses, especially our impulses toward identifying others as Others, white characters as good versus Indian characters as evil (i.e., with our own racist tendencies). He does this in the very Socratic manner of tempting us to commit ourselves to one position, and then subtly exposing us to the fact that our original simple commitment conflicts in very complex ways with other commitments that we have, e.g., commitments against racism, against dehumanizing others, against random acts of violence, against revenge.

I have suggested that there is something in Ethan which resists finding Scar, that some part of Ethan does not want to confront what Scar means to him—which would account for why the search takes so long (five years) and for why in the end it is not Ethan but Mose who actually finds Scar. When Ethan finally confronts Scar they are presented as standing close and face-to-face; their words even seem to mirror each other's. It is a scene that is as close to a physical enactment of Aristotle's description of two friends perceiving each other, and hence seeing in the other a part of themselves to which they would otherwise be blind, seeing their own reflection in the other, as I can imagine.[18] The irony, however, is that these two people are bitter enemies, which makes the scene a kind of Fordian extension of Aristotle. Where Aristotle describes how we can be made aware of our own goodness as it is reflected in our friend, Ford shows how we might be led to see our own evil through a confrontation with our enemy. The two move into Scar's teepee, his home, and Scar tells a tale of the murder of his family and of the need for vengeance that is virtually identical to Ethan's own story.

It is then that Scar says that for this he has taken many scalps. He has one of his wives (it turns out to be Debbie herself) show them the war lance with five scalps on it. Later, when Marty suspects that Ethan plans to kill Debbie rather than save her and expresses his concern, Ethan tells him that one of the scalps on Scar's war lance was Marty's mother's. Ethan's intent seems to be to incite in Marty the same hatred and desire for vengeance that he feels. It is a puzzling scene—how could Ethan possibly have recognized Marty's mother's scalp—that connects with another puzzling scene earlier in the movie. Very early in the movie Ethan denies that there is any special connection between himself and Marty. "I just found you is all." Here, however, he is able to recognize Marty's mother from a few strands of hair, which suggests a pretty intimate knowledge of her. There is a scene between these two scenes, when Ethan and Marty have been stymied in their search and have returned to the Jorgensons' ranch. Ethan and Marty are getting ready for bed in the bunkroom. They start to argue about whether Marty will continue searching with Ethan or stay behind at the Jorgenson's ranch and take care of what are now Ethan's cattle. Marty insists on continuing with the search and Ethan says, "Marty, there is something I have to tell you. . . ." Marty angrily interrupts him saying he knows what Ethan is going to say, but it is pretty clear that Marty does not know what Ethan was going to say, and neither do we. We never do learn what Ethan was going to say. Clearly it was something to make Marty more willing to stay behind at the ranch. It seems possible that it had something to do with Marty's mother, perhaps even something to do with Ethan and Marty's mother. What it was, though, the movie never says and we will never know.

To return to the scenes that follow the encounter with Scar, there are two scenes involving the mouth of a cave that seems inescapably symbolic. The cave symbolizes, as a womb metaphor, a kind of death/rebirth for Ethan, a return to a more innocent condition after the confrontation with, and then being routed by, Scar and his braves. It also becomes the scene of Ethan's attempt to make a home and a family of his own,[19] a home that is spacious and natural compared to the confined home of his brother, and a family out of the adoption of the part-Indian Marty as his own son, which serves as an acknowledgment not only of Marty as someone valuable to him, but also of his own Indian-like nature. This may be a moment of an even deeper acknowledgment of Marty but again we will never know because Marty will refuse this overture of family by Ethan. It is appropriate that he does so because, although wounded and apparently softened (with respect to Marty) after his confrontation with Scar, Ethan still refuses to acknowledge Debbie as a legitimate relative, as his, which signifies his continuing self-deception and need for revenge. In the end it is Marty and not Ethan who kills Scar. If this were a movie about vengeance then that would be a terrible failure. The fact that Marty kills Scar for relatively good reasons, i.e., in self-defense while rescuing Debbie, saves Ethan from his own worst side, and so allows for Ethan's redemption through an act of mercy and love. Ethan then completes his own savage tragedy by scalping the dead Scar. In this, the final acknowledgment of his own similarity to Scar, this expression of his own raw savagery, he is set free to finally embrace Debbie rather than kill her.[20]

In *The Searchers*, Ethan and Marty traverse a vast and complicated landscape. What prompts them to this traverse, this search, may be a kind of sickness, a kind of madness, but it is an important kind of sickness. How important depends on how far we are willing to go to understand it. Ethan's restlessness and roaming can be read as an analogue for the disquiet that we all feel from time to time about the uncertainty and potential for violence that is in the world, that is in us. The sickness is not the disquiet, but our attempt to ignore it or avoid it by means of a displacement that is really a self-deception. This is what Wittgenstein refers to as the sickness or the madness of philosophy (in the bad sense). The remedy, the way toward a kind of health, the way home, is by coming to know the landscape of the world, to know what to expect from the world, and, more importantly, from ourselves. The problem of coming to know ourselves, our own landscape, is a philosophical problem. We may help ourselves resolve this problem by paying attention to the way, in a movie, that a man learns it his duty to deliver a girl back to her community.

What is it, finally, that makes it possible for Ethan to embrace Debbie rather than try to kill her? It is my contention that the search for her took so long in part because he did not really want to find her. He did not want to find her because he did not know what to do if he did. He was always of two minds, driven by love as much as by hatred, although he himself seemed to be unaware of this conflict. He was himself lost, lost to himself, and so kept losing the trail of Debbie. It is a characteristic of being lost that one does not know how to get home. What got him lost in the first place was an unwillingness to acknowledge certain things about himself, certain feelings he felt, certain commitments he had, certain choices he had made and the consequences of those choices. This refusal of acknowledgment meant that he carried within him a storm of violent conflicts, conflicting emotions, conflicting commitments, conflicting desires. His refusal to acknowledge these conflicts meant that he had no control over them. That is why the violence so inevitably followed in his wake. The specific details of his life that haunt him, that he refuses to acknowledge, are only vaguely suggested in the movie. Perhaps he was once confronted with the choice between a family life (with Martha) and a life of violence (in war) and chose violence. Perhaps he was once actually married to a woman who was part Indian and saw her slaughtered by other Indians. Perhaps Marty is his abandoned son, given up when he gave up on the world of love altogether.

The details, in the end, are not that important. Ethan was a troubled man whose troubles presented him with the necessity of a search. He became a searcher, and followed the search to the bitter end, to the place where his hate had been leading him all along, to the scalping of Scar, the hated Other that was the dark mirror of his own self. Perhaps to his surprise, and certainly to our relief, he finds something other than utter darkness on the other side of this event. He finds in himself a new concern, or perhaps the acknowledgment of an old commitment, and he picks up Debbie and says, "Let's go home, Debbie."

The movie ends with an immensely poignant shot, looking, as in the beginning, from within a dark house (though not the same house), out across the distant dusty landscape at Ethan, once again alone, walking off in that distant direction. There is no question of his becoming one with the community—he won't—but there is also no question that he is not the same man as the one who rode into the dusty farmstead in the opening scene of the movie. He knows he has some genuine commitments to certain people, and he knows, if he ever has to go there, where home is.[21]

2

A The Usual Suspects Moment in Vertigo: The Epistemology of Identity

> —I have to go back into the past once more, just once more. For the last time.
> —Why? Why here?
> —Madeleine died here, Judy.
> —I don't want to go. I'd rather wait here....
> —I need you to be Madeleine for a while. And when it's done we'll both be free.
>
> —Scottie to Judy in *Vertigo*

> I'll get right to the point. I'm smarter than you. I'll find out what I want to know and I'll get it from you whether you like it or not.
>
> —Detective Kujan to Verbal in *The Usual Suspects*

Vertigo and *The Usual Suspects* share a similar epistemological trajectory. Both movies have central characters that are detectives who are confronted with puzzling, even mysterious narratives that they need to figure out. Described in these very general terms the plots of these two movies narrativize a situation that we all find ourselves in with respect to our lives. We are all detectives trying to solve the mystery of the meaning of our lives. Scottie (in *Vertigo*) and detective Kujan (in *The Usual Suspects*) are good detectives, they are good at figuring out puzzling narratives. Part of their strength as detectives derives from their self-confidence, from their conviction that they are good assessors of human motives and human situations. In particular, within the contexts of these two movies, they will be convinced that they know what is going on and how they can control the situations to their own desired ends.

As it will turn out, and in spite of their evident conviction, Scottie and Detective Kujan are both wrong in their assessments of the situations that they are in. I want to suggest that their errors stem from lack of a specific kind of self-knowledge. In short, they do not know who they are and so they do not know what they are doing. The problem is deeper than just an individual error on each of their parts. There is, in fact, a fundamental paradox about identity that makes the kind of self-knowledge that they need (that we need), in order to know what they (we) are doing, quite difficult. I see in *The Usual Suspects* and in *Vertigo* some indications of what the problem is and, at least in *Vertigo*, some suggestions about how the problem might be solved.

There is a moment in Bryan Singer's *The Usual Suspects*, very near the end, when the detective (Chazz Palminteri), after an intense but apparently successful interrogation of the small-time criminal Verbal (Kevin Spacey), notices an odd detail that captures his attention and seems to stick out. It is a piece of paper on the bulletin board behind the office desk upon which he recognizes a word, a name. It is a word that he recognizes from the story that he has so cleverly wrangled out of the apparently naïve and frightened Verbal. Then another word sticks out on the bulletin board that was an important part of Verbal's story; then another and another. Suddenly everything, the whole of the previous narrative, is transformed into something other than what he, Kujan, and we, the audience, had thought it was. When this change of aspect dawns on us, there is an immediate reshuffling of all the scenes of the film; all the values get retrospectively transformed. The experience is a little like that of watching the giant schedule boards in European train stations all of a sudden flip all of their panels to register the scheduling changes as trains arrive or depart.

It is clearly a more complicated switching of values than would be represented by a Wittgensteinian truth table, where the only values are true and false. It is not that all at once true values have become false and vice versa in *The Usual Suspects*. It is that we can find no way to begin to assess anymore what might be true or false. The values themselves have been transformed from the straightforward values of true or false to things impossibly ambiguous, complex, and elusive. The experience of this scene in *The Usual Suspects* is vertiginous. Our experience of the entire movie gets called into question. What have we actually been watching? Was any of it true? Is there any way that we can determine truth at this point, any criterion by which to distinguish the true from the false?

It is a complicated scene, philosophically and cinematographically, in its use of the power of the camera. This unfolding-of-an-aspect scene is created with point of view shots from the perspective of detective Kujan. On the first level, we, as the audience, experience this scene identifying with Kujan, hence, it is as though we were the detective making these discoveries. It is, however, a complicated scene for the character of the detective himself. Detective Kujan is smart. He is a good reader of signs and a good reader of people. He is able to put together the complicated story of what happened on the night of the

fire on the ship from a scattering of misleading pieces. He is also bullying and arrogant and too sure of his own immense superiority to the
apparently feeble Verbal. In these point of view shots we are seeing
through the detective's eyes as he is beginning to see through Verbal's
eyes. His dawning recognition of the origins of Verbal's story through
his ability to recreate Verbal's story from Verbal's perspective in the
room—by looking around and seeing what Verbal saw to create the
story that Verbal has just told him—is going to be radically destabilizing and decentering for detective Kujan. Not only was he duped, but he
was duped by someone by whom he thought he knew he could not be
duped. Presumably his shock would be on the order of the audience's
shock at the discovery in Neil Jordan's *The Crying Game* that Gil is
really a man. Not only is there the shock of the recognition that Verbal
was lying to him the whole time, but there is also the even greater shock
of the recognition that the fact of his shock reveals to him something
about himself.[1] It is a shock that the crippled and apparently harmless
Verbal could turn out to be, in fact, the vicious, bloodthirsty, and brilliant Keyser Söze. It is even more, and a worse sort, of shock to discover
that he, Kujan, is a dupe. Presumably, detective Kujan has believed himself to be a member of the class of brilliant masterminds for whom
others, other peoples' motives and their secret desires, are clearly
revealed. He believes himself to be matching his wits against the mastermind Keyser Söze (who he thinks is Dean Keaton, played by Gabriel
Byrne). In fact, he is one of those whose motives (to prove his intellectual superiority) and secret desires (this deep need for intellectual superiority) are quite evident to a real mastermind, like Keyser Söze, and so
subject to easy manipulation. This is a classic hamartia/hubris story. It is
Kujan's very strength, like Oedipus's, that is also his downfall. He is too
smart and too curious to know the truth to not see and understand the
signs, and all the signs ultimately point to his own guilt. In detective
Kujan's case it is the guilt of being naïve, stupid, and a dupe; of letting
the criminal go because he was outsmarted, and he was outsmarted
because of his arrogance, to which the criminal intentionally played.

This aspect is dawning for us, the audience, as well. The power of the
camera puts us into Kujan's point of view, into his head, just when he is
experiencing a major emotional and cognitive upheaval. We feel the double
shame of Kujan's humiliation and of our own. We did no better than he did
with Verbal's story. Our own arrogance has been on trial, has been played
to; our arrogance about our ability to read movies, to pick up on the
important signs long before the end, has been played to. We have been
duped, however, not so much by Verbal as by Bryan Singer, the movie's
director, who has played us for suckers. There is some pleasure here to be
sure. We like things to turn out to be a little more complicated than we

thought, especially if we get it. There is also, however, some anxiety. There is the question, what have I just been watching for the last two hours?

I do not regard *The Usual Suspects* as a tragedy in the classic sense, or, if it is, it is not detective Kujan that is the tragic character. If there is a tragic character in *The Usual Suspects* it would be Dean Keaton, who seems to be, in some sense, morally and intellectually superior to the other characters, and he dies (perhaps tragically) in the end because he is faced with impossible and conflicting moral choices. In many ways, detective Kujan is something of a fifth business in the movie, a figure necessary to draw out the story, but not really a part of the story at all. He is not a part of the story that we think of as the story. When what we think of as the story turns out not to be the story we think, Kujan becomes more central to the real story to which we now have access. *The Usual Suspects* may not be a classic tragedy, but it does have some of the forms that Aristotle associates with tragedy. I have in mind particularly *anagnorisis* and *peripeteia*, a recognition on the part of the protagonist and a reversal in the plot. For a tragedy to be edifying according to Aristotle, these formal components should lead to the experience of catharsis, the expelling of fear and pity via an experience of fear and pity. I understand the ethical value of the experience of catharsis to be that, after the cathartic experience, one is able to feel fear and pity more appropriately, although Aristotle is a little vague about this.[2]

It is a bit hard to conceive of how there *could* be a classic tragedy anymore, at least in the traditional sense of a story about an aristocratic man who is somehow by nature entitled to greatness and to be king, yet who falls due to cosmic forces of justice. *The Usual Suspects* is especially problematic as a classical tragedy since the most likely candidate for the tragic hero role is an avowed criminal, and in the end we find that there is no clear story or plot. In response to this apparent change in the form I would like to suggest an updating of some of Aristotle's terminology to more accurately reflect our contemporary culture. Instead of "pity and fear" as being the appropriate tragic emotions I would like to suggest the emotions of "anxiety and sympathy." Instead of the catharsis of traditional Greek tragedy, where an emotional purging yields moral clarity, I want to suggest that the more modern trajectory is based on the principle of the catapult, which will hurl us from a position of relative moral clarity to a place where values are ambiguous, complex, and elusive. The modern version that I am proposing is something like: through an increase in anxiety and sympathy with another who initially seems quite Other from us, a more appropriate attitude toward anxiety and sympathy (but not much understanding or clarity) is achieved. What one may begin to understand better are the limitations of one's own abilities to make sense of things—which, I suppose, does not make modern tragedies all that different from ancient Greek tragedies. From this perspective Kujan is also caught in a tragic trajectory, albeit in one that is less dramatic than the one in which Dean Keaton is caught.

Such an understanding can be empowering. There is an appropriate form of anxiety which is anxiety about the reliability of one's own fixed values. There is an appropriate sympathy that can be felt for others different from ourselves. This is empowering in our postmodern, multicultural world because defensive anxiety and the retention of reified values is so disempowering. It can help us to be flexible in a world of shifting values. The failure to feel sympathy for people different from ourselves will increase our feelings of isolation, vulnerability, alienation, and victimization, whereas an increase in sympathy for the (apparently) Other increases the possibilities of communication, understanding, and connection. Certainly there is a kind of systemic power, power granted by the system, for those who willfully hold on to traditional values. But in today's world where the systems themselves change so quickly, that strategy looks less and less indicated. A more genuine power comes from a responsive flexibility in our values and a willingness to be open in our sympathies. The catharsis that we experience will help us to realign our anxieties and sympathies to fit our complex, multicultural world.

There is a moment in Alfred Hitchcock's *Vertigo* that has an impact on the audience similar to the impact of the moment I have been discussing in *The Usual Suspects*, that causes the audience to reshuffle their ideas and values. It is the moment when the camera, in a very rare instance in the movie, takes up the point of view of Judy Barton (Kim Novak) and reveals Judy's own retrospective vision of the story we have just been watching. This moment reveals a very different version of the story from the version that we had been watching. What we see is not just what Judy sees, but what Judy sees in the private theater of her own mind, her recreation of the events of the movie we have been watching—this time from her perspective. What we learn is that there is a whole other narrative to all of the events that we have witnessed. What looked like a romantic/tragic unfolding love affair turns out to have been a manipulative scheme in which Scottie (Jimmy Stewart) is used as a witness to a murder. Another clicking over of the panels on the schedule board occurs. Madeleine was really Judy. Madeleine was never real, was never crazy, was never in the grip of a mysterious suicidal dead woman. It was all just Judy acting, pretending, making a useful dupe out of Scottie. This moment is a difficult one for Judy because of her conflicting emotions about the return of Scottie, but it is radically destabilizing, epistemologically, for us, the audience. Judy already knows all of this, but we had no idea, and so the transformation of all of the previous narrative values only happens for us. In this sense this scene from *Vertigo* is different from the scene in *The Usual Suspects*, but also more complicated.

This moment is purely Hitchcock's. It is a moment that is not in the original novel, *D'entre les Morts* by Boileau and Narcejac. It is also a moment that the people working with Hitchcock advised him against. Hitchcock discusses the movie in some detail in his interviews with Truffaut.[3] His defense for including the scene is explained in terms of his preference for suspense over surprise. The novel utilizes surprise: we find out at the very end that Judy and Madeleine are the same person. Hitchcock wanted to go for suspense, and so revealed this detail much earlier. What is the suspense about? Hitchcock frames his discussion of the suspense he wanted to generate in terms of a mother telling her son this story. Once the identity in the identities of Judy and Madeleine is revealed, says Hitchcock, the son will ask, "What comes next, mommy?... And Stewart doesn't know it, does he? What will he do when he finds out about it?"[4]

I find this account by Hitchcock quite remarkable, especially in light of the movie itself, a movie that I regard as a very adult movie, with very adult themes. First of all, to account for how he has set up the narrative of *Vertigo* in terms of a story that a mother would tell her young son is odd because the story of *Vertigo* would not seem to be a story that one would tell a young boy, especially if one were his mother. Hitchcock himself describes the story as about necrophilia. I find that description somewhat misleading, but certainly not altogether inaccurate. At the very least, there is a deep perversity that pervades the story. As Truffaut remarks, but does not particularly remark on (though it is to me a very remarkable detail), when Scottie saves Madeleine from "drowning" (Judy admits to be an excellent swimmer at the end of the film), he takes her "unconscious" body to his apartment and undresses her (so that, presumably, she can sleep and recover). What we can reconstruct in retrospect is that Judy was not unconscious but was only pretending to be. What we also know in retrospect (not so much at the moment of Judy's flashback memory, but later), is that Scottie is, as Truffaut says, a "maniac."[5] Scottie has a strange erotic obsession with Madeleine, especially with her clothes, as is revealed in the scenes where Scottie tries to recreate Judy as Madeleine by buying her a very specific *tout ensemble*. Now the scene of the erotically obsessed Scottie removing the clothes of the (to him) unconscious Madeleine while the presumably conscious Judy allows this to occur, becomes something, well, I am tempted to say horrendous, but deeply mysterious might be more appropriate.

The story of *Vertigo* is not a story one would tell a child not because it is so bizarrely untrue so much as because it is so strangely true. It is true about an especially bizarre and unspoken aspect of a kind of human love. It is a perverse story because after the revelation of Judy's version, the story is transformed from, turns away from (*perverse* is from the Latin for "to turn away from"), a story of conventional romantic love into a story of unhinged, obsessive manipulations, and not just on the part of Scottie. The acts of Gavin Elster (Tom Helmore) as well as of Judy, who sets Scottie up in this whole business, are equally obsessive. Minimally, what we can say is true in all of this is that it is often the case that in any narrative there is more going on than there at first appears, and that seems to be especially true in actual love relations, and that that is part of what this movie is about.

Of course, children's stories are often more complicated than they initially seem and about things more dark and sexual, as well. I am thinking of Grimm's fairytales and Bruno Bettelheim's reading of them in *The Uses of Enchantment*. Bettelheim's point is that fairy tales are meant, at least in part, to be instructional. They are meant to give information about how things go in this world, about things that the child will begin to experience soon. Many of the stories, according to Bettelheim, pertain to experiences that will occur when a child enters puberty. They are meant to be formative, to contribute to the development of a child's character. They are frequently about transformations, things appearing as one thing one moment and as another thing in another moment—frogs turning into princes and kindly old women turning into witches, beasts becoming men and men becoming beasts. My favorite is Bettelheim's analysis of the frog-prince story in which a small, shriveled, repellent creature, when kissed and stroked by the young princess, is transformed into a large, handsome, proud (one is tempted to say, swollen with pride) prince. It is a useful transformation for which to prepare a soon-to-be-adolescent girl, no doubt. To be instructed in, and so prepared for, the ways things get transformed in the world is to be empowered.

Hitchcock's precocious child asks, "What will he do when he finds out?" This question identifies exactly the source of the suspense that develops after the revelation of Judy's point of view. Suspense, however, is not the only emotion we experience at this point (if it is an emotion at all). Something radical has happened to the whole narrative. As Tania Modleski points out, there has been a dramatic bifurcation of our identification with the characters of the film.[6] Having once seen things from Judy's perspective we continue to do so, but we do not give up our identification with Scottie, although we now perceive him in a strongly qualified way. We look on with a certain amount of horror as he tries to transform Judy into Madeleine (feeling sympathy for Judy, now, and her experience). It is also hard not to prefer the refined and elegant Madeleine to the coarser and less subtle Judy, and so we also want Scottie to be successful in this transformation (feeling sympathy for Scottie and all that he has gone through). We, as it were, now know too much. We are morally in a very complex situation. Part of our suspense must surely be based on a desire to have this ambiguity and complexity resolved for us. We want to see what Scottie will do so that this tension, this insupportable uncertainty, will go away.

Interestingly, when the tension does break—when Judy not only is dressed as Madeleine, but even, finally, has put up her hair into its spiral bun, and presumably they have some kind of normal sex, and Judy is happy and hungry and Scottie, at last, looks relaxed—there yet lingers in the air a strange malaise. This cannot be the solution, and one gets a sense of it even in Scottie's banter, which is slightly off, as though he is slightly disappointed by this apparent victory of his fantasy over reality, as though he too senses that something is missing. This weirdly relaxed state will be, of course, only momentary. The repressed "real" will return soon enough, erupt, really, and Scottie will respond as the true maniac that he is.

Judy, unthinkingly (thinkingly? who knows?), puts on Carlotta's necklace. Scottie sees it in the reflection in the mirror and now experiences what we, the audience, have already experienced: all the panels on the value-schedule board click over. The entire narrative of his experience with Judy/Madeleine he must now recognize as a lie; the truth, however, remains occluded (he does not get as much information as we have). Our sympathies are in an extremely heightened state at this moment. We can understand what this must mean for Scottie, having already experienced it ourselves—and it is not even our narrative, or worse, our fantasy. We are also hypersensitive to what this will mean for Judy. We no longer see her as the beloved Madeleine, but now as the vulnerable lover who will do anything for Scottie's love in return. It is a poignant, fraught moment for everyone. It is a *peripeteia* moment, a turning point in which both of their fates rest on what Scottie does, how Scottie responds. Or, rather, in this more complex version of a tragedy, it is one of several *peripeteia* moments, moments in which all of the future seems to be contained. This moment is not, ultimately, definitive, nothing yet is inevitable. There will be several more moments ahead which can still determine the overall outcome of this narrative, moments in which the responses of both Scottie and of Judy will determine how things will go.

Initially, Scottie acts like a maniac. Only one thing seems to be important to him, not Judy, not Madeleine, but just the intent to get to the bottom of this story, to force Judy to give up the true narrative of what has been going on. He is a maniac in part because, as Dan Flory has argued, he is applying his rationalistic theories to the irrational.[7] He is a maniac in part because his need is so great, his abyss so near at hand. He is a maniac in part because he is so vulnerable. Scottie is frightening in a way that is different now than when he was trying to reconstruct Judy into Madeleine. That was a weird, psychological, conceptual fear. This is a visceral, physical fear that he inspires. He *looks* like a maniac now, and there is no telling what he might do in this condition. The growing fear is registered on Judy's face during the drive back down to the Spanish mission, but there is also concern and worry in her expression. In a crazed, maniacal fury Scottie brutally drags Judy up the tower stairs and recreates the plot on his own (he is an excellent investigator, sensitive to clues, alert to the workings of the deviant mind). After an initial bout, he no longer experiences the vertigo that crippled him earlier in the movie and he makes it to the top of the tower. His vertigo seems to be associated with an *epistemological* condition, one that has been transformed for him by this point.

What was the epistemological condition that contributed to Scottie's vertigo? There are just three scenes in the movie, prior to this final scene, in which the famous vertigo tracking-out/zooming-in shot occurs. The first is during Scottie's failed attempt to catch a fleeing criminal, when he fails to make a leap across two buildings that both the fleeing criminal and another police officer have successfully made. Scottie, hanging from a slightly improbable gutter, experiences his first bout of vertigo while the other police officer falls to his death trying to help Scottie. The second is when Scottie attempts to see whether he can overcome his vertigo in Midge's (Barbara Bel Geddes) apartment by climbing a stepladder. Just when he begins to proclaim confidently that he is cured, his vertigo strikes, and he falls into Midge's arms. Most traumatically, he experiences vertigo in the sequence when he is trying to follow Madeleine up the tower stairs in the final part of Gavin Elster's plan to murder his wife.[8] What narrative can be applied to connect what happens in these three apparently very different scenarios with Scottie's vertigo?

I want to suggest that Scottie's vertigo is a kind of emotional short-circuit that results from an epistemological tension, the tension between what he believes he is doing and what he knows that he is doing, between what he believes he wants to do and what he knows he wants to do. I am using "believes" here to signify that which is his conscious commitment in his actions, what he tells himself that he is doing. I am using "knows" to signify what he is less conscious of (though I do not think it is wholly unconscious), but what he really desires, what he really wants to do. My reading of Scottie's situation is that he does not really want to do what he thinks he wants to do, especially in the role of a police officer, and that he does not really know what he is doing, or, rather, really does know that he is not doing what he wants to do, although he refuses to allow himself to believe that. That ambivalence hinders his leap, and his failure to make the leap that two other men just made compels him to confront the

ambivalence that he does not want to admit to. Vertigo is not the problem, it is the solution. Of course he will feel terrible guilt about all of this.
He will feel guilty about the death of the police officer who tried to save
him, he will feel guilty about his failure to apprehend the criminal of
whom he was in pursuit, he will feel guilty about his own ambivalence
about upholding the law.[9] He will experience a completely debilitating
guilt over the death of Madeleine.

Epistemologically we can say that Scottie does not know what he
knows and does not believe what he believes. What he believes in is the
law and his place in the symbolic network. What he knows is that he does
not fit into his place very well and that he feels ambivalent about the law.
A similar epistemological and emotional confusion would naturally obtain
in his proving to Midge that he is cured of his vertigo. Since, at some level,
he knows that his vertigo is the solution saving him from having to perform his responsibilities as a representative of the law, he does not want to
be cured of it. Of course, there are also some responsibilities toward
Midge that he seems reluctant to perform, and his vertigo supplies a similar escape in that regard as well. There are several suggestions that the law
that Scottie is ambivalent about upholding is not just the law of the police.
Scottie's wearing of a corset, his vulnerability when he falls into Midge's
arms from the footstool, his mysterious incapacity for marriage with
Midge, his identification with Madeleine/Carlotta (having the same
dream), all suggest Scottie's discomfort as a pure or straightforward representative of the masculine figure in the symbolic network. In each case his
vertigo is his magic release from these responsibilities. He can become a
"wanderer," operating in an indeterminate zone that seems to be outside
of time and outside of the usual social laws, where "perversity" will no
longer be an applicable concept.

It is Gavin Elster who first introduces the idea of "wandering" in
the movie. It is a word that he uses to characterize the movements of his
wife, Madeleine. After describing some of his wife's symptoms to Scottie
he says, "And she wanders. God knows where she wanders." It is a
word that Madeleine herself will use and Scottie will adopt to describe
his own activities to Midge. The word "wander" comes from the Old
English *windan*, to wind or twist, which is the central metaphor in the
movie for this in-between zone that exists outside of ordinary tick-tock
time and ordinary social conventions. The twist in Madeleine's hair that
she gets from the portrait of Carlotta is a key, even a fetishistic, detail
for Scottie in his recreation of Madeleine from Judy. The sense of revolv-
ing, of winding around in a circle, characterizes the moments of the
most intense romantic/erotic attachment between Scottie and
Madeleine/Judy, first in the barn at the San Juan Baptista Mission and
again in Judy's apartment after she has been completely remade into

Madeleine (which includes a kind of return to that initial scene of intense erotic connection). Winding or twisting also invokes the phenomenon of vertigo itself, which is from the Latin *vertere*, "to turn," and this aspect of vertigo is especially represented in connection with the opening credits of the movie (and is somewhat ambiguously absent in the zoom/tracking shots used to represent Scottie's experience of vertigo). Vertigo is terrifying, but it is also a seduction, a siren call from the abyss. It is a call to which Scottie has proven himself quite responsive. It is as though what Scottie really wants is to give himself up to the vertigo, and that he comes closest to feeling that complete surrender when he is in Madeleine's passionate embrace. It is the desire to recover that sense of ecstatic release that makes him so ruthless in his determination to remake Judy into the figure of Madeleine. Without that hope, before he found Judy, his life was a kind of hopeless, barren wasteland. He drifted, but did not wander.

From what does Scottie want to be released? From what hold does he want to release his grasp? The first shot of the movie, after the uncanny opening credits, is of a hand grasping a ladder rung. Moments later Scottie will be holding on for dear life to a rain gutter suspended high above a street. We never see him escape from that perilous position and Robin Wood suggests that in some sense he remains suspended there for the entire movie.[10] I would say just the opposite, that the rest of the movie is about his fall. What is it that he was holding on to so desperately that he also so desperately wanted to let go of? To say specifically what Scottie is symbolically holding on to is to be more psychoanalytic than I want to be. Whatever it is it presumably has deep roots in the psyche of Alfred Hitchcock, since this image is repeated in film after film (just a few examples are *Rear Window*, *North by Northwest*, and *To Catch a Thief*). What I do want to suggest is that there is a socially constructed self that all of us hold onto, a self which is in some ways inconsistent with our "real" self, or other parts of our self, yet which we feel compelled to hold on to—terrified into holding on to—for the sake of our social life, for the sake of being socially acceptable, for the sake of our social future. We are holding desperately on to our place in the symbolic social network, and what is required of us to hold on terrifies us, demeans us, and oppresses us. A great seduction for all of us, I think, is the seduction of letting go, of "wandering." We would like to inhabit a space in which we are free of the social expectations and constraints—expectations and constraints that we ourselves have taken part in constructing. The question of where one wanders is a central concern. The sickness in Scotty is revealed not in his wandering, but in where he wanders, the way he is so powerfully compelled to work through a fantasy of love that is so traditional, so falsely romantic, so patriarchal.

It is just such a space, a space in which we can wander, that is created for us by movies. It is at the movies that we get to act out in imagination what we will not and cannot act out in our ordinary public spaces, in our ordinary public lives. Part of the allure of especially the first part of *Vertigo* is the allure of a double wandering. We are wandering with Scottie and Madeleine as we are wandering from our own lives at the movies. Of course, at the movies, at least at the movie *Vertigo*, we are wandering with a genius, since our wanderings are directed by Alfred Hitchcock.

The character of Gavin Elster is similarly complicated. An obvious connection to draw is between Elster and Hitchcock, since both are creators of the story of *Vertigo*, one from inside the film, the other from outside it. Both, similarly, work behind the scenes to construct the story we see and experience. Both seem to have ambivalent feelings about women. Both seem to deeply and profoundly know what we like in a story. The Gavin Elster character is remarkably insightful as a critique of an American type. Gavin Elster is a business magnate, very wealthy and very powerful. He seems to disdain his business and his power and expresses apparently heartfelt sympathy and concern for his wife. In fact, Gavin appears as more or less sympathetic in every scene we see him in in the movie. It is not until we see him pitch his dead wife's body from the top of the bell tower at the mission that we know that he is anything but kind and good. Of course he is, in fact, almost unbelievably evil, diabolical. He is also, clearly, brilliant. In the context of the movie, it is he who constructs the fake Madeleine, an almost irresistible mixture of beauty, death, and mystery, to lure Scottie into his plot. The American type is the apparently nice corporate executive who turns out to be both brilliant in the manipulation of other people and absolutely ruthless and corrupt. Tom Lay, of Enron, comes to mind. It is, in part, to escape from the control and manipulation of such people that we want to wander away to the movies. Of course, as Horkheimer and Adorno have pointed out, wandering away from the apparent social agenda can also be playing into the hands of those who control the social agenda. Scottie's wanderings play into Gavin's plans just as our going to the movies can play into the hands of, in Horkheimer's and Adorno's term, "the culture industry."[11]

There seems to be no way to escape the social agenda, the roles that others would have us play, the roles that others manipulate us into playing. One way to read the movie *Vertigo* is to see it in terms of people who are being forced into roles that they are not really comfortable playing, but from which they can find no escape. Scottie has responded to the social interpellation of the "big Other," (to use the Lacanian form employed by Slavoj Žižek) to the demands that he interprets the big Other as making on him, by becoming an officer for the big Other. The realization of his ego ideal would seem to be for Scottie living up to his nick-name, a reference to his being, as Gavin Elster says, "the hard-headed Scot." It is a nickname that has stuck to Scottie, no doubt, because it is an identity that he so plainly plays up to. He felt the demand that he be the hardheaded Scot before he became that via the signifier of his name. Gavin Elster certainly sees through this pretense. His whole plan depends on his assessment of Scottie's vulnerability to, as it were, wild imaginings. Presumably, it is the anti-Scot part of Scottie that is so attractive to the women in his life, as well. What Midge and Judy see in Scottie is not necessarily what Scottie would have them see. What attracts them is his quite evident vulnerability, the characteristic that Marian Keane, picking up an idea suggested by Stanley Cavell, attrib-utes to the actor Jimmy Stewart; his great ability to convey suffering.[12] These levels of identity are made very explicit within the context of the movie. When Madeleine is in Scottie's apartment (after he has "rescued" her from San Francisco Bay), she hears his official name, John Ferguson, and asks him what people call him. He says, "John. Old friends. Acquaintances call me Scottie." And we know that Midge has some additional nicknames for him, like Johnny-O.

Judy is the character most obviously forced into a role that she comes to despise and feel oppressed by, but she also exemplifies the complexity of our relationship to the roles we inhabit. Without her role as Madeleine she would not have met Scottie, or, even if she had met him, she would not have been able to attract him. Furthermore, when Scottie is dressing her up as Madeleine, and she knows exactly what he is doing, she goes along with it. She does it because she loves him. She does it because she can see that he *needs* her to. This seems to be a central reason for all of us in our trying so hard to fulfill the requirements of the role we inhabit, even though that role can be oppressive to our sense of who we are: because we feel such a strong need (from someone) that we do fulfill these roles.

In *The Sublime Object of Ideology*, Slavoj Žižek talks about the way our identities are formed in relation to the symbolic network, the big Other. The basic idea of Žižek's Lacanian analysis is that we hear, as it were, a call from the big Other to assume a specific identity, a symbolic identity within the symbolic network of society. Sometimes what we are being called to be is clear to us, but at other times the call is unclear and our interpretation of what we are being called to be is more on the order of a guess. In either case, however, what we are called to be necessarily does violence to who we spontaneously feel ourselves to be. To take our place in the symbolic network, to accept as a part of our identity the externally supplied signifier ("teacher," "police officer") is to begin to speak with a voice that is really, in a sense, not our own. We become channelers of the voice of that identity-space we occupy in the symbolic network. It is by means of this experience that we acquire an identity, and this experience is necessarily self-alienating. As Žižek says, "to achieve self-identity, the subject must identify himself with the imaginary other, he must alienate himself—put his identity outside himself, so to speak, into the image of his double."[13] To be a self one must identify oneself with some place in the symbolic network which is, of course, to be, to feel, alienated from one's "real" self (which does not actually exist except via one's role in the symbolic network). To be a self is to feel alienated from oneself. This is the paradox of identity. Scottie's "double" is the hard-headed Scot, the tough police investigator, which will become the very source of his self-alienation.

Part of the illusion involved in accepting this other identity as one's own identity is "the illusion of self as the autonomous agent which is present from the very beginning as the origin of its acts: this imaginary self-experience is for the subject the way to misrecognize his radical dependence on the big Other, on the symbolic order as his decentred cause."[14] His cause is "decentred" because the source of his motivations come from outside him, from the big Other, and not from his own center, not from himself. How does the big Other "cause" our actions? It causes us to act by means of the (more or less vague) expectations that we associate with a specific symbolic place in the symbolic network. We experience the big Other as an interpellation, as a call to be a certain way, to do certain things. Our initial response to this interpellation is, as Žižek says, a "*Che vuoi?*," a "What do you want of me?" We try to interpret the signs that will indicate what is expected of us and then respond to them appropriately with some particular ways of acting.

A way of coming at the epistemological question of how do we know who someone is, or, for that matter, how do we know who we are, is to ask the question, "*for whom* is the subject enacting this role? Which *gaze* is considered when the subject identifies with a certain image?"[15] Health, mental and emotional health, is to recognize that the source of the gaze, the source of the expectations of the other that one feels pressed to live up to, comes from oneself. The obsessional neurotic (i.e., Scottie, and perhaps others of us), however, experiences a gap, experiences the source of the gaze as from another, so that he ends up "experiencing himself as somebody who is enacting a role for the other, his imaginary identification is his 'being-for-the-other.'"[16] The irony here, the irresolvable paradox, is that, in some sense, the obsessional neurotic has a better grasp of a truth about his situation than the "healthy" person. We really are "being-for-the-other," our identities are constructed around a response to the desires of the big Other. What makes this not just epistemologically complicated but a paradox that is irresolvable is that the desires of the

Other around which we construct our identities are, ultimately, an unfathomable abyss.

Why are the desires of the big Other an unfathomable abyss? One reason is because the big Other does not really exist. The big Other is just a group construction around which we organize our identities and desires. Even if, however, we take, say, the desires of the mother as the paradigm of the desires of the big Other, they are still an abyss. Even if the mother knows what her desires are (and, really, she will not), we, in our formative infant condition, will be incapable of fathoming them. In the crucible of our initial experience of love (the love of the infant for its mother) the desires of the other will always be an abyss.

The abyss of the desires of the other, especially when they are of the mother, is terrifying to us. It is terrifying because we feel the demand and the desire to satisfy the desires of the other, but we do not know what the desires are and so have no idea how to satisfy them. This is an especially desperate situation in the case of the infant, who is so dependent upon the mother, and who is so disempowered by the mystery of her desire. The cruel irony of this is that in our maturity, when we are searching for love, for a person to fall in love with, the association of love with the experience of the abyss of the other's desire will become an expectation, so that without the experience of that abyss, love may not be possible. The only thing worse than not finding a person who seems to incorporate this abyss of desire (which will leave us disappointed, unsatisfied, feeling like this is not *real* love) is to find one who does (which will terrorize us with our impotence to understand, never mind satisfy, the desires of the other). This seems to be the trap that Scottie has fallen into. This seems to be precisely the trap that Gavin Elster has set for him: an abyss he can fall in love with in the form of a beautiful woman.

There is a solution—an evasion really—to this problem of the abyss of the desire of the Other. The solution is fantasy. As Žižek says, "The crucial point that must be made here on a theoretical level is that fantasy functions as a construction, as an imaginary scenario filling out the void, the opening of the *desire of the Other*: by giving us a definite answer to the question 'What does the Other want?', it enables us to evade the unbearable dead-lock in which the Other wants something from us, but we are at the same time incapable of translating this desire of the other into a positive interpellation, into a mandate with which to identify."[17] Fantasy constructs a kind of imaginary space in which one's own desires and the desires of the other meet in mutual reciprocal satisfaction. The ideal would seem to be two people who share the same fantasy. That is what seems to happen between Scottie and Madeleine. Madeleine's fantasy becomes, retroactively, Scottie's fantasy. Madeleine's fantasy turns out to be the fantasy that Scottie has always been searching for, but did not realize he had until he first sees

Madeleine. There is a sense, in Scottie's fascinated gaze upon first seeing Madeleine, his seeing her graceful glide through the space of Ernie's restaurant, that whatever Madeleine's fantasy was, that would become Scottie's fantasy. Of course, this is all helped by the fact that the fantasy of Madeleine is actually a constructed fantasy, constructed by the psychological mastermind Gavin Elster. But our fantasies do tend to be constructed by others, and by the big Other, especially, say, at the movies.

The problem with living in a relationship structured around a fantasy is that the fantasy is not real, and reality will inevitably intrude upon the fantasy. This is a problem, but not one without its own secret solution. To pose the problem as a question: is there some kind of knowledge that one can learn about one's own fantasies and about the fantasies of another that *is* based on reality and so can make possible a relationship that is stable *in* reality?

I am arguing that Scottie's vertiginous dilemma is a dilemma of identity, which I take to be the dilemma of how to figure out what one's own identity is and of how to understand one's identity in relation to another. A way of articulating this dilemma of identity is in terms of "voice." When one adopts an identity that has a place in the symbolic network one adopts a voice that is not one's own. We adopt the voice of the teacher or the police officer. The voice is not exactly given to us, so much as we construct it according to our understanding of what we think someone with this symbolic identity should sound like. Our speaking in this voice, when we express ourselves with this voice, will always cause us to feel some alienation, some sense of "This is not my voice." On the other hand, there is no means by which to articulate a counter or authentic voice. To speak is to speak in language, which is the language given us by the big Other.

There is a tension, therefore, between the expression/discovery/construction of one's own voice (which one senses primarily as an absence) and the expression/discovery/construction of the voice in us that responds to the need/desire (always somewhat vague) of the other or the (even vaguer) need/desire of the big Other. Michel Chion provides a fascinating vocabulary for articulating this tension. He speaks of the acousmatic voice, the voice without a body, and of the *acousmêtre*, "a special being, a kind of talking and acting shadow" that is the suggested but unseen body, the body that we would see if we saw the origin of the voice.[18] In cinema, the acousmatic voice is any voice that is not clearly associated with a specific body, the voice-over narrator's voice, the voice in the telephone, the voice from behind the screen (as of the wizard in *The Wizard of Oz*). I am primarily interested in a very special case of this acousmatic voice, namely, the case in which there is a body and the body has a voice, but, for some reason, the voice that is apparently coming from the body is not the voice that genuinely belongs to that body.

Chion discusses a situation like this when he talks about the phenomenon of "playback." Playback is similar to, but different from, dubbing.
In dubbing an actor reads over the lines of the original actor in a scene,
but in a different language (sometimes it is even the same actor rereading
the lines in the different language). Playback, however, is diegetic, it is
somehow part of the story of the movie itself. The voice of the demon
inside Regan in *The Exorcist* is an example of playback. Chion discusses
the example of Syberberg's *Parsifal*, in which another (unseen) person's
operatic voice (seems to) issue from the mouths of the actors we see. As
Chion points out, this version of the acousmatic voice creates the unique
problem for the actor of, as it were, living up to (acting up to) the intensity of the voice issuing from their own mouth. This combination of one
actor with another person's voice suggests, according to Chion, some deep
philosophical issues. "Syberberg's use of playback tells us...that there is
no homogeneity of body and voice, none in any case that the cinema can
show in a way that is real...; there is only a yearning...for unity, and the
cinema can show this yearning. It's even one of the things cinema is best at
telling us about."[19]

I interpret this idea of the "yearning for unity" to be a way of express-
ing the yearning for an integrated identity, the yearning to be, to know,
who one is. A way of describing this yearning is to say that it is a yearning
to have the voice that comes from one's mouth be one's own voice, and to
be able to recognize it as one's own voice. Cinema is a medium that *is*
especially and powerfully able to portray this yearning. Cinema combines
the visual and the audible with the power of the camera to direct our
attention toward very specific details, and the power of the camera to get
very close to a person's face so that their minutest expressions can be
noticed, so that any disparity between the voice and the person can clearly
be registered on film.

A way of framing one of the great themes of cinema is to say that the
plot of many great movies is about the search for the authentic voice, for
the voice that properly belongs to the body. *Citizen Kane*, for example, is
a movie preoccupied with voices, not least of which is the voice of Orson
Welles himself. A way of framing the question might be, do we ever hear
the voice of Charles Foster Kane between "The Union for ever!" and
"Rosebud"? This is to suggest that the search for the authentic voice is
not just a diegetic issue, the quest of the protagonist in the movie, but is
also a problem, a challenge, for the audience as well.

These issues are clearly pervasive in *Vertigo*. Most obviously there is
the question of Judy's voice. As Madeleine, the voice that comes from
Judy's body is Gavin Elster's construction—not just the words but also the
tone and manner. When Judy is Judy, however, it is still not her voice.
When Scottie finds Judy and pursues her to her room in the Empire Hotel,

the Judy that speaks to him is not the real Judy. It is Judy pretending to be the Judy she was when she first moved to San Francisco from Salina, Kansas. The voice that comes from Judy's mouth is not her authentic voice but an imagined reconstruction of her own earlier self. Interestingly, when we do hear Judy's real voice it is a voice of almost pure yearning. It first appears just before Madeleine is about to go up the tower. Madeleine's voice seems to take on a strangely urgent inflection and she says, first, "I love you too...too late...too late..." and then much more cryptically, "It's not fair, it's too late. It wasn't supposed to happen this way, it shouldn't have happened...!" And then, most cryptically of all:

> Madeleine: "You believe that I love you?"
> Scottie: "Yes."
> Madeleine: "And if you love me, you'll know that I loved you and wanted to go on loving you."

Of course, we, just like Scottie, are in no position to know what she is talking about because we do not know that this is really Judy's voice, not Madeleine's. Judy's voice also seems to emerge surreptitiously from behind the pseudo-Judy persona when she says,

> Judy: "Couldn't you like me, just me, the way I am?! When we first started out it was so good! We had fun! And you started on the clothes! I'll wear the darned clothes if you want me to! If you just like me!"

And then when she says a moment later,

> Judy: "The trouble is, I'm gone now. For you. And I can't do anything about it. I want you to love me. If I let you change me, will that do it? If I do what you tell me, will you love me?"

And it emerges at the very end of the movie, when Scottie has forcibly dragged her to the top of the tower. Her real voice, the voice of the Judy that has been through everything in the movie, pleading, begs Scottie to love her as she is, as the Judy she really is. A specter emerges from the shadows. Keane suggests that Judy sees the specter as the shadowy figure she will always be for Scottie, the not-Madeleine that she will always be, and so she leaps from the tower in horror and despair, which Keane frames in terms of a refusal and a declaration that she is not the ghost Scottie would have her be.[20]

After Chion, one could say that that would be the *acousmêtre*, the shadowy being she knows she would become if she were to continue in this relationship with Scottie. All that would remain of her would be a shadowy specter as Scottie relentlessly pursued the elusive voice of

Madeleine within her. In this sense, there is not much difference between her leap and her staying; in either case she dies.

It is, I want to say, a thing that Judy and Scottie have in common that they do not own their own voices. Scottie's own real voice seems to emerge as pure yearning, as well. With Midge, there is always a certain ironic tone, a vague evasion that suggests that he is never really present to her. Midge seems to be the one character in the movie who is close to owning her own voice, although her yearning, her counternarrative to her own words, is clearly indicated through the slightly odd from-above-and-from-her-right closeup shots showing her secret dismay at the discussion of her short engagement to Johnny-O in college.

Midge's role in the movie is a key to gaining some understanding of the depths of Scottie's psychological complexity. Some kind of incipient version of the plot of *Vertigo* seems to have occurred between Johnny-O and Midge when they were in college. The details are sketchy, but we know that they were engaged for a short time and then, for some reason, Midge felt compelled to withdraw from the engagement. The reason was not that she didn't love John; she admits to still loving him. So the reason must have had to do with something about the way Johnny loved her. One possibility is that Johnny-O's love was based on an insistent fantasy projection that made him vaguely maniacal and made Midge, in both self-defense and for the sake of maintaining some kind of relationship with Scottie, bail. She, as it were, felt compelled to leap out of the fantasy space in which Scottie would trap her and define her.

One way to read the uncomfortable scene in which Midge paints her own head and face into the portrait of Carlotta Valdez is to see it as an attempt by Midge to solve the problem of communicating with one's own authentic voice. Midge knows that her authentic voice (of yearning love for Scottie) cannot be heard by Scottie in the abyssal depths of his desire. He will only hear the voice that will fit into his fantasy space of love. I see Midge's self-portrait as her attempt to articulate her longing for Scottie in her own voice using a medium other than words, a medium that Scottie knows is peculiarly hers, the medium of paint. From this perspective, the painting is not, as Tania Modleski says, "a demystificatory act,"[21] but rather precisely a mystifying act, an attempt to inscribe herself into Scottie's fantasy space. It is also an act that expresses a profound yearning.

Midge's frustration with herself after seeing Johnny's reaction to the portrait is based on the fact that she knows that Johnny-O cannot stand to hear (and so cannot stand to see either) this real voice, her real voice. She knows that he cannot stand her real voice, in part, because her real voice will do violence to the fantasy to which he is so committed. It will do violence to his fantasy by its insistence on its status as pure fantasy. He does not want his fantasy seen because he does not want to see his fantasy as a fantasy. She also knows that for her to give voice to her authentic longing is to offer an exchange that she knows that Johnny-O cannot accept, an exchange of a real relationship with a woman for the idealized fantasy. This threatens their fragile relationship (which is based on her respect for and responsiveness to the fragility and tenuousness of the hold that Scottie has on his own identity). She has done what, no doubt, she has sworn to herself not to do; to try to speak to Johnny in her own authentic voice.

For all that, Midge does seem to be the one character in the movie most in control of her own voice. She has made her space for herself in the world (nicely represented by her apartment). She seems to know what her own voice sounds like and to know, for the most part, when and how to use it. She seems to make space for Johnny's authentic voice if he should choose to use it. If there is any hope in the movie, it is held out by Midge. It seems clear that if Scottie ever can find and use his authentic voice, if he can discover who he really is and so be able to accept the reality of another, Midge will be there for him, as she is even when he fails to do that.

Of course, Scottie does not own his own voice. None of the words spoken by the cool, objective, professional investigator Scottie are Scottie's real words, not when he is speaking to Gavin Elster and not even when he is speaking to Madeleine as part of his investigation. In those scenes Scottie is playing a role; it is his interpretation of his place in the symbolic network. It is only after their experience in Muir Woods, by the sea, that Scottie's real voice emerges, similarly full of yearning. (An irony of this scene by the sea, once one is paying attention to the sources of the different voices in a given character, is the complexity in the meaning of the words uttered by Madeleine, "I'm not mad. I'm not mad. And I don't want to die, but there is someone inside me, there's somebody else, and she says I must die...." She seems to be talking about Carlotta Valdez, but, in retrospect, this could be Madeleine talking about Judy, or Judy, acting as Madeleine, talking about Madeleine, or just Judy giving her own meaning to the script she has been given by Gavin Elster.)

The trauma of Madeleine's death seems to convince Scottie of what he must have always suspected (and what Midge already knows, although she momentarily forgets/hopes is not true), that it is useless to try to use one's own voice in this world. It is not clear for how long he remains silent, but we see him, hear him, break his speech-fast when he first finds Judy. Every word he speaks to Judy is raw with yearning, and Judy feels that as plainly as we do.

Judy has the same problem that Scottie has (and Midge has as well), which is the problem of having a space in which to speak with one's own voice. Judy and Midge have come to know something because they have been able to acknowledge something, something that Scottie does not know because there is something that he cannot acknowledge. What both Judy and Midge know is something about what their authentic voice wants to say, and so they can see something about the relationship between their authentic voice and their fantasy space. They have come to know these things through the acknowledgment of their love for Scottie as Scottie, as a man who yearns for a unity with his voice. Both Midge and Judy know what they would say if they could say it. They would say, "Scottie, I love you, in all of your vulnerability. Love me in all of mine!" Scottie does not know, is afraid to admit, what he would say if he could say it, so he does not know who his authentic self might be. Not knowing that, he does not know what he really wants and so cannot genuinely love.

It is Scottie who yearns to fall. He yearns to fall in love, but he does not know what real love is so he does not know how to fall in love. To really fall in love is a way of falling into the discovery of one's own authentic voice, since it is to discover something that one really wants. Scottie is also terrified of falling. He is terrified of the abyss of the desire of the other in which he fears the total loss of his self. Of course, the self that he has so desperately been holding onto is not really *his* self; it is the self conferred upon him by the big Other, with all the rights and responsibilities associated with that conferral, rights and responsibilities that are driving him crazy and alienating him more and more from himself. Neurosis is characterized by the repetition of a pattern of behavior. Scottie repeats the pattern of, at a key moment, refusing authentic love. He tempts others to fall for him in the hopes that he will fall in return, but then he never allows himself to fall. So I guess Robin Wood is right after all. Scottie *is* forever perched on the edge of the precipice, is left clinging to the gutter, caught in the vertiginous desire/fear of falling.

It may be that the experience with Madeleine was so traumatic for him because she fell before he could complete the pattern. He needed to return to the tower with Judy, by this reading, specifically to repeat the appropriate pattern. Judy's fall is a kind of capitulation to the insistent inevitability of Scottie's desire. She falls because she sees that he will insist on it.

Judy and Midge both know what they would say and they know that they cannot say it. This gives them some perspective on the relationship between identity and desire that Scottie cannot get. Žižek, in *The Metastases of Enjoyment*, describes the genuine possibility of love as follows:

> Here we find the inescapable deadlock that defines the position of the loved one: the other sees something in me and wants something from me, but I cannot give him what I do not possess—or, as Lacan puts it, there is no relationship between

what the loved one possesses and what the loving one lacks. The only way for the loved one to escape this deadlock is to stretch out his hand towards the loving one and to 'return love'—that is, to exchange, in a metaphorical gesture, his status as the loved one for the status of the loving one. This reversal designates the point of subjectivization: the object of love changes into the subject the moment it answers the call of love. And it is only by way of this reversal that a genuine love emerges: I am truly in love not when I am simply fascinated by the agalma ["treasure"] in the other, but when I experience the other, the object of love, as frail and lost, as lacking 'it', and my love nonetheless survives this loss.[22]

This is a change that both Judy and Midge have been able to make with respect to Scottie. Knowing something about their own authentic voice (which is a voice of yearning), they understand something about the discrepancy between what one desires and what the other can give. They were each of them the object of love for Scottie (I am speculating on the experience of Midge in college) and were able to see what they could not give and so acknowledge what they could not expect in return. In spite of their understanding that Scottie would not supply the satisfaction of their fantasy desires, they loved him anyway. They loved him for his inability, his lack, his weakness. They loved him *for* his desperate attempt to shape a fantasy space for his desires. Since Scottie never knows enough about himself to know that he cannot fulfill the fantasy desires of either Midge or Madeleine or Judy, he cannot see that they will never satisfy his fantasy desires. The consequence of this is that his fantasy desires go unchecked. He creates a fantasy abyss that is bottomless and into which three women more or less symbolically leap. Two leap to their death, and one, Midge, leaps to a kind of purgatory of suspended friendship.

The climatic *peripeteia*, the dramatic turning point for Scottie and for us, is apparently the moment when Scottie recognizes the necklace that Judy is putting on as the necklace that once belonged to Carlotta Valdez. I say apparently because I think that this is a misrecognition that is based on a repression. The real source of the anxiety for Scottie is when the real Judy starts to talk about her very real hunger for "one of those big beautiful steaks" at Ernie's. My reading is that this is just a little too much reality for Scottie. His fantasy space is in severe jeopardy. The necklace is just the placeholder for this psychological intrusion of the real into his fantasy space. At some level he must know that the woman he has just made love to is the same woman he made love to earlier as Madeleine. (Obviously, I am filling in some ellipses that are suggested but not actually in the plot that we are given.) Judy's very real hunger does violence to his fantasy image of the ethereal Madeleine, and he was going to explode one way or another. It just happened to be the necklace. We, of course, repress this along with him. We *want* him to be sane enough to sustain a real relationship with Judy, even though we may suspect that he cannot.

The lesson of all this seems to be that self-knowledge will mean acknowledging that at one's core there is no positive self, just a sense of absence, a sense of yearning. The self that we construct from this central lack will be a *bricolage*, an assemblage of parts taken from the big Other, from the desires we read in the gaze of others that we try to satisfy, from the fantasies that get constructed for us by the symbolic network, which includes the movies. Emotional and psychological health, by which I really mean philosophical health (having a healthy epistemological perspective), involves recognizing and acknowledging that one's self is just this *bricolage* around this particular vortex of yearning. Versions of obsessional neurosis develop when one has the illusion that one has a core self that is substantive, hence of which one can actually give, and a sense of the yearning as not being one's own, but from some other, represented in the unsatisfied gaze of the unrecognizable other. Once one is convinced that there is a definite thing that one is expected to provide to the big Other, and that one *should* be able to provide it, one is lost. From that perspective misrecognition is inevitable. Interestingly, this is a position of both hubristic, narcissistic overconfidence and a position of perpetual terror and sense of inadequacy. This accounts for the misrecognitions of the two detectives Scottie Ferguson and Agent Kujan. This also gives some insight into the emotional and psychological instability that demanded those misrecognitions.

Both movies, both *The Usual Suspects* and *Vertigo*, end quite darkly. Both end with the suggestion that we will not figure things out in time. Both end with the suggestion that our misrecognitions will doom us to a life of remorse, to a life filled with the sense of missed chances. If these are tales of darkness, can they point us in the direction of some light? Can these movies be read as cautionary tales?

The Usual Suspects is a slighter movie and I do not see much helpful wisdom in it other than to try to avoid being too arrogant, which will be mostly wasted wisdom on both the wise and the arrogant. *Vertigo*, however, is a much more complicated movie. Its darkness is more complicated and its very, very vague suggestion of hope is also more complicated. Its wisdom seems to be a very un-American type of wisdom, and so, to that degree, insofar as it is Americans going to see it, I suppose it is hopeless. Its wisdom seems to be that the primary impediments to the possibility of self-knowledge or of reciprocal and lasting love are a sense of autonomy, of having a substantive identity, of being something. The suggestion seems to be that the stronger position, the acknowledgment of the ultimate substancelessness of our identity, is the one that generally appears to be the much weaker. Even more darkly, the movie seems to suggest that even this stronger position is virtually powerless against the sometimes too powerful illusions of autonomy, positive identity, and of being something. The stronger position involves the ego-deflating acknowledgment that insofar as we are anything, we are nothing particularly original; that our identities are deeply dependent on material from the big Other; and that the sources of our motivations are more externally than internally driven. It is only when we can begin to appreciate that about ourselves that we will be able to see the beauty and the heroism in the struggle of others to try to make their voice their own, and to love them, in their attempt, for their necessary failure.

3

The American Sublime in Fargo

> Aside from those more obvious considerations touching Moby Dick,
> which could not but occasionally awaken in any man's soul some
> alarm, there was another thought, or rather, vague, nameless horror
> concerning him, which at times by its intensity completely overpow-
> ered all the rest; and yet so mystical and well nigh ineffable was it,
> that I almost despair of putting it in a comprehensible form. It was the
> whiteness of the whale that above all things appalled me....
> —Melville, *Moby Dick*

The Sublimity of Whiteness

Fargo begins with a blank field of whiteness. It is an undifferentiated, pervasive blankness, not unlike Anaximander's primordial *apeiron*, meaning,
literally, "the unbounded," from which all things come and to which all
things go, according to some unrecognizable principle of justice. From out
of this whiteness, which will turn out to be a snowstorm, will emerge first
a bird and then a car hauling a trailer. I take this initial blankness to be a
visual trope for the sublime. I read the movie as a whole to be a kind of
commentary on peculiarly American ways of encountering the sublime. I
will call this the American sublime, but that describes more a particular
attitude toward the sublime, a particular way, or ways, even, that the sublime manifests itself because of particular American attitudes about it.

    The bird I interpret to be an omen. It is a bad omen for Jerry
Lundegaard, the driver of the car, but it is a good omen for us, the viewers
of the movie. It is a good omen for us because the fact of an omen—something that calls attention to itself, something that by its very presence
seems to suggest some meaning, which the bird at the beginning of *Fargo*
does seem to do—is an indication that the movie that will follow will
require interpretation, will have meanings to be interpreted, and it is
always a good sign when a movie suggests that about itself early on.

    This idea of an omen invokes another idea that I want to raise, ini-
tially, in relation to the music in this opening sequence. Omens suggest a

mythic context, a situation in which the invisible gods reveal their workings in visible signs. The melody of the opening music (by Carter Burwell) is a theme that will recur throughout the movie, accompanying different scenes with different characters. Modulations in the tone and intensity of the way the theme is played will also function as a sign, a sign indicating something about the internal condition or mood of a character or characters. In the opening sequence, for example, this theme suddenly surges to a level of great intensity as Jerry's car comes over the rise in the highway, suggesting a sense of the largeness, of the heroic proportions of the undertaking on which Jerry has embarked. That initial thundering accompaniment introduces Jerry to us. The music that accompanies Jerry just a few scenes later, after he has been not only humiliated by his father-in-law but also cut out of his own deal, is, by contrast, rather comically delicate and lugubrious. The music signals Jerry's change of mood from feeling like a hero to feeling more like a defeated mouse.

What is amusing here is not the fact that Jerry is beaten down and depressed. His mood seems appropriate to what he has just suffered. What *is* a little bit funny is the disparity between the heroic largeness suggested by the initial music and the pitiful smallness that is in fact Jerry. What we realize later is that that early music was not God's view of Jerry, or the movie's view of Jerry, it was just Jerry's view of Jerry, a view that Jerry himself can only sustain when he is all by himself. In our very first view of Jerry, in his floppy hat and beige parka, he strikes us as a comically unlikely hero. He is not a hero; there is nothing heroic about him except occasionally in his own imagination. As Jerry drives down the highway toward Fargo, North Dakota, and the music surges, we also hear the clanking of the trailer chains. They are a counterpoint to the heroic-sounding music and they signal Jerry's true condition: he is really as imprisoned in his chains (what William Blake calls "mind-forged manacles") as Marley's ghost in Dickens' *A Christmas Carol*.

The opening moments of the movie are, for the audience, not unlike an encounter with the sublime itself. We are confronted with a visual scene—the blank whiteness and the inscrutable bird and car—of which we can make no sense, in which we can find no point of reference, determine no rational order. The scene threatens a certain violence to our imaginative abilities to construe a plausible narrative. We must wait, somewhat passively, and hope that some pattern will emerge. The movie is not just about the sublime, but is sublime in itself, or, at least, has its sublime moments, its sublime aspects, so that it will be teaching about the sublime on two levels, narratively and experientially. The initial encounter with the sublime will be an encounter with something that will not make sense to us and it will be our confusion in the presence of this thing that will provoke our anxiety.

Rob Wilson, no doubt influenced by Melville's whale, describes in his book *American Sublime: The Genealogy of a Poetic Genre*, the American sublime as "Founded in a mythology of detextualized whiteness. [T]he American sublime comprises, on some primary level, the all-too-poetic wish for a phantasmic blank ground, or *tabula rasa*...."[1] In the American fantasy of self-creation, we both long for, and are terrorized by, the fantasy of a clean slate. This is symbolized by whiteness, the whiteness of the whale Moby Dick, the whiteness of the snowstorm in the beginning of *Fargo*. Whiteness is an appropriate symbol because it seems endlessly significant and yet never reveals a final, determinate meaning. The American myth of radical self-transcendence depends on the sense that it is possible to leave one's old self behind to create a new and improved self from scratch. The infinity of possible selves to choose from, or at least the mythic promise of such choices, and the distinct possibility of failure, makes the prospect of having to choose daunting and even terrifying. The dynamics of this kind of encounter with the sublime are outlined in Kant's third Critique in the *Critique of Judgment*, published in 1790.

Kant describes the sublime as a subjective phenomenon that occurs inside us, not outside us in some object (as Kant says, "Sublimity...does not reside in anything of nature, but only in our mind....")[2]. The experience of the sublime itself involves the encounter with some phenomenon, some object, that defies the ability of our imaginative powers of mind to present some delineated idea of the thing. This experience of an inability of our own mind is distressing to us. Kant says, for example, "the feeling of the sublime may appear, as regards its form, to violate purpose in respect of the judgment, to be unsuited to our presentative faculty, and as it were to do violence to the imagination."[3] The experience of the sublime seems to violate our sense of purpose because our encounter with it is an encounter with something that defies by its very nature—its enormity and indeterminacy—all of our notions of what can constitute a purpose. Kant distinguishes a mathematical sublime, in which the cognitive or conceptual faculty of the mind is confounded, and the dynamical sublime in which our desiring faculty is confronted by a force or an object that would overwhelm it. In both cases, however, the basic trajectory of the sublime is that of a confrontation with something that would seem to defeat us, that is therefore terrifying to us, and which yet leads us to realize something about ourselves that shows us that we are not defeated. We realize that we have powers that are immune to the apparent immediate danger of the sublime object. The conclusion of the experience of the sublime is a feeling of aesthetic pleasure.

The pleasure of the sublime is in the discovery of these powers that we possess. It is an *anagnorisis*, in Aristotle's sense, "a change from ignorance to knowledge."[4] This discovery aspect of the sublime might seem to make it a mystical concept. It seems to be a kind of knowledge that depends on one's having had a certain kind of experience which cannot be articulated in any clear way to someone who has not had that type of experience. I take it, however, to be no more mystical than Aristotle's notion of the pleasures of virtuous actions, which are similarly occult to those unfamiliar with the virtuous dispositions themselves. You can only know the pleasure of being generous by being generous, and generosity to the ungenerous will look like a kind of stupidity. That does not make generosity mystical, it just affirms the necessity of a kind of training. Just as we will need training in order to recognize generous actions and so become generous ourselves, we will need training in the sublime in order to be able to recognize the possibilities of increased power imminent in certain kinds of anxiety-provoking situations. Movies can help to teach us this lesson, if we can learn to learn from them.

Harold Bloom, in his essay on the American sublime in *Poetry and Repression*, picks up a passage from late Emerson (1866) that Bloom claims characterizes the American sublime. Bloom quotes Emerson saying, "There may be two or three or four steps, according to the genius of each, but for every seeing soul there are two absorbing facts,—*I and the Abyss*." Bloom then says, "the American sublime equals *I and the Abyss*."[5] I find this a provocative suggestion, and I want to unpack it a bit, especially in light of Kant's account of the sublime, to try to find a way of characterizing the Americanization of the sublime. The problem we are left with after Emerson's and Bloom's reference to the Abyss is to say what this Abyss is. Since, for Kant, the sublime is ultimately a subjective response, i.e., something about us, not something about objects in the world, what characterizes a given experience of the sublime will depend on what we bring to the experience. The question that this raises for me is whether there can be said to be something about us as Americans that would make for a peculiarly American Abyss, and hence a peculiarly American sublime.

I suggest that the features of the American Abyss derive from features of the American myth: the myth of newness, of being traditionless; the myth of moral purity or innocence; the myth of the wild West which is a myth of open spaces, of closeness to nature, of a certain comfort with violence. Another aspect of the American myth, which is also part of the American Abyss, is the myth of the American dream. I take the idea of the American dream to be based on the idea of self-creation, including the idea of the self-made person—one who pulls him- or herself up by their own bootstraps, to be a self-made millionaire before turning thirty, to transcend, by his or her own powers, the limitations of class, prejudice, tradition, and her or his own past. This version of the American sublime is consistent with Kant's analysis of the sublime, both mathematical and dynamical, as an encounter with something that the mind feels attracted to and threatened by and which it cannot completely fathom.

In "The American Scholar," Emerson speaks of an ancient oracular wisdom that says, "All things have two handles: beware of the wrong one."⁶ Whatever the American sublime is it would seem to be one of those things that has two handles. I see the movie *Fargo* as exploring the two ways of grasping the American sublime. *Fargo* explores the two handles of the American sublime by, as it were, pitting against each other two characters that grasp it by its two different handles. I see the character of Jerry Lundegaard as enacting the wrong way to grasp the American sublime and the character of Marge Gunderson as enacting the right way.

In *Fargo* the character of Jerry Lundegaard, played by William H. Macy, seems to have had an encounter with a manifestation of the American sublime. Within the context of the movie the experience is characterized not in terms of terror (the usual term for an encounter with the sublime), but as "trouble." As Jerry says, "I am in a bit of trouble."⁷ He has summoned two men, Carl Showalter (Steve Buscemi) and Gaear Grimsrud (Peter Stormare) to the bar King of Clubs to initiate his plan to get out of trouble. Just what trouble he is in is never made completely clear, although, for all that, it is clear enough: Jerry is failing at the American dream. It remains unclear, however, how clear Jerry's trouble is to Jerry. When one of the men he meets at the bar asks him, "What kind of trouble are you in, Jerry?" Jerry replies, "Well, that's, that's, I'm not gonna go inta, inta—see, I just need money."⁸ It may be that Jerry's trouble is too complicated to explain, or too personal (although it is hard to imagine a problem more personal than having one's wife kidnapped for the ransom money, which is his solution), or it may be that Jerry does not really know what his trouble is. It may be that all he really knows is that he needs money, and he is even wrong about that. Jerry is not good at reading signs, is not good at interpreting situations—especially his own.

Jerry Lundegaard is a salesman. Selling is the underside of the American dream of limitless buying and endless consumption. The desperation of selling is the reality beneath the dream. To fail as a salesman is to fail doubly at the American dream, and Jerry is nothing if not a bad salesman. He has trouble selling anyone anything. Some of the most painful scenes in the movie are of Jerry trying to sell people things: the two men on his plan, the couple the Truecoat undercoating for their new car (which they had already explicitly declined), his father-in-law on his plan for buying a lot, the policewoman Marge on his casual innocence and on his status as a salesman. The moment he begins to try selling something people begin to feel suspicious.

In, I will say, fear and trembling, Jerry has decided to give up selling and to make a play for the American dream by other means. It is at that point that we see him driving through a snowstorm, across the vast open spaces of Minnesota, hauling what he has to offer in exchange for his chance at the American dream, a "Brand-new burnt umber Ciera"[9] that he has stolen from his own car lot. He's heading for Fargo, North Dakota.

I take "Fargo" to be a name for the location where one encounters the sublime; it is more a state of mind than an actual physical location. Like the Chinatown of Roman Polanski's *Chinatown* or Mordor in *The Lord of the Rings*, it is the place that will take you in when you have to go there, but at an extremely high price. Most likely it will simply destroy you. It is the place of the forbidden, at the outskirts of society, which, I believe, is how people in Minneapolis, Minnesota, actually regard Fargo, North Dakota. Not only is Jerry Lundegaard from Minneapolis, but so are the creators of the film, the Coen brothers. For everyone, however, there is presumably a Fargo, a place where children are told not to play and which even adults tend to avoid, unless it is to do things out of sight of the regular members of the town society.

Marge Gunderson is Jerry Lundegaard's opposite in her approach to the American sublime. She exemplifies a peculiarly American kind of healthy-mindedness. She grasps the American Abyss with an unflinching openness that is as undaunted as it is self-reliant. There seems to be no aspect of the sublime that she cannot face, from death and mutilation, to craziness and sexual deviance, to a bag of squirming worms. Her first confrontation with a messy dead body looks problematic since she seems to get sick, but it turns out that the problem is only morning sickness. When it passes, she is ready for breakfast. She is pregnant, and that condition is a kind of objective correlative for the positive potential of encounters with the sublime. Emerson's word for the condition of pregnancy is genius.[10] To come to the sublime in the right way is to come at it with the potential for radical transformation, the potential for radical creative production.

What the sublime will demand of us is an acknowledgment of the limitations of our own powers and a recognition that there are things about the world that we cannot understand. Simone de Beauvoir in *The Ethics of Ambiguity* describes what she calls the "serious man."[11] The serious man takes all values as fixed and certain. Jerry Lundegaard is a serious man, in Beauvoir's sense. He takes values, as well as the world, as ready made, fixed, and determinate. He denies ambiguity. His refusal to acknowledge ambiguity and indeterminacy is a sign of his own lack of self-knowledge. He accepts what Jean-François Lyotard, author of *The Postmodern Condition*, calls "the sublime in capitalist economy,"[12] which is the idea of "infinite wealth or power." He accepts this as a real thing, a thing that he believes he understands and has a right to. He is also terrorized by this idea because he sees his father-in-law as possessing it, but can find no way to get it for himself. Instead of acknowledging the ambiguity and indeterminacy of this idea, Jerry attempts to clutch at it, grasping after what he does not understand. It is not, however, an idea that can be grasped, and he will be destroyed by what he does not understand. Marge is not serious in this way and does not clutch or grasp. She will confront and acknowledge a fundamental indeterminacy.

Marge is the real hero of the movie *Fargo* and I think her character in the movie is meant to have heroic, mythic dimensions, even though she does not seem very heroic or mythic at first. Marge can be seen as a kind of Midwestern and female version of Leopold Bloom from James Joyce's explicitly mythic novel *Ulysses*. *Ulysses*, one of the great novels of the twentieth century, follows the events in a single day in the life of Leopold Bloom. The events of Bloom's day are quite ordinary—he gets up and has breakfast, goes to the bathroom (the outhouse, really), walks around Dublin, goes to a funeral, suspects his wife's fidelity, and finally returns to bed with his wife. All of these scenes, however, are correlated with the events of Homer's epic poem *The Odyssey*, in which Odysseus undergoes many mythic adventures in his attempt to get home to his wife Penelope. In *Ulysses*, Joyce seems to be suggesting that there are mythic contours underlying all of our on-the-surface-ordinary lives. The novel ends with a monologue by Leopold's wife, Molly. From her monologue we learn that Molly affirms her life and her marriage to Leopold, as she says, over and over, "Yes."

Like Leopold, Marge does not make her entrance into the narrative until the narrative is well underway (not until scene nine on my DVD scene list, out of a total of twenty-three scenes). As with Leopold, we first see Marge getting up in the morning and eating breakfast, and, as in *Ulysses*, *Fargo* will end with the character in bed with her spouse. I will suggest that the underlying mythos of Marge's story will be—like that of Leopold Bloom and Odysseus—the problem of how to get back into bed with her spouse and to affirm her marriage. What will make this a narrative will be the many impediments she will have to overcome to achieve that end, with puzzles to solve and things to learn before her final affirming and happy return to bed will be possible. That the Coen brothers may have actually thought of these connections with Homer's *Odyssey* and Joyce's *Ulysses* is given some credence by the fact that two movies after *Fargo* they made *O Brother, Where, Art Thou* which begins with an explicit acknowledgment that it is based on Homer's epic poem, and it is an updating of that poem much like Joyce's *Ulysses* is.

Two major impediments to Marge's final return to bed will be Carl and Gaear. Carl Showalter and Gaear Grimsrud are like emissaries of the American sublime, summoned up by Jerry in his desperation. Like Dante's demons in cantos twenty-two and twenty-three of *The Inferno*, and with similarly peculiar names, they are Nemesis to the humans by whom they are invoked, and, comically, each other's own worst enemy. A strangely troubling scene is the one in which Jerry's kidnapped wife, Jean Lundegaard (Kristin Rudrüd), stumbles wildly through the snow, trying to run away from Carl and Gaear when her hands are tied behind her back and her head is covered in a bag. Showalter bursts into laughter at her, and, I am somewhat horrified to say, I started to laugh too. I take this scene to be emblematic of the human condition from the perspective of the sublime. Her running around blindly is, presumably, what most of what we do would look like to the sublime. We are comic in our struggles, in our blind and constrained attempts at escape.

Read in a Dantean mode, so that what is depicted is viewed as a kind of externalization of her own internal, subjective experience, Jean, like her husband Jerry, is confused and terrorized by the sublime. Read in this way, this scene suggests that she was always stumbling around wildly and blindly in the face of the sublime, driven by fear rather than interest or attraction. She certainly chops vegetables with a manic fury that is frightening. The arrival of Carl and Gaear just make this implicit fact narratively explicit. Insofar as the scene is comic, however, it is comic in the way Dante's *Inferno* is sometimes comic: dangerously comic, seducing us into assuming that we may be superior, only to remind us later of the real horror and terror of the situation (here, it is when we discover that she has been fairly arbitrarily murdered). There is, ultimately, a self-recognition in our laughter and that is made clear when we are reminded of the fatality of the condition.

There is a similar bittersweet comedy in the pitifulness of Jerry's whole plan to have his wife kidnapped in order to get ransom money from his father-in-law, apparently so that he can start his own car-lot business. In some sense, it seems clear that Jerry loves his family and is even doing this for his family, for his wife and son. It bypasses the poignancy of an American tragedy like Arthur Miller's *Death of a Salesman*, however, because instead of a noble, if pitiful, gesture of *self*-sacrifice as occurs in Miller's play, in the movie *Fargo* the father chooses to sacrifice his *wife* for the money instead. The *Fargo* story is both funnier and sadder, since it is so much closer to what people are doing everyday, not literally, perhaps, but at the level of our relationships; we sacrifice them to make more money, ostensibly for the sake of those same relationships. Jerry's reduction to a naked, quivering, terrified wreck at the end of the movie can similarly be read as an exteriorization of his emotional condition throughout the movie. That, presumably, was what it always felt like to be Jerry, and by the end of the movie we can see that that is the case quite plainly. It also seems clear that the source of terror, the incarnation of the sublime in the lives of Jean and Jerry, is Jean's father, Wade Gustafson (Harve Presnell). Wade is even more serious, in Beauvoir's sense, than Jerry, and he will be similarly undone by a confrontation with an indeterminacy that he will insist on seeing determinately, as inferior and weaker than himself.

For me, one of the great challenges of the movie is the character of Marge herself. Initially I found her very compelling and attractive, but also a little bit repellent and even frightening. I found her frightening because of what struck me as the blandness of the life she had chosen for herself. She is obviously very smart and capable, and yet she seems to want nothing more than a good buffet and some conversation about duck stamps. The banality of it was terrifying to me.

Slavoj Žižek, from a psychoanalytic, Lacanian perspective, says, "...we can acquire a sense of the dignity of another's fantasy only by assuming a kind of distance toward our own, by experiencing the ultimate contingency of fantasy as such, by apprehending it as the way everyone, in a manner proper to each, conceals the impasse of his desire. The dignity of a fantasy is its very 'illusionary,' fragile, helpless character."[13] I think this is a very interesting idea. It is impossible not to respect Marge for her dignity, and the challenge is to accept her fantasy as it is for her, even if we cannot share it. This is itself a confrontation with the sublime. It is a confrontation with the arbitrariness of my own fantasy, and so the arbitrariness of everything about me, which is a way of thinking that does violence to my imagination. And yet, that is exactly what the challenge of the sublime, the bearing witness to an indeterminacy, the acknowledgment of ambiguity, requires. This level of subtlety strikes me as quite intentional in *Fargo*. "Fargo," in the end, is not just a word for what is dark and forbidden in America; it also represents a vision of America that is sublimely hopeful and meaningful. It is pointing to powers we possess that we may not yet have discovered. It is a word for a vision of America that is not just sublime, but that transcends the sublime, or, in Emerson's words from "Experience," "a new yet unapproachable America."[14] To see Marge anew, if still unapproachable, will be my final task.

Nature and Tools

> Men suffer all their life long under the foolish superstition that they can be cheated.
>
> —Emerson, "Compensation"

I take the foregoing reading of *Fargo* to be initial. It is initial because there is too much emphasis on being passive and receptive, and not enough emphasis on active doing and making. It could hardly be an *American* sublime if all that is required is a passive receptivity. It is initial because, ultimately, it fails to come to grips with the character of Marge, which is a failure to come to grips with the sublime itself. Insofar as

Marge represents the right way to come at the sublime, if she remains a mystery, then the sublime will remain a mystery. In a sense, we have yet to move much beyond Jerry's strategy for dealing with the sublime. Jerry's strategy is an aleatory one. For him the sublime is fundamentally mysterious. His mind can gain no purchase in it, and so he can devise no strategy better than a wild and improbable gamble with it. It is like fate for him, similarly mysterious and unpredictable, and, consequently, it will be fatal for him and for those whom he loves. Jerry's gamble has about as much chance of success as his playing the Minnesota state lottery, which is another, much more popular, strategy for taking on the sublime (and one with much less severe consequences if it fails than Jerry's strategy, although it is similarly irrational). Of course, such strategies are irrational only if there is a clearly better strategy available. We must go farther than we have so far gone if we are going to take the proper measure of the American sublime, or of the Coens's movie *Fargo*.

I take the great American treatise on the metaphysics of the sublime to be John Dewey's *Experience and Nature*. Dewey himself does not identify the subject of that work as the sublime, but it is a book about the "aleatory" nature of our existence, and about the strategies that we might employ to improve our chances. This is how Dewey describes the human condition: "Man finds himself living in an aleatory world; his existence involves, to put it baldly, a gamble. The world is a scene of risk, it is uncertain, unstable, uncannily unstable. Its dangers are irregular, inconstant, not to be counted upon as to their times and seasons." Dewey concludes, "man fears because he exists in a fearful, an awful world. The world is precarious and perilous."[15] This is an acute description of the initial moment of the sublime. We, as human beings, have lived individually and communally, temporarily and interminably in this moment. This condition is not the experience of the sublime. It is the experience of the world as more terrifying than pleasurable or aesthetic.

That we need not exist interminably in this moment, in this condition, takes a discovery. To make this discovery can be a somewhat arduous and painstaking undertaking, and it will take time. What the discovery is a discovery of is that there is another aspect to nature, to things in nature, that is initially invisible. It will take a certain amount of undergoing, training, practice, discipline in order to be able to perceive this aspect of things in nature, but once one has, nature itself is transformed, and access to the sublime is opened. What makes the invisible aspect of nature visible, what empowers us to be able to work with the invisible in the visible is, Dewey says, the empirical method.

A primary physical manifestation of the empirical method being employed is tools. "The first step away from oppression by immediate things and events was taken when men employed tools and appliances."

Dewey defines a tool as "a thing in which a connection, a sequential bond of nature is embodied."[16] This is an appropriately pregnant definition of a tool. It suggests that our human connection to nature is manifested in our connection to our tools, which are themselves embodiments of connections to nature.

To use a tool is to respond "to things not in their immediate qualities but for the sake of ulterior results. Immediate qualities are dimmed, while those features which are signs, indices of something else, are distinguished."[17] Insofar as anyone has ever used a tool successfully they have worked with the invisible in the visible, the unseen in the seen; they have demonstrated the knowledge of nature as a mixture of the precarious and the predictable.

Given this account of tools, the way a person handles a tool will be a sign of their bond—or lack of bond—with nature. The ability to use tools well will indicate a person's ability to work with the unseen in the seen, with the tendencies of things, as opposed to simply being reactive with the immediately given and seen of things. The way tools are used is certainly significant in the movie *Fargo*. Two scenes will serve to illustrate some differences between Jerry and Marge, revealed in the way they use their tools. Jerry is not a man without a plan, he is just a man with a very bad plan. To say that Jerry has a bad plan is just to say that he is not a good reader of the tendencies of things. He is especially bad at reading the tendencies of people.

A wonderful scene in *Fargo* is the scene in which Jerry, after being outwitted, manipulated, and essentially cheated by his father-in-law and his father-in-law's lawyer—cheated out of his, Jerry's, own admitted-by-all-to-be-good plan to buy a car lot—goes outside and finds his own car completely encrusted in ice. Jerry gets out his ice-scraper and begins to go to work on the windshield of the car. He starts scraping, slowly, numbly, then faster and more furiously, but it is all ineffectual. Finally a kind of madness erupts and he starts beating the windshield of his car with the ice-scraper. This is a man who is out of touch with his tool.

This scene is so wonderful because it completely captures and reveals Jerry's world as he experiences it. It reveals his frustration, his anger, and, most of all, his helplessness with respect to nature, with respect to the manifestations of nature such as the ice on his car or the iciness towards him and his plans in his father-in-law's heart. For Jerry, nature is not sublime; it is terrifying. It is terrifying because he has not discovered how to watch for the tendencies of things, or how to test and verify tendencies in experience once he has detected them. Not understanding this, he does not know how to work with things, how to bring to fruition the latencies that are there in things that require nudgings and coaxings to be drawn out and made actual manifestations. Insofar as he lacks such an understanding of nature,

nature remains purely precarious and aleatory. To go to his father-in-law
for assistance was pure gamble, as is his backup plan of having his wife
kidnapped. There is in Jerry's evident quiet desperation the suggestion that
he does not have much faith that either plan will work. His is not the
excitement of one with a perceived solution, but the gloomy fatalism of one
for whom the workings of the world are fundamentally mysterious.

Presumably, what Jerry aspires to be is to be like his father-in-law,
Wade. It is an ironic aspiration since, as we will see, he already *is* like his
father-in-law. There are tools and there are tools. Jerry's father-in-law has
achieved more mastery over more complicated tools than Jerry has, but he
is not nearly the master he (or Jerry) thinks he is. The tool he thinks he
has mastered is money and the power that money yields, but in this he is
grossly mistaken. Wade believes that the power that money yields is coter-
minus with his will. Money, like all things in nature, however, has its own
logic and tendencies. Wade would certainly seem to understand some of
these with respect to money, but the point or purpose of money remains
opaque to him. An early sign of this is Wade's clear intent to control the
family of his daughter and son-in-law by means of the power of his
money. This is made clear in the dining scene where Wade expresses his
contempt for the leniency granted to his grandson, and his implied threat
to Jerry that "Jean and Scotty never have to worry."[18] —which explicitly
leaves Jerry out of that promise of financial security. Wade's refusal to
help Jerry buy his own lot seems to be really about insuring Wade's own
power and control over the family by keeping Jerry from becoming finan-
cially independent.

Wade uses money as a club to bully people and to aggrandize himself.
These are things that money certainly can do, but other things have their
own tendencies and using money against these tendencies is like using a
hammer to drive in screws: the screws may go in, but the hold will not be
lasting. The negative consequences of Wade's bullying Jerry are to drive
Jerry to go to desperate lengths to try to recover some self-control and
self-respect. Wade's bullying is, in some sense, what compels Jerry to come
up with his bizarre alternative plan of having his wife kidnapped in order
to get some financial autonomy from Wade (ironically, with Wade's own
money). The consequences of this plan will be as bad for Wade as they
will be for Jerry, if not worse.

Wade's misconceptions about the power of money are made clear in a
much less subtle way later in the movie when he insists on making the
ransom exchange with the kidnappers himself. Wade thinks he is just
going up against a couple of petty hoodlums. He thinks the power of his
money will enable him to take control of the situation and bully the kidnappers the way he does his son-in-law, Jerry. What Wade does not know
is that what he is really going up against is the "perilous and precarious"

in nature. Of course, he has always been going up against this, and his money has been a pretty good hedge against it, but it is not the bulwark he thinks it is, and there is not much that money can do when the "perilous and the precarious" really come calling.

The encounter with the kidnapper Carl Showalter is a potential encounter with the sublime for Wade. It is an encounter with the initial moments of the sublime, but it will never achieve its fruition in true sublimity because Wade will be shot down before that fruition can be realized. Emboldened by a false sense of his own power, wielding a gun (a tool he is ill-equipped to use), having misread the real tendencies and powers of money as well as misreading the tendencies of a desperate criminal (who will behave quite differently, although, ultimately, not that differently, from his son-in-law, whom Wade has also misread), Wade will make of a potential encounter with the sublime a tragedy. Ultimately, Wade knows no more about money than Jerry does about his ice scraper, and he uses his money as ineffectually. A situation which, if well handled, would potentially bring reconciliation and reconnection with his family (a situation which is really a replaying of his previous relationship with Jerry and his family), yields instead death and tragedy. Wade believes that the best use of money is to hold onto it and to threaten people by withholding it. That is not the best use of money, and everyone suffers from his ignorance. Wade's tragedy has this similarity to a classic Greek tragedy: The very thing that made him so successful with money will also be his downfall (his *hamartia*, or tragic flaw). His apparent strength, a certain arrogance and conviction about what the power of money is, is also the place of his greatest ignorance. The Greeks called this *hubris*.

In striking contrast to Jerry and Wade is Marge. Her most striking use of a tool is the use of her gun near the end of the movie. Shane's line, in the movie *Shane*, that "a gun is just a tool,...as good or as bad as the man [sic] who holds it" expresses a very Deweyan sentiment, and Shane himself will be revealed as what he is by his use of his gun, how he uses this tool. He will be revealed to be what he is, a gunfighter, a shootist, and a killer. What Marge is will be similarly revealed through her use of her gun.

After finally tracking down Grimsrud and coming upon him as he is feeding the last of his partner, Carl Showalter, into the wood chipper (Grimsrud as the purest representative in the movie of the sublimity of nature dis-integrating the unified whole, the temporary integrity, of Carl— what nature will do to us all), Marge attempts to arrest him. Grimsrud resists; he throws a log at her and then runs. She orders him to halt, draws her pistol, orders him to halt, fires a warning shot, orders him to halt, fires at him but misses, fires again, and hits him in the leg, which brings him down. Holding her gun on him, she approaches him as he lies face down in the snow. She puts handcuffs on him and takes him to the police cruiser.

Not only is Marge an expert, even an amazing, markswoman with a pistol—bringing down a running man by shooting him in the leg at fifty feet or more—but she uses her gun non-fatally to arrest a vicious killer. In her hands the gun really is a "peacemaker." We are fearful for her being up against this psychotic killer and we are amazed, at least I was, at the apparent aplomb and self-control she demonstrates in doing it. We are amazed because we would be so afraid. She is not afraid, or not so afraid, presumably because she knows things, understands things, that we do not. She knows about the tendencies of this man, and of criminals in general. She knows about her own tools, her authority as a chief of police and her gun. She knows the cold and the deep snow and how fast and how far a man can run under such conditions. And she knows her own skill and that she can shoot a man if she has to, in the leg, while he is running, if she has to. She knows, in short, how to work this situation, how to work with the tendencies of the things in the situation, in order to have the situation yield the outcome she desires: the apprehension of this killer. And that is what she does.

The tool of tools, for Dewey, is language, and, again, it is in the use of the tool that character is revealed. Jerry's use of language is halting, hapless, and unpersuasive. In language as in other things, Jerry seems to aspire to be like his father-in-law. He attempts to speak with an authority that commands peoples' submission, to bend people to his will with his words, and he always fails miserably. It is as though Jerry thought that if he had some of Wade's money he could command some of Wade's authority with words. This is a terrible misreading of that from which genuine authority issues, and of how to get it. The only authentic communication Jerry is really seen engaging in in the course of the movie is when he whispers fearfully to his wife about whether her father, Wade, is staying for dinner. In that brief transaction we see Jerry openly anxious, openly sharing his anxiety with his wife, who seems to recognize his anxiety but is helpless to be very reassuring in the shadow of the presence of her father.

Marge, on the other hand and somewhat ironically, has a wonderful way with words. I say somewhat ironically because her language initially strikes one as being a bit limited. Her words are folksy, idiomatic, and she speaks with a decisively Midwestern accent. But once one gets used to her manner of speaking, once one begins to recognize her aptitude, her fluency with this tool, one's attitude toward her language, and toward her, begins to change. Not only does she use words remarkably effectively, but there is not an inconsiderable amount of poetry in her speech. Her effectiveness in using language is shown in her ability both to extract important information from others and to give information, while simultaneously being reassuring, understanding, supportive, and considerate. The poetry comes in the way she speaks.

A telling scene that illustrates Marge's use of language comes early on in Marge's investigation of the first murders, when Marge is talking with one of the other Brainerd police officers, Lou. Marge is driving; Lou sits next to her.

> Marge: You look in his citation book?
> Lou: Yah...
> Lou:...Last vehicle he wrote in was a tan Ciera at 2:18 a.m.
>   Under the plate number he put DLR—I figure they
>   stopped him or shot him before he could finish fillin'
>   out the tag number.
> Marge: Uh-huh.
> Lou: So I got the state lookin' for a Ciera with a tag startin'
>   DLR. They don't got no match yet.
> Marge: I'm not sure I agree with you a hunnert percent on
>   your policework, there, Lou.
> Lou: Yah?
> Marge: Yah, I think that vehicle there probly had dealer plates.
> DLR?
> Lou: Oh...
> Lou: ...Geez.
> Marge: Yah. Say, Lou, ya hear the one about the guy who
>   couldn't afford personalized plates, so he went and changed his
>   name to J2L 4685?
> Lou: Yah, that's a good one.
> Marge: Yah.[19]

Part of what makes this sequence of dialogue so wonderful in the movie is just Frances McDormand's way of saying the lines. She says them with a lilting, rolling cadence that has a real flow to it that is wonderful to hear. "I'm not sure I agree with you a hunnert percent on your policework, there, Lou," with the "there" there just for the rhythm of it. The scene carries more than just the pleasing sound, however; here Marge enacts with Lou what she will later do with Grimsrud. She has arrested and redirected a negative or harmful movement in the gentlest, most considerate and caring way possible. Marge just does see more of what is going on than most other people. She uses language to get information and connect with people, but also to help empower people to see things more clearly themselves.

Both Wade and Jerry must already have more money than Marge and her husband Norm have, but their lives are still much less secure than Marge's and Norm's lives are. When Ralph Waldo Emerson, a precursor to and an influence on Dewey, said, "Men suffer all their life long under the foolish superstition that they can be cheated"[20] he must have had some particular men, or people, in mind. Certainly some people are cheated. Emerson was writing in a time when slavery was an American "institution" and women could not vote. People are cheated. Yet just as people are cheated, not all people think of themselves as being cheated, or as cheatable, and so do not suffer under the superstition that they can be cheated. Just as certainly there are people who labor their lives long under the weight of the suspicion that someone is going to cheat them, or that they are in fact being cheated every day. The only truth to this suspicion is that by the very suspicion itself they are cheating themselves every day.

In his essay, "Nature," Emerson says, "property, which has been well compared to snow,—'if it fall level to-day, it will be blown into drifts to-morrow,'—is the surface action of internal machinery, like the index on the face of a clock."[21] Property compared to snow gives a new and even more particular resonance to the opening of *Fargo*, which begins in a snowstorm (as well as to the pervasive presence of snow throughout the film). One might say that the particular form of the initial moment of the American sublime in which Jerry is lost, by which he is terrified, is that one concealed under the surface of property. Following the example of Wade, Jerry has put all of his faith in the putative powers of property. But the actual objects of property, the car, the lot, the big-screen television, are just the surface manifestations of currents and powers that remain unseen, and which have a logic of their own. To be the real master of property one must understand these undercurrents and the directions toward which they will tend. To attempt to "own" property in the absence of such knowledge is to dive into an abyss that will appear to be purely chaotic, which is exactly what Jerry does in *Fargo*.

What laws govern the logic of property I cannot claim to know myself, but there is a hint of what they may be in Emerson's critique of Napoleon, whom Emerson dubs "the man of the world." After praising Napoleon for his strengths, Emerson turns to Napoleon's great weakness. In the concluding paragraph of the essay Emerson says, "It was the nature of things, the eternal law of man and of the world which baulked and ruined him; and the result in a million experiments will be the same. Every experiment, by multitudes or by individuals, that has a sensual and a self-ish aim, will fail.... As long as our civilization is essentially one of property, of fences, of exclusiveness, it will be mocked by delusions.... Only that good profits which we can taste with all the doors open, and which serves all men."[22] I interpret Emerson's suggestion here to be that property sought or held with selfish aims will not, in the long run, avail. The corollary to this would seem to be that property is well used when used for the good of others, generously and inclusively. Emerson's critique is not so much of property *simpliciter*, but of regarding property as an end. He says, speaking critically, "our civilization is essentially one of property," and I take this to be his critique of the American dream generally. The appropriate attitude to have toward property is to see it as a means to other goals, a potentially powerful means, but merely a means, of little inherent value by itself. The transformation of the chaotic and terrifying undercurrents of property into something tractable and satisfying is something neither Jerry nor Wade can effect.

To be able to do this is part of the American sublime, the transformation of the potentially awful and terrifying into the satisfying and useful for some future purpose. It is the transformation of the horrible into the aesthetic. It is a description of this transformation that pervades the classics of American philosophy, in the works of Thoreau and Emerson, James and Dewey. It is profoundly futural, and so revolutionary, coming out of America's severance with its own past by means of its own revolution. It is a transformation that is like a pregnancy, an immediate appreciation that is also fraught with future possibilities.

What Jerry Needs

> ...philosophy is inherently criticism, having its distinctive position among various modes of criticism in its generality; a criticism of criticisms, as it were.
>
> —Dewey, *Experience and Nature*

What Jerry was lacking, what Jerry really needed, was not more money or more property but more philosophy. That goes for his wife, his son, and his father-in-law as well. Every activity, to be done well, requires criticism, some process by which errors can be corrected and performance improved. Criticism is essentially a measure of how well one is using one's tools, whether or not one is reading the tendencies of things rightly and using one's tools to their best effect given those tendencies. For every activity there are appropriate criticisms, and, within the public space, you can get a sense of this by looking, for example, at the *New York Times*. For business criticisms look to the business section, for art criticisms look to the arts and leisure section, for political criticisms look to the first section.

As important as such criticisms as these are, they are limited by the scope of the enterprise they are criticizing. They give no metaperspective for the activities they are criticizing. Business criticism is important for understanding how to improve the efficiency of one's business, but it does not provide any help with the problem of what one should do with an efficient business. Wade has a lot that he could teach Jerry about how to make money, but what he does not know about is what to do with the money he has made. What is needed is a criticism of criticisms. What is needed is philosophy.

When Dewey speaks of philosophy he does not mean what it is generally taken to mean in most academic circles, i.e., the abstruse reasoning about first principles or final ends. Rather he means an idea of philosophy that is consistent with his idea of empirical method and an open, questing attitude. Dewey takes the proper task of philosophy to be "liberating and clarifying meanings."[23] Meanings are imprisoned and occluded by routine, convention, social norms, cultural practices, traditional assumptions, and by habits in general. Meanings are liberated and clarified when someone is able to step out of their habitual ways of experiencing things in order to see things in new ways, from a new perspective, so that the unseen tendencies in things and situations will be revealed.

Science is best suited to the criticism of meanings that are true and false, but there are meanings that do not resolve themselves into propositions that can be judged true or false. As Dewey says, "Poetic meanings, moral meanings, a large part of the goods of life are matters of richness and freedom of meanings, rather than of truth." Here is where the work of philosophy comes in. It is at this level that philosophy as the liberating and clarifying of meanings becomes coextensive with "social reform."[24] Social reform, like individual reform, is a matter of learning to see the possibilities in things that are not immediately apparent. It is a matter of the expansion of meanings.

Dewey's conception of philosophy, like his conceptions of experience and of art, is profoundly democratic. He is consistently critical of any notion of philosophy (or of art or of experience) that puts it out of the reach of virtually anyone. Philosophy "has no stock of information or body of knowledge peculiarly its own.... Its business is to accept and utilize for a purpose the best available knowledge of its own time and place. And its purpose is criticism of beliefs, institutions, customs, policies with respect to their bearing upon good."[25] Not *the* good—as Dewey makes clear, it has no special access to that—but good insofar as intelligence and experience can understand. By this account of philosophy, workers talking over lunch about the corporation they work for, its proper ends and improper, are talking philosophy. Neighbors talking about improvements to their community are talking philosophy. Families talking amongst themselves about how to decide how best to spend a summer vacation for the best outcome for all are talking philosophy. Jerry's problem was that he had no one with whom to talk philosophy, no one with whom to compare ends and strategies. He had no one to whom he could tell his plan, and so no one who would ask him if there were not more important things in the world to do than risk his whole family for a car lot.

Dewey distinguishes the merely aesthetic from the artistic. "Both involve a perception of meanings in which the instrumental and the consummatory peculiarly intersect," but "in the esthetic object tendencies are sensed as brought to fruition," i.e., we sense them having been brought to fruition already, whereas the "artistic sense...grasps tendencies as possibilities; the invitation of these possibilities to perception is more urgent and compelling than that of the given already achieved."[26] The merely aesthetic yields a sense of satisfaction at the perception of a tendency brought to an apparent fruition, but art has an urgency because one senses the potential for a fruition suggested by the art, a fruition not yet *fully* realized. The fruition will depend in part on our continued interaction with the artwork, and with our own lives, to realize the potentialities contained in the artwork.

Dewey offers this definition of art: "Art in being the active productive process, may thus be defined as an esthetic perception together with an *operative* perception of the efficiencies of the esthetic object."[27] In viewing an artwork (or listening to an artwork, or, I suppose, dancing an artwork), one perceives in the artwork the very process that Dewey has been describing as the experimental method in experience being enacted. That is, in the artwork tendencies of things are identified and worked with to reveal trajectories that will themselves reveal future possibilities.

This is an excellent description of the Coen brothers' movie *Fargo*. *Fargo* is all about revealing the hidden tendencies in things, in people, and in situations. Watching the movie *Fargo* yields both immediate pleasures and future possibilities for greater wisdom and understanding. Certainly it functions as social critique, as well as reflective analysis on the human stories it narrates—which is to say that it is philosophical. These issues themselves are somewhat hidden in the narrative itself, so that they need drawing out, they require discovery. For the movie to really be philosophical it has to be discussed philosophically, but the materials for a philosophical discussion are replete within the movie itself, if we but have the eyes to see them. Initially, the movie might strike one as being rather horrifying. It is, after all, about terrible things—murder, desperation, a family subject to terrible, if not exactly arbitrary, physical and emotional violence. But the horror and the terror need only be an initial, if necessary, stage in our experience of the film. If we reflect on the film after watching it, if we open ourselves to the lessons that it has to teach us, if we actively study the film, being selective and directive in our investigation of the film, and, most important of all, if we talk about the film with others and about what we think we may have found there, the film itself can be transformed from something horrible and terrifying into something edifying and empowering. The film itself can become another example of the American sublime.

How to Sublime: Marge

> The world of the happy man is a different world from that of the unhappy man.
> —Ludwig Wittgenstein, *Tractatus Logico-Philosophicus*

Perhaps the most sublime experience of all is the abyss of other people. Marge's abyss is not just American; it seems to be a peculiarly Midwestern, Minnesota abyss. One way to characterize this is Marge's insistence on a kind of outward cheerfulness, even when what she is doing or feeling may not be cheerful at all. There is something unsettling in that. Another indication of this abyss is Marge's immense appetite. A scene that is quite revealing on several levels, is the scene at a buffet. There is an awkwardness in this scene that I think is quite suggestive. First of all, simply the huge portions Marge serves herself are discomforting. Then, when Marge announces her plans to go to Minneapolis, her husband Norm (John Carroll) seems surprised and Marge herself seems evasive, staring down into her food. Of course, when she goes to Minneapolis it turns out she makes a date to meet with Mike Yanagita (Steve Parker) at the Minneapolis Radisson, which is what I am guessing she is being evasive about at the buffet. The buffet scene seems to be open to several levels of interpretation. Now Marge's appetite seems less healthy and robust and more of an attempt to fill an emptiness that she feels in her life with food. This new suspicion about her can reflect back to our first images of her, when a peculiar look is registered on her face as she sits on the edge of her bed, as Norm gets up to make her breakfast and hacks and coughs. We start to get a whole new read on Marge. As gentle and sweet as Norm is, he also seems a little boring, and maybe she is thinking that too, although you would never be able to tell from her explicit external behavior.

I have tried to suggest that Marge is deeper than she originally seems. Initially I mean by that that she is more unhappy, more complex, has more issues going on with her than is readily apparent from her external ways of acting. At first Marge seems more or less impervious to the sublime. As I have suggested, grisly murders, prostitution, and bugs do not seem to phase her. Through it all she seems to remain quite cheerful. I have also suggested that she is in denial about some things and is refusing to admit even to herself her own suspicions and doubts. It is this denial that will lead her to miss the signals clearly sent out by Jerry Lundegaard in her first interview with him. These doubts will lead her to call Mike to arrange to meet with him. I believe she thinks this meeting is innocent, although it is the only time in the movie we see her in make-up and feminine clothes. She even touches her hair before going in to meet him.

The pivotal scene of Marge confronting the sublime, of her figuring out *how* to sublime, occurs just after the scene with Mike, when she learns that Mike is not who he said he was. "Oh, geez. That's a surprise!" she says, and I think she is more surprised by her own response to this news about Mike than she is to the news itself. I think that for the first time in the movie Marge is really confronted with the sublime, the fact of an indeterminacy that she had thought was clear and determinate. She is so surprised because of her own denial about what she was looking at and looking for. After this revelation she has to do some processing. She has to do some philosophy. She thinks, she eats some Hardees, she thinks a little more, and suddenly something is registered on her face. She goes back to see Jerry Lundegaard, this time meaning business.

What she is doing in those intervals is what Cavell calls, "subliming."[28] She is confronting this indeterminacy, tracing its outlines as far as she can. It is not only Mike who has turned out to be other than he appeared, but *she* is other than she thought she was. She eats because she is anxious. She is anxious because she feels herself to be lost, incomplete, out of control. An aspect of the world has suddenly opened up to her that she had not seen coming. What happens to her at that moment is a shift in perspective. The trajectory of this shift in perspective is one from feeling lost and helpless in the face of the unfathomable to suddenly being aware with great clarity who one is and what there is for one to do. What makes this shift of perspective possible is a sudden detachment from that which is so anxiety provoking, which is a detachment from one's own fear, which is a detachment from oneself. Paradoxically, sometimes it is only upon becoming detached from oneself that one can come to understand who one is and what there is for one to do. With respect to Marge, she may not be able to figure out the strangeness of the world, and Mike's craziness may remain unfathomable, but now that she is prepared to see the strangeness she can see the strangeness in the earlier behavior of Jerry Lundegaard, the car salesman. She still has her job to do, her, if you will, vocation, and now she can see more clearly than before how she has to do it.

This invocation of her vocation brings us back to Kant's conception of the sublime. Kant says, "our imagination, even when taxing itself to the utmost on the score of this required comprehension...betrays its limits and inadequacy, but still, at the same time, it exhibits its proper *vocation* of making itself adequate to the same as law. Therefore, the feeling of the sublime in nature is respect for our own *vocation....*" [my emphases].[29] What the sublime reveals to us, what it has revealed to Marge, is something about our, her, own vocation in the world. Our proper vocation, according to Kant, is to respond to the world rationally, i.e., according to law. In her encounter with the sublime Marge is reapprised of her vocation, which, being a police officer, applies to her doubly. This is not something that simply happened to her, but something she has also done. She has looked into the heart of her own abyss, which is also the abyss of the world. She has strained to discern its bottom and has found it bottomless as far as she can tell. But in this straining she has come upon something that is not bottomless, something about herself, something about what she has to do. And she goes and does it.

This is subliming. Subliming begins with a confrontation with radical doubt, with uncertainty and the acknowledgment of indeterminacy. There is a heroic attempt to make sense of this indeterminacy. Finally there is a shift in perspective, a detachment from one's current perspective, which begins to open up a sense of another possible perspective. Into the vacuum created by giving up the commitment to that first perspective flows a new sense of what remains for one to do as part of one's new perspective. You realize you have another purpose, another vocation, than making sense of the unfathomable. The world may remain mysterious, but a sense of order in one's own life becomes overwhelmingly present to you and that feeling is deeply pleasurable. That feeling is the feeling of the sublime.

The sublime, as I understand it, will inevitably end in a sense of beauty, a sense of the world as beautiful. That which had seemed so ominous and threatening earlier has been transformed into an object that has provided an opportunity for me to realize something about myself, about my own powers and my own purpose in the world. Once the world no longer appears as threatening our mood has changed. We feel once again in control of our own lives and from that perspective the world reveals itself as beautiful. We already have achieved the detachment, the disinterest, and now the frightening specter has been recognized as harmless, which leaves us with the aesthetic pleasure of beauty. Marge, like all of us, had a natural propensity for seeing the world as beautiful, although her confidence in that perspective was shaken. In the end, she recovers that perspective and the world is once again beautiful to her.

After her encounter with the sublime, with her sense of her natural powers restored, Marge solves the case and once again reigns in the forces of the sublime, specifically and literally by arresting Gaear Grimsrud. He, and the sublime itself, may remain a puzzle to her, but it is a puzzle that she can let go of because she has other things to do. On an overcast day in the middle of a Minnesota winter, a day in which Marge has just witnessed a man feeding another man into a wood chipper she says, "There's more to life than money, you know.... Don't you know that? ... And here ya are, and it's a beautiful day.... " And I think she really means it.

The experience of the sublime is really a transitional experience. It is what lifts us up out of our anxiety and confusion. The real wisdom is not so much in the sublime as on the other side of the sublime. It is to see the ordinary world as extraordinarily beautiful. This recognition will obviate the imperatives of money and of the power that money can give. This represents a shift in perspective from a quantitative measure (how much do I have, how much do I need, how much can I get) to a qualitative measure (how beautiful it all seems!). This is a move to an aesthetic perspective on the world. An aesthetic view of the world is the view of the world of the artist. This is the deeper reading of Norm. He is an artist. He is not without aspirations, his are the highest aspirations: to appreciate the beautiful in the world. It is a view of the world that Marge had lost for a short time, but which was restored to her after her encounter with the sublime. With that is restored her deeper appreciation of her artist husband, Norm.

What does Marge know that Jerry does not know? Why does Marge find her way home and back into bed with her husband and Jerry will not get back to his wife? Marge knows how to sublime and Jerry does not. Which means that Marge does not take her values or herself so seriously that she cannot learn from what she encounters in the world, especially when things turn strange. She is able to detach herself from her commitments on one level in order to be able to see new relationships, new trajectories at a higher level. She is, in short, open to interpretations, which is a way of saying that she is open to philosophy. What Jerry needs is some philosophy in his life. He is terrified by his father-in-law, and the success and power that Wade wields ruthlessly. If he could have just *talked* to someone about his situation and his plan he may have gained a better perspective on the limits of Wade's success, and the craziness of his own plan.

To look into the abyss, to face the very thing that terrorizes us, takes both faith and courage. We must trust that somehow we will have the resources to survive confronting the sublime, and then we must have the courage to act on that trust. Marge has both of these qualities and so will not be undone by an encounter with the sublime; she will learn from it. After this, she will be different from what she was at the beginning of the movie and she will feel differently about what she has. What she has is no different from what Jerry had, and on the material level, probably much less. What she has that Jerry did not have and does not have is a different perspective. But that is quite a lot, and with that what she also has is a home to go to, a husband waiting for her there, and a bed to share with him where he will tell her that he loves her and she will tell him that she loves him too, and together they will eagerly await the birth of their child in just two more months.

4

Visions of Meaning: Seeing and Non-Seeing in Woody Allen's Crimes and Misdemeanors

> Ophthalmology: a branch of medical science dealing with the structure, functions, and diseases of the eye.
> —*Merriam-Webster's Collegiate Dictionary*, 10th Edition

Crimes and Misdemeanors begins with the character Judah (Martin Landau), who is an ophthalmologist, at an award banquet. He is giving a speech in response to a humanitarian award that he has been given. He explains his early attraction to ophthalmology by telling a story about his father. He tells a story about a story that his father told him, a story about the "eyes of God." He says, as part of his story, "I remember my father telling me, 'The eyes of God are on us always!' The eyes of God! What a phrase to a young boy! Unimaginably penetrating and intense eyes, I assumed. And I wonder if it was just a coincidence that I made my specialty ophthalmology?" The appeal to the eyes of God is an appeal to seeing and being seen, specifically, to having be seen those parts of us that other people mostly cannot see. We think of the eyes of God as being able to see into our soul, by which we mean that God can see into our deepest motives, desires, and intentions. The idea of the eyes of God is the idea that God can see our deepest secrets.

Some people have more secrets than others. Socrates more or less claims not to have any secrets when he says in the *Apology* that "in any public activity I may have engaged in, I am the same man as I am in private life."[1] I take Socrates to be exceptional in this regard, and, for all that, if one considers his famous irony, he seemed to keep the biggest secret of all in both his public and his private life. For Aristotle, we are mostly bad secret keepers since Aristotle thought that who we are is displayed in how we behave, that our souls are largely revealed through our

81

actions. The invocations of Socrates and Aristotle make clear the area of our concern, namely, morality and ethics. That is, what is more or less difficult for us to see in others (and, perhaps, especially in ourselves), but which we think of as open to the eyes of God, is the ethical condition of the soul. I say more or less difficult because, following Aristotle, the suggestion in the *Nicomachean Ethics* is that if you are a stranger to generosity, say, you will not be able to recognize either opportunities for generosity for oneself, or the acts of generosity of others. Generosity itself will be invisible to you. On this model, what we will be able to see will be constrained by the limits of our own goodness.

With respect to ethics, what there is to see is literally invisible, but, if we have the eyes to see it, it is epiphenomenally or emergently evident. That is, what we might literally see is a person placing their hand on another person's shoulder. A suspicious person may see some form of opportunism in that, while a generous person may see it as the act of generosity it may really be. There is no one thing in the act itself that would be a definitive signal of generosity, but a myriad of subtle signs may be clear indicators if one knows how to read them, if one knows how to see them. To see the generosity is to be able to do something like seeing into a person's soul. It is to see their consciousness, their real intentions, made manifest in their actions. It is the basis of what makes ethical understanding and behavior possible.

I want to argue that this idea of learning to see what is literally invisible is a role that can be played out in art. Arthur Danto in *The Transfiguration of the Commonplace* tries to capture what it is that gets conveyed in a work of art. He comes up with the idea that it is, at least in part, something like a "style," a "way of seeing things," something internal and central to the artist's whole perspective, that gets externalized. Danto describes it in this way; "It is as if a work of art were like an externalization of the artist's consciousness, as if we could see his way of seeing and not merely what he saw."[2] One way to describe the movie *Crimes and Misdemeanors* is to say that it is all about seeing, about vision, about being able to see.[3] Following Danto, one could say that the challenge presented to us by a work of art, a movie, say, is to be able to see from a certain perspective, to find, as it were, a perspective from which to see.

Perhaps the most important postmodern question of all for us is the question of ethics, whether there is anything inherently desirable in the good, or anything that can be called inherently good, which is a version of the question of where the meanings are. Of course, this is also a very old question and one that can be framed in terms of seeing. The underlying image of Plato's *Republic* is one of seeing and being seen. In book two of the *Republic*, Glaucon raises the question of the Ring of Gyges, a ring that can make its wearer invisible and so invulnerable to moral or ethical scrutiny.[4] The central question of the *Republic* from then on becomes the question of whether or not it is in anyone's real interest to use the ring. With the ring a person could do anything with impunity; one could do the things one might want to do but does not do for fear of exposure. With the ring there would be no fear of exposure since, literally, one cannot be seen. So the question is, would the ring make any difference to the good person? The Ring of Gyges is not just a story either. There is certainly a modern (and, I suppose, ancient) version of that ring: it takes the form of great wealth and social position. In the context of *Crimes and Misdemeanors*, Judah has this version of the ring and he uses it.

I do not mean to claim that *Crimes and Misdemeanors* is as great a philosophical text as Plato's *Republic*, but I do want to claim that it can be seen as a kind of philosophical text, and that, just as Plato's *Republic* was addressing issues especially pressing to fourth-century Athens, *Crimes and Misdemeanors* is addressing issues pressing to the late twentieth- and early twenty-first-century United States.[5] The socio-political contexts are different and the answers to the problems raised will be different (and differently presented), but the importance of the questions and the moral seriousness of their treatment seem to me to be similar.

Metaphors of vision and perspective are pervasive in the film. Judah is an ophthalmologist; Lester is a television producer; Cliff is a film producer; Ben the rabbi is going blind and wears increasingly darker glasses; Judah needs glasses, but does not usually wear them; Cliff needs glasses and wears them, as does Louis Levy, the philosopher; Halley wears glasses at first, but not later. Judah attempts to avoid being seen, i.e., found out, by having Dolores, the woman with whom he is having an affair, murdered. Cliff believes that he sees Lester's true nature, and tries to convey what he sees in the film he makes about Lester (comparing Lester to, among other things, a braying ass and Mussolini). Halley will tell Cliff that he is wrong about Lester, that, in effect, he really cannot see Lester at all (and, because of who Halley is, we are tempted to believe her).

The theme of knowing, for which seeing is a metonymy, is also pervasive in the film. Judah pretends not to know what he is doing when he calls his brother Jack (to "take care of" his problem with Dolores), but claims to know all about his wife's, Miriam's, values and feelings. That knowledge is neither affirmed nor denied in the context of the movie, but if Judah's relationship with Dolores is any indicator, his knowledge of his wife is dubitable. He does not seem to know Dolores, the person, at all, but sees her only as a past pleasure and current problem, a threat to the comfort of his life. Cliff thinks he knows Halley, as well as Lester and Louis Levy. In each case his supposed knowledge will prove quite faulty. Clearly, part of the problem of knowing is seeing, being able to see, which, when it is a question of seeing a person's character, their goodness or badness, requires a level of understanding of good and bad in oneself. Such self-awareness is not only very difficult, but also, in this postmodern age, very complicated.

Self-awareness, the sense of one's own goodness or badness, is so difficult in the postmodern period because of the way the very notions of goodness and badness have been contextualized, historicized, deconstructed, and undermined. The question of seeing oneself depends on the question of how one is to judge oneself, of how one is to begin to understand oneself, which requires some place, some perspective from which to make such judgments in the absence of some overarching moral prescription. I take Nietzsche as proposing a relevant and provocative solution to this problem.

For Nietzsche, the way of the philosopher and the way of the artist are very similar. Both have a kind of intuition about other levels of reality beyond the apparent one and an idea about how one might inhabit a reality different from some given one of which one might find oneself a part. In the first section of *The Birth of Tragedy*, Nietzsche speaks of what he calls the "beautiful illusion" of our dream worlds and he will compare the experience of the philosopher to that of our ordinary experience of dreaming. He says of dreams, "But even when this dream reality is most intense, we still have, glimmering through it, the sensation that it is *mere appearance*." This sense of experiencing what seems to be real but is an illusion, and which one is aware *is* an illusion, is also characteristic of the philosopher. Nietzsche says, "Philosophical men even have a presentiment that the reality in which we live and have our being is also mere appearance, and that another, quite different reality lies beneath it."[6] The liminal possibilities of transcendence (of, say, self-transcendence) and creativity are most availabe to those who can acknowledge this "mere appearance" of apparent reality.

In section five of *The Birth of Tragedy* Nietzsche invokes a figure that would seem to resemble whatever is invoked by speaking of the "eyes of God." Nietzsche refers to it as "the true author": "we may assume that we are merely images and artistic projections for the true author, and that we have our highest dignity in our significance as works of art—for it is only as an *aesthetic phenomenon* that the existence of the world is eternally justified." The suggestion here seems to be that what is ultimately available to us, what there is ultimately for us to know about ourselves, has something to do with our own dignity, and that that is possessed and revealed only aesthetically. It is only by finding ourselves or, rather, creating ourselves as artworks, through what Nietzsche refers to as the "mirror of illusion," that we can begin to speak of any justification, or genuine awareness, of who we are. At the end of section five Nietzsche goes on to say, "Only insofar as the genius in the act of artistic creation coalesces with this primordial artist of the world, does he know anything of the eternal essence of art; for in this state he is, in a marvelous manner, like the weird image of the fairy tale which can turn its eyes at will and behold itself; he is at once subject and object, at once poet, actor, and spectator." [7] It is a weird beast indeed that can turn its eyes and behold itself, and yet the suggestion is that it is only insofar as we do do that that we are ourselves justified, that we are like the primordial artist of the world, that our lives have any real meaning at all.

The plot of *Crimes and Misdemeanors* is quite complicated. The overarching plot involves an interweaving of a number of subplot lines which eventually converge at the end of the movie. An excellent way to summarize the various subplot lines is given by Dianne Vipond in her essay "*Crimes and Misdemeanors*: A Retake on the Eyes of Dr. Eckleburg." Vipond suggests that the movie can be seen as, in her phrase, a "labyrinth of doppelganger relationships." [8] Vipond describes two basic triadic doppelganger relations. For Judah there are two possible versions of himself as represented by his brother Jack, (Judah's dark side), and the rabbi, Ben, (Judah's spiritual and righteous side). For each of these there is also a shadow version from Judah's childhood; his Aunt May correlates with the "whatever you can get away with, might makes right" philosophy of Jack, and his father Sol correlates with the "God over truth" philosophy that is also represented by Ben. The other triadic doppelganger relation has the film producer Clifford (played by Woody Allen) at its center, with Louis Levy, the existential philosopher, representing a kind of atheistic, yet profoundly spiritual affirmation of the world and life based on love; and Lester, Clifford's brother-in-law, representing a kind of shallow, egoistic materialism and love of fame. Taking Danto's suggestion seriously, I take these triadic doppelganger relations to be, themselves, expressions of the director's, that is, Woody Allen's, own consciousness, and so each is also, ultimately, a doppelganger for the director of the film *Crimes and Misdemeanors*.

In this sense, Woody Allen as the artist who has created the film is telling a story about these characters, which is also, in some sense, a story about himself. The film is, then, both a story about these characters in these situations and a visual instantiation of the Nietzschean monster that has eyes that are able to look at itself. *Crimes and Misdemeanors* is a public work of art created by a famous movie director, but the artistic process itself, as Nietzsche suggests, is one that anyone might engage in, and, I want to argue, one from which everyone stands to gain great benefits. To make this latter point I will turn to some ideas in John Dewey's *Art as Experience*.

John Dewey, like Nietzsche, finds the justification of our lives, and the discovery of meaning in our lives, in an artistic or aesthetic process, what he calls "having an experience." As I have explained earlier (in the intro-duction), to have an experience for Dewey is to weave the various strands of what happens to us into a kind of narrative, and it is the resultant nar-rative that defines and determines the meaning in our lives. *Art as Experience* is a kind of training manual for how to engage in this narra-tivizing activity. The most significant step in this narrativizing process is "re-flection." An experience begins with what Dewey calls an "impul-sion," which is just a kind of surge in the organism as a whole toward some action. An experience then has the following course: "Impulsion from need starts an experience that does not know where it is going; resistance and check bring about the conversion of direct forward action into re-flection; what is turned back upon is the relation of hindering con-ditions to what the self possesses as working capital in virtue of prior experiences. As the energies thus involved re-enforce the original impul-sion, this operates more circumspectly with insight into end and method. Such is the outline of every experience that is clothed with meaning."[9]

It is through reflection that end and method get identified. To discover the end and method is to have one's experience "clothed in meaning." A lifetime of such experiences would be a meaningful life. When an experi-ence is "clothed with meaning" a transformation has taken place. Dewey says, "Experience is the result, the sign, and the reward of that interaction of organism and environment which, when it is carried to the full, is a transformation of interaction into participation and communication."[10] If anything can be taken as a basic postmodern desideratum, a postmodern good simplicitur, it seems to me it would be something like a way toward "participation and communication." I see in *Crimes and Misdemeanors* the suggestion of just such a way, although the way is implicit, enacted in the film as a whole, rather than standing out as an explicit message within the film.

The explicit message at the end of *Crimes and Misdemeanors* is dis-turbing. The message seems to be just the opposite of that for which Plato seems to argue in the *Republic*. Plato argues there that virtue is its own reward, that the Ring of Gyges would be of no interest to the truly virtu-ous person, and that the bad (basically, anyone who would use the ring) suffer the most. In *Crimes and Misdemeanors*, the good seem to genuinely suffer, and the bad seem to genuinely thrive. Clifford, the apparently much more attractive suitor, ethically speaking, fails to win Halley, while the pompous and apparently shallow Lester wins her love. Judah, the master of the Ring of Gyges, has used the ring, that is, his wealth and social standing, to cover up adultery, fraud, deceit, and murder, and he, after a bit of soul-searching, seems to thrive. He seems to have come out of the experience without remorse, but with his family, career, and social posi-tion intact. It is all quite troubling.

There is, however, a very interesting conversation at the end of the movie between Clifford and Judah. They are at the wedding of the daughter of the rabbi, Ben. Each for his own reason has withdrawn from the rest of the wedding celebration and they stumble upon one another. They sit and talk. Judah tells Clifford a story, which he suggests as a potential plot for a movie. The story Judah tells is his own story. It is of a very successful man who commits a murder but is able to cover it up; after awhile, one morning he wakes up and finds the whole sordid affair behind him, no longer a source of anguish or pain. His life goes on; he thrives as never before. (It is interesting that as Judah speaks of this very successful man with a secret, the film immediately cuts to a shot of Lester.) Clifford is dissatisfied with Judah's ending to the story and proposes a different, more tragic ending, an ending in which the protagonist takes responsibility for his crime and turns himself in. There is no resolution as to which of these scenarios is superior or more plausible. In some sense it is left to the audience to decide.

As Vipond argues in her essay, this scene has the character of a "metafiction."[11] That is, a character in the film suggests to another character in the film the plot for a movie that parallels the plot of the movie that the character is in fact in. This creates a complex matrix of meanings. The story that the character Judah tells is a story of a very successful man who has a terrible secret, and this secret itself is complicated since it is a secret about something he did to keep something else he had done secret. Within the context of the film, we, the audience, know this story to be true, although it is presented as just a story, as a proposal to the other character, Clifford, who is a filmmaker, for a film he could make. Of course this story, which is a true story within the context of the film, we take to be a fictional story because it takes place in a film, which itself is supposed to be a fictional realm (at least in this instance). What further complicates this situation, however, is that, in some sense, the story as a suggestion for a film does have another layer of truth to it since, in fact, the *Ur*-character or the original source of the character of Clifford is Woody Allen, who will actually make a film of the story that Judah has told. It is, in fact, this film, *Crimes and Misdemeanors*.

There is, then, a considerable amount of self-reflexivity within the film itself. There is a sense of both self-awareness and self-revelation. The story itself is a story about secrets, about things that are seen and things that are not seen, and about how one is to deal with such things. The story the character Judah tells is about that, but, of course, the whole film, *Crimes and Misdemeanors*, is about that as well. Presumably, we all have secrets, things that we would have kept from the eyes of others, and things that we do more or less successfully keep from the eyes of others. Is there something in the way the story is told in *Crimes and Misdemeanors* that can shed some light on how one might think about the things one has done, the secrets one would keep? How one might look to the future given who one has become?

The self-reflexivity of the film, its self-consciousness, the way it seems to see and reveal things about itself, engages Danto's suggestion about art as the externalization of the artist's consciousness. Danto's analysis of an artwork, however, is more complicated than just the suggestion that we see something about the artist in the artwork. For Danto, an artwork is transfiguring, a transfiguring mirror; but what gets mirrored and transfigured is not something in the world, but, ultimately, oneself, the audience of the artwork. Danto says of such mirrors, "mirrors tells us what we would not know about ourselves without them, and are instruments of self-revelation. One has learned something about oneself if one can see oneself as Anna [Karenina], knowing of course that one is not...." That is, in an artwork, which may be something like the artist's consciousness externalized, what one sees is some way one's own consciousness might be; one sees oneself transfigured through the reflection of oneself in the artwork, who one would be, what one would look like, if one thought and saw things like that. Danto goes on to say, "Art, if a metaphor at times on life, entails that the not unfamiliar experience of being taken out of oneself by art—the familiar artistic illusion—is virtually the enactment of a metaphoric transformation with oneself as subject: you are what the work is ultimately about, a commonplace person transfigured into an amazing woman."[12]

What we see, then, in an artwork, is something like possibilities that exist for our own future ways of being, ways of being that are different from the way we are now. In *Crimes and Misdemeanors*, the *Ur*-subject, for which all of the other characters are, in some sense, dopplegangers, is the creator of the film, Woody Allen. If we look at the film as a kind of externalization of the consciousness of Woody Allen, then the film becomes for us a kind of objective correlative for the reflections that Woody Allen might be entertaining about his own possible future ways of being. Certainly, there are suggestions of connections between the characters in the movie and Woody Allen its creator. Lester describes himself as a filmmaker who never finished college but now knows of college courses on the existential themes in his films, which is, of course, true of Woody Allen. Louis Levy's existential musings on finding meaning and significance in an apparently meaningless universe echoes themes raised in many of Allen's own movies (as the character Lester suggests). The spiritual issues raised by Ben and Sol are always just on the other side of the existentialism in Allen's movies. There are obvious connections between the Clifford character and Allen, suggested, in part, by the fact that Allen plays the character in the movie. That Allen had a large secret that he was, no doubt, wrestling with like the character of Judah in the film is, at this point, in the public domain, and certainly the science of seeing is part of his business as a filmmaker. How other characters in the movie, such as Halley, Barbara, Clifford's niece and wife connect with Allen's consciousness is more obscure, and none of these connections is really clear. What does seem clear, however, is that there is some relevance to Danto's suggestion about an artwork as the artist's consciousness externalized when we are talking about the artist Woody Allen and his film *Crimes and Misdemeanors*.

What is important for us as the audience in our experience of the film is, following Danto, the possibility of our seeing ourselves mirrored in it and our being transfigured by it. What one sees, what one experiences, is the exploration of a variety of different narratives, a variety of different ways of connecting the events of a life into the narrative of an experience. Woody Allen's exploration of such narratives becomes an opportunity for us to engage in that process as well. Woody Allen's explorations become our explorations. What the variety of possible narratives yields is not necessarily a single, decisive narrative, but rather a narrative of complexity, a narrative of being a person who sees the world and its possibilities complexly. Complexity itself not only yields more choices for oneself, more choices about who one is, who one would be, but also the ability to see more in the choices of others. Complexity increases our abilities to, as Dewey recommends, participate and communicate. As Dewey says, in praise of increased complexity, "The designs of living are widened and enriched. Fulfillment is more massive and more subtly shaded."[13]

Plato's *Republic* concludes with the idea that "justice by itself is best for the soul itself, and that soul must do the just things, whether it has Gyges' ring or not."[14] That is, if one knows what the just thing is one will do it, whether one has Gyges' ring or not. For Plato, the only reason some people do not act justly is because they do not know what the just thing is. It is a problem of ignorance (and, of course, for Plato, most people are ignorant in this way). One might say that it is a problem of sight, of being able to see hence to recognize the just thing. The conclusion of *Crimes and Misdemeanors* is considerably more ambiguous on the Ring of Gyges problem. It seems to me, however, that Allen's ethical message is different from Plato's. The good, for Allen, is not some abstract, metaphysical Form that is there for us to know and which, if known, would settle all disputes, but rather just the imaginative process, the narrativizing process that explores the varieties of ways of being and thinking that are available to us. This is the process in which art engages us. This is a process that can transfigure us. It is the process to which Allen, with an almost ferocious determination and intensity of hard and persistent work, has devoted his life.

I am arguing that Woody Allen is attempting to act as a kind of ophthalmologist for the eyes of the soul. That is, what we need to have tested is our ability to see certain kinds of moral possibilities, which is to say, certain life possibilities, that might be available to us, and that these moral possibilities are best rendered narratively. Unless we are able to see the narrative possibilities that are available to us, unless we can project possible ways of being narratively into the future, unless we can, as it were, live futurally or proleptically, our lives will simply be determined by what has happened to us in the past. I see Woody Allen as engaging in just that kind of activity in his making a movie like *Crimes and Misdemeanors*, and I see the appropriate response for us the audience as trying to follow the process out with Allen and for ourselves, as a kind of practice for doing it by ourselves with our own lives. The suggestion in Dewey's *Art as Experience* is that it is only in having "experiences" that we find meaning in our lives, and that it is in narrativizing the events of our lives that we have "experiences." In the narrativizing lines of *Crimes and Misdemeanors* we are transfigured into narrativizing beings, and, if Nietzsche and Dewey and Danto and Allen are right, in narrativizing is where the meanings are.

Sander Lee, in his chapter on *Crimes and Misdemeanors* in his excellent book *Woody Allen's Angst: Philosophical Commentaries on His Serious Films*, argues for a final reading of the film rather different from the one that I propose here.[15] Our analyses have many points in common, but our readings of the ultimate, overarching philosophical significance of the film are quite different. Lee argues that, although apparently ambiguous and commonly misinterpreted, the ending of the film really suggests a very positive and specific moral message. Lee focuses on the voice-over soliloquy by the Louis Levy character that accompanies the ending of the movie. The soliloquy ends, "...It is only we, with our capacity to love, that give meaning to the indifferent universe. And yet, most human beings seem to have the ability to keep trying, and even to find joy, from simple things like the family, their work, and from the hopes that future generations might understand more."[16] Lee sees in these lines from the Levy character the promise of, as Lee says, "the elements of a Sartrean existential analysis of the possibilities for authentic moral projects in an indifferent universe in which all meaning springs from the ways in which we exercise our ontological freedom and take responsibility for our acts."[17] As a consequence of this Sartrean idea of freedom and moral responsibility, Lee sees Clifford's condition as still essentially hopeful (even though he has lost his wife, his girlfriend, his one paying job, his mentor, and with his mentor's suicide, the raison d'être of his movie), and Judah's condition as damned (even though Judah retains his family, his job, and his social position and seems to be not only pretty happy, but almost entirely free of remorse).

Interestingly, Woody Allen himself denies this interpretation of the relative conditions of Clifford and Judah. In a response to a question specifically about this issue, Allen responded to Lee saying, "You are wrong about Judah; he feels no guilt and the extremely rare time the events occur to him, his mild uneasiness (which sometimes doesn't come at all) is negligible."[18] I agree with Lee (and Plato) that the artist is not always the best judge of what she or he has produced, but in this case I want to argue for Allen's having more complex motives and a more complex moral understanding than Lee attributes to him.

For Lee, given his reading of the final events of the film, the movie resolves itself into a fairly unambiguous lesson about the moral life and human good. The title of Lee's chapter on the film is taken from a line spoken by Judah's father, Sol, in the movie; "If necessary, I will always choose God over truth!" Lee's conclusion, and the conclusion of his essay on *Crimes and Misdemeanors* is:

> Only by blinding ourselves to the so-called "truth" of the "real world" can one create a meaningful life. If the universe is fundamentally indifferent to our human capacity to love and create meaning for our lives, then we have absolutely no reason for choosing truth that destroys life's joy over the fulfilling subjective values we can create for ourselves. In this sense, Sol is right when he proclaims, "If necessary, I will always choose God over truth!"[19]

I find this conclusion to be both less optimistic and less complex than an interpretation of the film that is consistent with Allen's own suggestion about the ultimate condition of the Judah character. I take Lee's reading as less optimistic because it suggests the necessity of some kind of self-deception, the necessity of some kind of *refusal* to see that will be demanded of us in order to live either a moral life or a happy life or a meaningful life. This suggests a fairly dark evaluation of our actual circumstances in the world. I see in the suggestions of Nietzsche and Dewey the possibility of meaning and happiness as a consequence of seeing, as a consequence of honesty about oneself, about one's condition, and about the way the world is. All of which raises, it seems to me, a rather larger question about the nature of art and morality and meaning, and, I think, the real difference between Lee's reading of the ending of *Crimes and Misdemeanors* and my own.

My reading of the ending of the film, and of the film as a whole, turns on the idea of the Deweyan idea of the role of narrativizing in our lives. The idea is that the narrativizing of the events of our lives into something like stories, stories that conform to Aristotle's definition of a drama as having a beginning, middle, and end, and which, upon reflection, generate meaning and significance in our lives. In his essay "The Storyteller," Walter Benjamin attempts to get at what the essence of storytelling is, and what storytelling can mean to us in this modern, postmodern age. He distinguishes what the storyteller does from what the historian does. Benjamin says of the historian, "The historian is bound to explain in one way or another the happenings with which he deals; under no circumstances can he content himself with displaying them as models of the course of the world."[20] That is, the historian is all about drawing unambiguous conclusions. She or he is about providing information, which is all about being "understandable in itself."[21] Benjamin refers to the storyteller as a "chronicler," and describes what the chronicler does as being just the opposite of the project of the historian. He says of the chronicler, "they have from the start lifted the burden of demonstrable explanation from their own shoulders. Its place is taken by interpretation, which is not concerned with an accurate concatenation of definite events, but with the way these are embedded in the great inscrutable course of the world."[22] Benjamin gives as an example of the chronicler's art a story from Herodotus's *Histories*. It is the story of the Egyptian king Psammenitus who is beaten and captured by the Persian king Cambyses. Psammenitus watches with stoic passivity as his daughter is reduced to a maid getting water from a well, he watches as his son is marched to his death, but upon seeing a lowly, impoverished servant among the ranks of the prisoners, he breaks down and wails and beats his head. No more information is given. Benjamin cites various interpretations of what has happened such as Montaigne's that the king was overfull of grief and so it took just a bit more to send him over the edge, or the alternate explanation that grief only gets released in relaxation, and to the king the servant was a relaxing from the tension of witnessing the blows to his family, and there are other possible interpretations. Benjamin endorses none of them and says only, "Herodotus offers no explanations. His report is the driest. That is why this story from ancient Egypt is still capable after thousands of years of arousing astonishment and thoughtfulness."[23]

I see Allen with his film *Crimes and Misdemeanors* as acting as a storyteller in a similar mode. The whole point is to give a truthful account of how events can unfold in "the great inscrutable course of the world." To suggest an ultimately unambiguous moral lesson is to suggest that the aim of the work was directed at a relatively lower artistic goal. To insist that there is an unambiguous moral to the story is to underestimate, it seems to me, Allen as an artist, and his audience as able interpreters, as able proto-storytellers in their own rights. My own reading of the ending of the film is that it presents a lesson in the activities of narrativizing and interpreting themselves. Each person must produce his or her own interpretation of the events of the film, just as each must produce his or her own interpretation of his or her own life and the world in which we all live.

Some, perhaps many, will be put off by Allen's own apparent moral status. The revelations about Allen's own complicated moral life raise the question of whether ethical and moral lessons can be learned from someone whose own life seems to be so morally dubious. To me, such an attitude is as suspect as that of one who would condemn Sophocles' *Oedipus Rex* because it reveals Sophocles' moral degeneracy. Honesty, openness about the complexity of moral issues (or about health issues or about financial issues) is the most difficult thing for us to get from other people, and perhaps from ourselves. Complicity in the morally reprehensible is a widely enough shared condition that any honest messages we can get about that condition should be welcomed. I certainly do not see *Crimes and Misdemeanors* as glorifying infidelity and murder, any more than I see *Oedipus Rex* as a recommendation for incest. I see both the film and the play as artistic texts that are confronting the fact of these as temptations and difficulties that we all face in one form or another. That is not to say that there is no immoral art. I think that there probably is. It is to say, however, that all great art will inevitably lead us into areas that are morally ambiguous, and will not show us any obvious or easy way out.

It is in the construction of such stories, of such interpretations, that meaning and significance, real meaning and real significance I believe, get generated in our lives. There is no call not to look. If anything, it is exactly looking that is called for. It is, in some sense, in the confrontation with "the great inscrutable course of the world" that the possibility of finding significance and meaning opens up. To avoid the truth is to give up all hope of living a life that one can ever bear to look at and reflect upon with honesty and satisfaction. Of course, the truth that we find will have its dark aspects, and may very well be ad hoc, historicist, contextual, and emergent from the stories we ourselves have generated, but it will still have emerged from the honest confrontation with the nature of the world and our place in it, and so will be as much of the truth as we may ever know.

5

Oedipus Techs: Time Travel as Redemption in The Terminator and 12 Monkeys

Only through time time is conquered.
—T.S. Eliot, "Four Quartets"

I'll be back.
—*The Terminator*

The Terminator and *12 Monkeys* share a specific form of time travel that makes possible a kind of redemption for the protagonists of those films. This redemption can be described as a kind of recovery of, or perhaps, a creation of, meaning for their lives, which would seem to have been unavailable to them without this form of time travel. The form of time travel that engages the plots of these movies involves a movement from the future to the past that ends in the past. The problem of redeeming one's life, of finding a way to affirm one's life as one's own, is a perennial one, but one that has a certain urgency today in this rapidly changing, high technology, postmodern world. Anxiety is natural. The question is, is there some good way to deal with the anxiety? I see the movies *The Terminator* and *12 Monkeys* as suggesting some answers to this question, some, as it turns out, very philosophical answers. These answers will engage the philosophies of Nietzsche and Heidegger, and of contemporary theorists like Jean-François Lyotard, Harold Bloom, and the neo-pragmatist Richard Rorty.

There is an intimate connection in the structure of these two movies.[1] The primary similarity is in their basic plots: a man travels back in time in order to save the human race, meets and falls in love with a woman in the past, and dies in the past. This scenario may seem banal enough, the common fodder of Hollywood science fiction films, but, in fact, I think this very structure engages some fairly complicated philosophical ideas that have a great intuitive appeal. These movies serve to introduce these ideas on a mass level in a way that is quite accessible and pleasurable, yet still deeply provocative and philosophical.

I see these movies as not only coming out of, and so reflecting, a historical context, that is, late twentieth-century postmodern American culture, but also as providing some guidance, in a fairly wild narrative form, for how we might come to grips with our own individual relation to that culture. Part of why I think that these movies are so exciting to watch is because they are playing out tensions and anxieties that we already are experiencing, but for which we have no narrative structure by which we understand them. These movies both enact these tensions and anxieties and show a kind of allegorized solution to them. Freud thought that dreams were the mind's way of working through subconscious and unconscious tensions and anxieties. Psychoanalytic dream interpretation was a way of drawing these subconscious and unconscious tensions into consciousness so that they could be dealt with and worked on more effectively. I think that there is a similar attraction for our minds in movies. That is, our mind responds to movies in much the same way it responds to dreams: it considers them as a way of working through certain cognitive and emotional difficulties that we are consciously or unconsciously experiencing by means of a narrative structure. I want to try to make some of the issues that subconsciously preoccupy us, or, in the movies, covertly engage us, and treat them as consciously present and overt. I will interpret these movies, not from a psychoanalytic perspective so much as from a philosophical perspective, which is, after all, the older, hence more experienced tradition from which to draw. My intent is to trace some of the deeper emotional and cognitive lines in these movies through an appeal to some explicitly philosophical analyses. I see these two movies as dealing with a similar human dynamic, one that engages the questions, what is the nature of our contemporary condition, and how can we best come to terms with it?

In his *The Postmodern Condition*, Jean-François Lyotard describes certain contemporary social dynamics, specifically, capitalist dynamics, in terms of vectors of power that exercise a kind of terror over the majority of the populace in the service of the "system." The system is just the social network, or some part of the social network, that is governed by what Lyotard refers to as the "decision makers." The decision makers legitimate their power through their "optimizing the system's performance—efficiency."[2] Lyotard calls this "the logic of maximum performance." This logic leads, according to Lyotard, to a kind of "terror." Lyotard says of this terror, "By terror I mean the efficiency gained by eliminating, or threatening to eliminate, a player from the language game one shares with him. He is silenced or consents, not because he has been refuted, but because his ability to participate has been threatened (there are many ways to prevent someone from playing). The decision makers' arrogance...consists in the exercise of terror. It says: 'Adapt your aspirations to our ends—or else.' "³ This description of this particular form of "terror" has considerable resonance, and it is, it seems to me, a largely repressed terror. We do not want to think of ourselves as victims, and we can ill afford to dwell on the tenuousness of our positions if we are going to maintain the kind of efficiency that those positions demand. We act as though we were not terrorized, though, in fact, the submerged mood of our everyday lives will be a kind of repressed terror.

I will argue that this form of terror exercised by, in Lyotard's formulation, the "decision makers" has a subtler corollary within each of us individually, as I believe Heidegger argues persuasively. That is, the arrogance that Lyotard attributes to the decision makers is a kind of arrogance each of us may manifest toward ourselves (as well as toward others) insofar as we are living inauthentically, and it is with this arrogance that it is the most pressing for us to come to terms. It is the arrogance that comes with our acceptance, conscious or unconscious, willing or unwilling, of this attitude of the importance of efficiency, the arrogance that comes with the adoption of the attitude of what Heidegger will call the "they." The "they" is the ideal of public ordinariness to which we all, in our public identities, aspire. It is characterized, according to Heidegger, by "*averageness.*" Our "they" identity emerges in our "Being-with-one-another," in our social associations. Heidegger says the following of our "they" identity:

> This Being-with-one-another dissolves one's own Dasein completely into a kind of Being of 'the Others', in such a way, indeed, that the Others, as distinguishable and explicit, vanish more and more. In this inconspicuousness and unascertainability, the real dictatorship of the "they" is unfolded. We take pleasure and enjoy ourselves as *they* take pleasure; we read, see, and judge about literature as and are as *they* see and judge; likewise we shrink back from the 'great mass' as *they* shrink back; we find 'shocking' what they find shocking. The "they", which is nothing definite, and which all are, though not as the sum, prescribes the kind of Being of everydayness.⁴

Herbert Dreyfus, interpreting Heidegger in *Being and Time*, associates the "they" with norms, norms we are mostly unaware of, norms we mostly do not know comprise our identities, at least not until we experience their breach. In the breach of these norms we feel anxiety. We flee that anxiety by means of an attempt to conform more precisely to those norms, to escape into the "they."⁵ It will be precisely this attempt to escape into "theyness" that will be the primary impediment to our own self-knowledge, as well as to the knowledge of, and care for, others.

There are various levels of terror in this postmodern world: systemic terror, wielded by employers and systemic decision makers in general, our own internalized forms of terror; and, ultimately, terror by nature itself, which can threaten elimination at any time through, for example, disease and death. There is an almost Darwinian dimension to these forms of terror, a kind of selectivity at work. The threat of nature is part of the struggle for survival that we share with all living things. It is as if the post-modern capitalistic systems have learned a lesson from nature and have adopted an institutionalized form of terror similar to nature's own—similar to, but not the same as. It is not the same as because where nature, through sex, encourages differences, new permutations, and radical mutations, institutional systems have a horror of differences because of their internal-ized conception of efficiency. People who behave "differently" diminish efficiency like a cog that is missing a tooth.[6] As Lyotard suggests, social and economic systems, unlike nature, do not encourage differences; difference itself becomes a primary criterion for elimination. In nature, differences are a species' primary defense against elimination when environmental condi-tions change. Since, from the perspective of the species, there is no telling what environmental changes may ultimately occur, there is no telling which genetic mutations, and which phenotypes, may prove most effective for a species' survival in the future. Sex generates differences because differences are what best guarantee the survival of the species under changing environ-mental conditions. Of course, nature can be pretty brutal about differences too. Reproduction is more about sameness than it is about differences, even if sex, as a particular form of reproduction, is more about differences.[7]

We have adaptive strategies of our own, which we employ within con-texts where there are tensions between conformity and individuality, and these strategies also engage notions of survival and fitness. The question of difference, the question of our being different and that of how to react to others who appear to be different from us, therefore, is personal as well as systemic. What postmodernism, as well as neo-pragmatism, but also Heidegger, Nietzsche, and certain Hollywood movies, have to teach is something about embracing rather than fearing differences, differences such as complexity and individual autonomy that respond uniquely to a given context.

Sarah Connor (Linda Hamilton) in *The Terminator* (and somewhat less obviously, Catherine Railly (Madeleine Stowe) in *12 Monkeys*) is an apparent misfit, someone who struggles where others seem to move with ease, especially when it comes to the use of machines and technology. She bumbles her roommate's Walkman cord in their bathroom, she punches in at her work time clock late, she confuses orders as a waitress, her answering machine serves to give other people a means for avoiding her, she tries to make calls on broken phones, and she seems completely ill at ease in the nightclub Tech Noir. When Kyle (Michael Biehn) tells her, "You've been targeted for termination," this is, in some sense, exactly what we have already been afraid of for her. If nature doesn't do it, it looks like decision makers in the system will. Furthermore, it seems to me that this fear that we feel for her, and that she presumably feels for herself, is a fear any one of us may feel for ourselves at any time, that somewhere, behind closed doors or metaphorically in nature's unfolding, the same words are being spoken about us.

The Terminator (Arnold Schwarzenegger) functions as a kind of metaphor for the forces that deliver all of these various forms of terror. That is, the Terminator is the inexorability of nature in the form of cancer. It is the threat of our elimination by the "decision makers" from those language games to which we belong and to which we hope to continue belonging. It is also in us as an internalized source of terror, as our own internalized capitulation to an inauthentic conception of efficiency. When the Terminator says, "I'll be back." We know it will be, and we have a pretty good idea what will happen when it returns. The Terminator's human appearance but machine nature makes it a perfect reified analog for the "logic of maximum performance"—a logic that is as merciless and nonhuman as nature itself. It is the embodiment of the postmodern terror. As Kyle says of the Terminator: "That Terminator is out there. It can't be bargained with. It can't be reasoned with. It doesn't feel pity or remorse or fear; and it absolutely will not stop. Ever. Until you are dead." There's efficiency for you.

This idea of a postmodern terror in *The Terminator* works as a kind of analogue for a subtler form of this condition which, in *Being and Time*, Heidegger calls "anxiety" (*Angst*). *The Terminator* is a movie about fleeing an embodied terror. For Heidegger, what most of us spend our lives fleeing is anxiety, our own internalized version of the Terminator. Heidegger describes this in terms of "Dasein's [i.e., a human being's] fleeing *in the face of itself* and in the face of its authenticity."[8] What we flee is not something that is in the world, according to Heidegger, but the confrontation with our own anxiety, which is a confrontation with ourselves. The anxiety is in response to our "thrownness," the fact that we find ourselves in the world, or, as Heidegger says, "That which anxiety is anxious about is Being-in-the-world itself."[9] The problem with our Being-in-the-world is that we find ourselves in a world that we did not make, with roles assigned to us that we did not choose. We are born into a particular society, into a particular gender, class, family, and body; and all of these with particular challenges and responsibilities, and none of them freely chosen by us. These roles, when looked at from within the mood of anxiety, seem to belong to us only accidentally. The meaning of my life, of who

I am, suddenly seems not to be intrinsic, either to me or to my situation. The suspicion that there is no meaning, that I am simply replaceable, is the source of my anxiety. As Piotr Hoffman puts it in "Death, Time, History: Division II of *Being and Time*," "Being a member of the public world I can easily be replaced ('represented') by another person. Somebody else could have filled the position I occupy in society; somebody else could have been the husband of the woman I married, the father of her children, and so on."[10] Our response to this premonition, to this anxiety, is to flee into "theyness." We try harder to belong, to take seriously the various roles in which we find ourselves. We attempt to flee our anxiety by running from oursleves.

We flee our anxiety but we should not. Anxiety is a kind of double-edged sword. As Hubert Dreyfus explains, "anxiety both motivates falling into inauthenticity—a cover-up of Dasein's true structure—and undermines this cover-up, thus making authenticity possible,"[11] or, as Heidegger says, "anxiety as a basic state-of-mind is disclosive." That is, if we can confront our anxiety, our anxiety will disclose something to us about our real condition. Anxiety is a mood (*Stimmung*), which is the expression of a way of being in a context, or an attunement (*Befindlichkeit*). If we become attuned to our attunement, to our mood of anxiety, the feeling is of uncanniness. As Heidegger says, "In anxiety one feels 'uncanny'." By "uncanny" Heidegger means a sense of "not-being-at-home."[12] (In German "uncanny" is *unheimlich*, literally, not-at-homeness.) In anxiety, our "not-being-at-home" in the world is forcefully made present to us. That is, we are confronted with the lack of intrinsic meaning in our lives. In this sense, most of us are, at a deep level, Sarah Connor in our not-at-homeness in the world. In our everydayness we flee this uncanniness, we flee into "theyness," but it comes after us, not unlike the Terminator itself. "This uncanniness pursues Dasein [i.e., human beings] constantly, and is a threat to its everyday lostness in the 'they'." In this flight Heidegger describes us as "falling into the 'they'."[13] We have fallen away from our authentic self, which is our only hope for feeling at home in the world, at home with ourselves.

In *The Terminator*, I find this sense of being pursued and the uncanniness of it best conveyed in the musical leitmotif that is associated with the Terminator. The "boom boom boom boom; boom boom boom boom" of the score is a frightening simulacrum of our own heartbeat, which is a powerful and inescapable reminder of our thereness, as well as of the someday not-to-be-there of our death. This theme, with its reference to our own heartbeats, it seems to me, emphasizes the everydayness and the closeness of what the Terminator represents. In *12 Monkeys*, the uncanniness is conveyed in the symbol of the 12 Monkeys itself, and the way it points to our animalness on the one hand, and to a kind of human craziness on the other—both of which are elements of our lives that can frighten us into flight. That is, some of the most powerful shots in *12 Monkeys* are of animals inhabiting spaces that we think of as peculiarly and exclusively human. These shots evoke the uncanny. Similarly powerful, and similarly uncanny, are the scenes in the insane asylum, and the theme of madness in general. It is madness that directs the radical sect of the 12 Monkeys, and it will be another kind of madness that will drive the scientist to release the virulent virus into the atmosphere around the world. With such specters haunting us, with such possibilities to face if we are going to face our own anxiety, no wonder we flee into "theyness."

Sarah Connor is very much lost in "theyness"—as, interestingly, are the pseudo-toughs on the promontory where the Terminator first appears, and the blustery and self-sure police in the police station. There are many forms of conformity and flights from one's own authentic self. Sarah Connor, with the help of Kyle, as well as Catherine Railly with the help of James Cole (Bruce Willis), will do much better than these trying-to-be-tough guys or even than the police who try to deal with the forces represented by the Terminator with posturing and violence (which, on this allegorized reading of the film symbolizes the violence they do to themselves in their flight from authenticity).

As has been suggested, the solution to the problem of this latent anxiety, of this repressed sense of the uncanny, is, ironically, through anxiety. Anxiety is most a problem for us when we respond to it with flight from ourselves, our flight from our own anxiety is about not being our own self. This is what Heidegger calls "inauthenticity." Inauthenticity, for Heidegger, has to do with a loss of one's sense of one's true self and derives from an attempt to escape from anxiety into "theyness." The beginning of a solution to this condition of inauthenticity is a new anxiety. This new anxiety is a solution to the problem because it begins to move us away from our descent into "theyness" that was our original strategy for dealing with the anxiety. This anxiety results from the confrontation with the ever present possibility of our own nonbeing, which is to say, the ever present possibility of our own death. For Heidegger, the way to authenticity, which is to say, the way to freedom *from* "theyness," and *to* our own individual destiny, is through the confrontation with, and the acknowledgment of, our own death. It is our death that is the one thing in the world that is intrinsically and uniquely our own. What this confrontation will entail is seeing our life as a whole, that is, our life including its conclusion in our death, which will necessitate the acknowledgment of our death as an inescapable part, and limit, of our life.

The Terminator and, somewhat more ambiguously, *12 Monkeys*, can be seen as narrative, if interpretive, enactments of the process that leads to what Heidegger describes as a "Being-towards-Death." I will try to show this in a passage from *Being and Time* that I choose not quite at random, but as one of many passages that might have served as well:

> Only an entity which, in its Being, is essentially *futural* so that it is free for its death and can let itself be thrown back upon its factical "there" by shattering itself against death—that is to say, only an entity which, as futural, is equiprimordially in the process of *having-been*, can, by handing down itself to the possibility it has inherited, take over its own thrownness and be *in the moment of vision* for 'its time'. Only authentic temporality which is at the same time finite, makes possible something like fate—that is to say, authentic historicality. [Emphases are Heidegger's.]

Heidegger calls this authentic historicality in the individual "resoluteness." Of this resoluteness he says, "The resoluteness which comes back to itself and hands itself down, then becomes the repetition of a possibility of existence that has come down to us. Repeating is handing down explicitly— that is to say, going back to the possibilities of the Dasein that has-been-there."[14] Heidegger's all but impenetrable vocabulary notwithstanding, I take what he is describing here to be a fairly precise description of the plots of *The Terminator* and *12 Monkeys*.

Both plots follow a person who is essentially futural. In these two movies, that is presented as a literal fact about them. The protagonists are in a past that they have arrived at from the future by means of a time machine. This is a kind of narrative objective correlative of the philosophical insight that Heidegger is advocating about the appropriate attitudinal stance one should take with respect to oneself. More subjectively, each of us has a kind of time machine in the form of our imagination. We can, in our imagination, go into the future and imagine our own dying and death in order to begin to understand the implications of our death to our life. We can then, as it were, return to the past, but now transformed by our "shattering" experience of the confrontation with our own death. We will be different, we will be, subjectively, more futural. I understand that to mean that we will be more attuned to the urgency of being in the present moment because we understand how precious this moment is in light of the inevitability of our own death, which will mark the end of all moments for us. The confrontation with our own death shatters our arrogant narcissism, the false and constructed self-importance we seek in our aspirations to be a "they."

The behaviors of the protagonists, Kyle Reese and James Cole, demonstrate more (Kyle) or less (James) resoluteness because of a vision that Kyle and James have had of their lives, which includes their having-been and their own deaths. They are both motivated by a strong sense of their own authentic historicality, which Heidegger calls fate or destiny, and their resoluteness is manifested in their willingness, even their commitment, to live a repetition of their lives. In what could be taken as an accurate description of both Kyle's and James's resoluteness, Heidegger says, "Resoluteness constitutes the loyalty of existence to its own Self. As resoluteness which is ready for anxiety, this loyalty is at the same time a possible way of revering the sole authority which a free existing can have—of revering the repeatable possibilities of existence."[15]

It is in the nature of time travel that moves from the future to the past and ends in the past that it necessarily entails an endless repetition of that life. To will that repetition, to see that life as the life that you will be repeating infinitely, is to have achieved that moment of vision that Heidegger describes, and to realize that attitude of resoluteness or steadiness that characterizes, for Heidegger, authentic Dasein. There is no absolute freedom from the "they." There is only one's own synthesis of the various options available to one, given one's particular "thrownness" into the world, among and as part of the "they." It is what one does with one's various possibilities that will make one's life authentic or inauthentic. What authenticity will come down to is something like a kind of style, a comportment, a readiness to read one's own moods so that one can be most responsive to the possibilities any particular situation may present.[16] One's resoluteness, one's intensity derives from one's intention to remain responsive to one's moods, to anxiety, to the endlessly repeated possibility of one's life in the face of one's own death.

Willing a life endlessly repeated points inescapably to Nietzsche's conception of the eternal recurrence. Nietzsche's problem is the same as Heidegger's: How is one able to find one's life to be genuinely and originally one's own, and how does one find a way to affirm that life? For Nietzsche, as for Heidegger, who was certainly strongly influenced by Nietzsche, the solution to these problems begins with the attempt to conceive of one's life as a whole, and to see and acknowledge the connection of one's present to the past and to the future. Nietzsche describes the successful outcome of this attempt as *amor fati*, love of fate.[17]

While there is considerable controversy over how to interpret Nietzsche's conception of the eternal recurrence, I find Alexander Nehamas's treatment of the concept in his *Nietzsche: Life as Literature* compelling. Nehamas says of Nietzsche's theory, "The eternal recurrence is not a theory of the world but a view of the self."[18] Nietzsche's view of the self, according to Nehamas, is that the self is just the sum total of all of our experiences and actions: "there is ultimately no distinction to be drawn between essential and accidental properties at all: if any property were different, its subject would simply be a different subject."[19] According to Nehamas, Nietzsche's conception of the eternal recurrence is really about affirming our lives in every minuscule detail of their unfolding. To will anything to be different is to will not to be who one is, which is to be defeated by one's life instead of a creative affirmer of it. To be a creative affirmer of one's life will take, of course, great conviction and energy, one might say resoluteness. It will take calling good what others call bad. It will take being an individual and affirming, or rather, creating through one's affirmation, one's individuality. Nietzsche reserves the possibility of success in this for some future creature, the *Übermensch*, but he is clearly recommending it to us all. Kyle and James seem to be prototypical *Übermenschen*. They each, more or less, know how their life is going to go and each chooses it, not once, but, by returning in time to a time in which they will die, they choose it an infinite number of times. This is a choice each makes, to leave a time in which they live lives largely indistinguishable from other lives; through a kind of persistence—say, a resoluteness—of vision about their own lives, their own destinies, they affirm a creative, very individual life by their own willing and resoluteness. *The Terminator* and *12 Monkeys* can be seen as enactments of Nietzsche's conception of the *Übermensch*'s relationship to his or her own life and the world, their *amor fati*, that is, their love and affirmation of their fate, of their lives as they are, in a very Hollywood science fiction movie.

The fact that these movies are very Hollywood science fiction, very American in their brashness, violence, and even kitschiness, leads me to a final theoretical suggestion before drawing a conclusion from these attempts to watch *The Terminator* and *12 Monkeys* philosophically. It will be useful at this point to reinvoke Harold Bloom's idea of what he calls the "American Sublime." For Bloom, artistic creativity is associated with repression, with a sense of belatedness that gets repressed in order that the works of the fathers might be repeated with a kind of impunity, and thereby original works are once again produced through a kind of repetition. What drove the Freudian and Romantic creative productions was a vision of the sublime. According to Bloom, the American Sublime represents a deeper repression than the European sublimes of Freud and the Romantics,[20] and a more extreme expression of the repetition that becomes meaning, and the meaning that makes us who we are. To understand each new version of the sublime, such as the American Sublime, Bloom says that the following question must be asked: "What is being repressed? What has been forgotten, on purpose, in the depths, so as to make possible this sudden elevation to the heights?"[21] Bloom takes Emerson to be the originator of the American Sublime and answers this question for Emerson: "What Emerson represses is *Ananke*, the Fate he has learned to call 'compensation.' His vision of repetition is a metonymic reduction, an undoing of all other selves, and his restituting *daemoniza-*

tion renders him solipsistic and free."[22] What Emerson represses is his own belatedness, but not in order to recreate the figure and works of the father, which Bloom attributes to the classical European pursuers of the sublime, but to refuse to acknowledge the father altogether, to repeatedly affirm his *own* spontaneity (this is what Bloom means by daemonization) and hence to find himself, as Bloom says, "solipsistic and free." For Bloom, all rhetoric is defensive, all meaning, as he says it is for Emerson, is "concerned with survival." "What holds together rhetoric as a system of tropes, and rhetoric as persuasion, is the necessity of defense, defense against everything that threatens survival, and a defense whose aptest name is 'meaning.'"[23] This is a form of pragmatism. The trope that Bloom attributes to Emerson, and which becomes the basis of the American Sublime, is the trope of self-begetting. This, says Bloom, is "the distinguishing mark of the specifically American Sublime....Not merely rebirth, but the even more hyperbolical trope of self-begetting...."[24]

In *The Terminator* and *12 Monkeys*, time travel into the past becomes the mechanism of this very trope. Both Kyle and James are implicitly self-begetters insofar as each is and becomes who they are by virtue of the role each plays in their own development. Kyle is the literal father of John Connor, who then becomes Kyle's spiritual (and possibly literal) father; and for James, it is the witnessing of his own death that becomes the dream that is his presentiment of what he needs to do to become what he is. And this cycle of self-begetting is endlessly repeated by this particular form of time travel so that the anxiety of precursors, the fear of derivativeness which Kyle or James might feel, is effectively quelled by the enactment of their own self-begetting through the mechanism of time travel. The power to be who one is is realized. In this way the characters Kyle Reese and James Cole enact what Bloom has identified as the American Sublime. What both Kyle and James bring is not, strictly speaking, violence, but meaning. That is, ultimately, *The Terminator* and *12 Monkeys* do not celebrate macho violence so much as they celebrate inventive strategies for creating meaning in one's life. In both movies, all of the proponents of violence as a solution to what confronts them are portrayed pejoratively, especially the punks and the police in *The Terminator* and the various versions on the mad scientists and radicals in *12 Monkeys*. Violence is and always has been the false solution to the problem of our American identity, to the problem of our belatedness as Americans. For Bloom, the real solution, the peculiarly American solution, to the problem of our belatedness, which I take to be just a more particular version of Heidegger's conception of "thrownness," will have to do with finding a way to be responsible for our own identity in spite of our thrownness, in spite of the fact that we find ourselves in a world with no clear idea of what to make of it or of ourselves.

How does watching these movies help us to make something of that fact? Wittgenstein's formulation of this problem is to ask, what is the axis of our real need?[25] We cannot rely on an answer to this from the institutionalized social systems, because their only criterion for determining value is, shortsightedly, their own internalized conception of efficiency, which terrorizes us. The way to escape from this terror seems to be to find what is genuinely ours. According to Rorty, certainly influenced by Heidegger, this will emerge from a state of anxiety.

Rorty's form of the hero is the "liberal ironist." His description of an ironist goes well for the characters of both Sarah Connor and Catherine Railly: "The ironist spends her time worrying about the possibility that she has been initiated into the wrong tribe, taught to play the wrong language game. She worries that the process of socialization may have given her the wrong language, and so turned her into the wrong kind of human being. But she cannot give a criterion for wrongness."[26] Both Sarah Connor and Catherine Railly seem to be very uncomfortable with their social roles. Both manifest concerns that are regarded with suspicion by other, more centrally placed, members of the society. I am thinking in particular of Sarah Connor's experience in the police station and Catherine Railly's interactions with her colleagues on the subject of James Cole.

One way of reading these films is to see the female and the male characters and their experiences as mirroring one another, but as in a funhouse mirror. Both are versions of Rorty's ironist: from anxiety they emerge as individuals who are idiosyncratic, critical, receptive to alternative ways of perceiving things, and, ultimately, *creators* of alternative ways of perceiving things. The central female characters in *The Terminator* and in *12 Monkeys* enact this drama of self-realization through finding something beyond themselves, but idiosyncratic to themselves, to which they are committed, and which for them is simply love. In this sense, if the finding of one's authentic self is what these movies are most deeply about, then the real protagonists of the dramas are the women in the films. They are the ones who enact the drama of the recovery of one's authentic self in more like real everyday terms that we all can imitate. The time machine for them, which is to say, that which forces them out of their "theyness," to confront the submerged anxiety of their past so that they can live futurally (i.e., embrace their Being-unto-Death), is their encounter with a man who holds out to them the possibility of a kind of care or love. And so the real time machine, what may serve for us as a kind of Heideggerian version of a time machine, is not the mysterious science fiction invention; the science fiction invention is a kind of objective correlative for the epiphenomenon of the receptive encounter with another person in whom the possibility of love for you resides, all of which can occur in the glance of the eye (an *Augenblick*).

For Heidegger, what occurs in the person who comes to grips with their own anxiety is something like a transformation, a gestalt shift, and it occurs in an *Augenblick*. It is, as Dreyfus says, "the moment of transformation from falling to resoluteness."[27] What is seen is, ultimately, a projection, which is what understanding consists of for Heidegger. What is projected is the sense of one's own genuine possibilities, one's own genuine possible future ways of being. This is a kind of discovery of the possibility of one's own authentic commitments. For Kyle this seems to have been triggered by the photograph of Sarah Connor, who looks, somewhat sadly, directly out of the photograph. For James it was triggered by the witnessing of his own death, and even more significantly, by the glance of the eye of Catherine Railly. Catherine, in her love for him, seeks out his childhood self, and in her glance holds out the future possibility of love to him.[28] In both instances, what initiates the possibility of the transformation to authentic being is the possibility of love that is first offered in a glance of the eye to their past and future selves. So, for the male heroes as well as the female heroes of these two films, the real initiator of the trajectories that will follow is the encounter with a sense of the possibility of, and so the search for, a kind of love.

I say that the male protagonists and the female protagonists mirror each other, but as in a funhouse mirror, because of the specific kind of trajectory their search for this love will take. The women in the two films have to confront and overcome obstacles like skepticism, social disapproval, and the coming to terms with their own possibilities with respect to the future, to understand a set of possibilities that they alone are responsible for configuring, but all of which happens in relatively realistic everyday terms. The men, on the other hand, must travel in time machines, run, fight, and shoot their way to the same goal. This, it seems to me, is the kitsch version of the American Sublime. It is a lesson taught twice, and once with a hammer, because even in our terrorized state, we recognize and love the romance of the autonomous, spontaneous, strong, self-made, self-created hero.

Of course, this romance of the autonomous, entirely self-reliant hero contributes to our terror. It is part of the cultural landscape that we find ourselves thrown into, hence feel compelled to try to live up to, hence are terrorized by. It is a cruel irony of Western male identity that our aspirations to "theyness" can only be met through asserting our emotional autonomy, our emotional unconnectedness, from others. I never said that going to the movies wasn't a mixed bag. Certainly, there are risks to run at the movies. I just insist that the risks are worth running, although it is best to be prepared for them with some philosophy.

With some philosophy, *The Terminator* and *12 Monkeys* can lead us to an ancient wisdom that is also a very recent wisdom. It is a wisdom about the possibility of redemption through transcendence, and of transcendence through an acceptance of one's particular circumstances, which includes an affirming acknowledgment of one's own death. When one has been shattered by, but also has accepted the reality of, one's own death, then one becomes futural. It is only then that one really chooses one's future, as opposed to having a future foisted onto one by the "they." It is only in being futural that one can authentically be in a moment and know its real value. To be in the moment is to be prepared in a moment, in an *Augenblick*, to recognize the authenticity of another. This is how one's life acquires authentic meaning (as opposed to "they" meaning). It is how one becomes what one is. The philosophical lesson contained in the narratives of these two movies is that one becomes an authentic self through a creative, or moral, or personal, act, but an act that is chosen and is chosen out of love. As the original Oedipus says in Sophocles' *Oedipus at Colonus*:

> . . . one word
> Frees us of all the weight and pain of life:
> The word is love.[29, 30]

6

Into the Toilet: Some Classical Aesthetic Themes Raised by a Scene in Trainspotting

Hope it's not too big bring on piles again. No, just right. So. Ah!
Costive one tabloid of cascara Sagrada. Life might be so.
—Leopold Bloom, thinking, in *Ulysses*

Things of the body. Aristotle was not averse to considering them. As he says in *Parts of Animals*, "...if men and animals and their several parts are natural phenomena, then the natural philosopher must take into consideration their flesh, blood, bone, and all other homogeneous parts; nor only these, but also the heterogeneous parts, such as face, hand, foot, and the like."[1] A few pages later Aristotle tells a story about Heraclitus. Aristotle is admonishing against squeamishness and says, "We therefore must not recoil with childish aversion from the examination of the humbler animals. Every realm of nature is marvelous: and as Heraclitus, when the strangers who came to visit him found him warming himself at the fireplace in the kitchen, is reported to have bidden them not to hold back from entering, since even in the kitchen divinities are present)."[2] One might say as well, also in the bathroom. If, as Lakoff and Johnson claim in their work in *Philosophy in the Flesh*, "The mind is inherently embodied,"[3] then, perhaps, greater attention needs to be paid by current philosophy to things of the body.

In *Ulysses*, Joyce describes Leopold having a bowel movement after which Joyce has the thought run through Leopold's mind (not without irony), occasioned by a piece in the paper that Leopold is reading while relieving himself, "Print anything now."[4] One might think the same about what gets into movies these days after watching Danny Boyle's *Trainspotting*. It is a movie filled with disturbing and horrific episodes, most of which have to do with bodily functions gone awry, or just too

109

intimately considered. A focal scene for this theme in the movie is the episode that involves the movie's protagonist, Renton, having to make an emergency bathroom stop and being compelled to make use of what is labeled in the film as "the worst toilet in Scotland." To briefly fill in the details, Renton is a heroin addict who has decided to give up his addiction. In preparation for the traumas of withdrawal he has taken some precautions, one of which, by chance, ends up being the use of two opium-filled suppositories. He, somewhat unwisely, inserts the suppositories as soon as he procures them, and then must walk back to his apartment while they begin to take effect. It is on the return trip that the suppositories begin to do their work and Renton must make use of the first toilet he can get to.

In the scene that I would like to focus on, Renton enters a bar, and finds the way to the toilet which involves a strangely long passageway through a very dank, dark, underworld-like back storeroom to an even more liquid, say, swamplike men's room. He finds quick relief, but then remembers the essential suppositories, now extruded. To the viewers' considerable alarm, he immediately hops off the stool in order to plunge his hands down into his own fecal mess to recover the lost suppositories. The groping through the opaque effluvia is not immediately successful, and as Renton extends his reach down into the toilet, the film shifts to a kind of surreal dream sequence. He slips into the toilet entirely, sneakers last; on-screen we see a kind of heroic dive and underwater swim through pristine, but not undangered waters (he swims past a spiked land mine). Through the crystalline waters Renton can see the precious white tablets nestled among some rocks and swims down to recover them. After that he emerges from the toilet and the bathroom sopping wet to make his way home.

What does this scene have to do with truth and beauty? Well, I actually think a lot, but, as we shall see, there will be some differences of opinion with respect to what constitutes truth and beauty. My intention is to show how this scene from *Trainspotting* not only invokes some classical aesthetic theories, but also that it manifests some of the aspects of human experience that aesthetic theory has long striven to characterize and describe. The reference to "classical" is meant to invoke the Greeks and it is with them that I will start. My strategy is to survey several quite different lines of thought with the intention of tracing their convergence to a focal point that is meant to illuminate some features of art, human experience, and the movie *Trainspotting*.

In the *Poetics*, Aristotle famously, and famously cryptically, describes the experience of tragedy in terms of "catharsis." Catharsis, literally, a purging, following Bernays' interpretation,[5] can refer to either a medical/physiological purging by means of aperient or laxative, or a religious/spiritual purging to rid the soul of some accrued pollution by means of ritual observations. To which of these ideas of catharsis Aristotle refers is not completely clear, but in either case, the idea of catharsis by means of tragedy is certainly meant symbolically. Aristotle himself never unpacks this symbolic notion of catharsis. What Aristotle says about tragedy, however, is that, "through pity and fear it achieves the purgation of these emotions."[6] The idea here seems to be that through the experience of an excess of fear and pity, fear and pity are somehow expelled from us, leaving us both calmer and wiser after the experience, and that this experience is somehow the point of tragedy.

I would like to begin to explore this symbolic description of the effect of tragedy on us as a kind of purging in terms of the most primitive form on which this symbol is based, the phenomenon of purging by means of an aperient. The notion of catharsis at this level invokes the necessitating condition of constipation. Constipation, in the sense of an unhealthy or unwanted retention of material, can be easily translated into the symbolic mode as a psychic retention that is similarly unhealthy or unwanted.

To apply these initial steps to the situation in the movie *Trainspotting*, the character Renton is, in fact, physically constipated because of his heroin use, which could also be viewed as a kind of objective correlative for a psychic constipation, and he is in need of an aperient for both forms of constipation. For Aristotle, there is a fairly explicit connection made between the physical object, i.e., the play, and psychic health, which is the result of the cathartic experience that results from watching the play. Of course, for Aristotle, the point of the play is not that the protagonist experience catharsis, but that the virtuous (or, at least, basically virtuous) people in the audience do. In the movie Renton employs some opium-filled suppositories. Within the context of the movie the suppositories are a necessary aperient for Renton's physical condition, but also a remedy for his psychic condition. The movie itself, if it is to be effective along these Aristotelian lines, will, in turn, function as a kind of aperient for us, the audience of the movie, to restore us to a condition of less-retentive health.

What, then, is the psychic correlative to the physical condition of constipation, a condition presumably both Renton and we, the audience, suffer from to a greater or lesser degree? Well, according to Aristotle, what must be purged are the emotions of "pity and fear." What do we pity and what do we fear? That is to say, what are the sources of these unhealthily stored responses? One might say that the answer to this question is simply, life. Or, perhaps one might say with more precision, life within the context of a society, or, in other words, social life. Social life is not only fraught with many anxieties, about money, job, food, shelter, love, other people, sickness, and death, but also with a great deal of necessary retention of our emotional responses of, for example, fear and pity, as well as hostility, envy, erotic desire, and all sorts of non-erotic desires.

Negotiating this tangled web of physical need, emotional response, and necessary emotional retention (or repression, following Freud) is an extremely difficult task, especially when conditions in the world conspire against the successful satisfaction of our various needs in these various areas, as they certainly do for Renton (and for most of us). As Renton says, talking about being a heroin addict, "We're not...stupid." And he is more or less right about this. That is, he is operating in a near impossible context, a context in which no strategy will be particularly effective, hence any strategy will be just about as effective as any other. At least the strategy of heroin provides a temporary cessation of the pain and a modicum of pleasure, or as Renton says, "People think it's all about misery and desperation and death and all that shyte, which is not to be ignored. But what they forget is the pleasure of it."

The fact that Renton is a drug addict and that the aperient, the drug, he uses is opiated, and so is a drug-filled drug, is worth pursuing. Aristotle traces the development of the tragedy as emerging from the festivals of Dionysus, and especially the dithyramb portion of those festivals. Dionysus was the god of wine and drunkenness, or at least that is one part of his domain. He is associated with the ancient mother-earth cults, Demeter, and the dark forces of nature, generally. It is this sense of the Dionysian that Nietzsche makes so much of in *The Birth of Tragedy*.[7] Camille Paglia associates the Dionysian with Plutarch's *hygra physis* or liquid nature, and she says, "Dionysian liquidity is the invisible sea of organic life, flooding our cells and uniting us to plants and animals....I interpret Plutarch's *hygra physis* as not free-flowing but contained water, fluids, which ooze, drip and hang...."[8] Liquidity is a pervasive theme in *Trainspotting*, not only in toilets, but more centrally in the movie's fascination with the liquid form that heroin must take for it to be injected. In addition, Renton's experience in the bathroom is a veritable recreation of the primal Dionysian swamp that Paglia describes.

For Nietzsche, the ancient Greeks were trying to negotiate the very demands that life in a society forces upon us that I listed above, and to do so with a minimum of illusion and a maximum of enthusiasm for life. As Nietzsche says about the Greek attitude toward the arts, specifically as they were represented in the figure of Apollo, it is "the arts generally, which make life possible and worth living."[9] The Dionysian by itself, that is, nature in its rawest form is too much for us, a "'witches' brew' of sensuality and cruelty."[10] The force in us opposed to that of the Dionysian is the Apollonian, the force of the human intellect and imagination. The Apollonian represents a constructed illusion that we interpose between nature and us, a "transfiguring mirror"[11] that is the basis of art. This transfiguring mirror makes the horrible beautiful; it transforms the absurdity of life into something eminently desirable. Too much

Apollonian, however, leads to an anemic "healthy-mindedness." That is, illusion that we do not see as illusion, a kind of absolute blindness to the Dionysian, makes us vulnerable to the Dionysian. We are weakened by a loss of enthusiasm for life and alienated from ourselves and others by our insistence on our own separate individuality, what Nietzsche calls, following Schopenhauer, the *principium individuationis*.[12] Too much of the Dionysian, and we lose touch with our own personal sense of ourselves. We experience the "mysterious Primal Unity," with other people and all things, but we lose our sense of our individual self; we lose our *principium individuationis*. Without a sufficiently strong sense of ourselves, we begin to lose track of ourselves and begin to court death. What Nietzsche prescribes is a healthy balance of these two forces.

Nietzsche, and somewhat derivatively, Paglia, both see the truth of art and the art of truth as stemming from the necessary negotiation between dark Dionysian forces and light Apollonian construction, that is, the construction of illusion, of an art to live by, that will apotropaically control these Dionysian forces. Pure Apollonian is anemic and life-threatening because in its hyperrational denial of the Dionysian it makes itself susceptible to the Dionysian. Pure Dionysian is life-threatening because one loses the point of one's own *principium individuationis*, even to the point of neglecting one's own life. That leads to the choice of death, which is more or less the description that Renton gives for his choice to be a heroin addict at the beginning of the movie. Life requires, and art seeks to establish, the two mixed in the proper proportion. Achieving this appropriate mix will necessarily involve the expulsion of some proportion of whichever of the two one has in excess—that is, a catharsis.

Renton is a kind of paradigm of Dionysian excess, and his life conforms to this pattern in terms of its chaos and complete disorder. Interestingly, ironically, it will take a kind of descent into the Dionysian to cure his Dionysian sickness and, homeopathically, to restore some Apollonian order to his psyche and life. He will need some opiated suppositories.

I will be making some claims for the universality of Renton's condition of ill health. I will not insist that the condition is always exactly similar to Renton's, although his does seem to be emblematic of the *Zeitgeist*, especially for those, say, under thirty. But, certainly, the problem as often goes to the other extreme, as Nietzsche diagnosed his own times, and the retention, then, seems to be more on the order of the Apollonian—too much order, too much control, too much illusion. But first I want to briefly examine the Greek paradigm that opposes this Aristotelian and later Nietzschean ideal of health as a kind of emotional balance, namely, Plato.

In the *Republic*, Plato explicitly refers to poetry as a kind of drug and as a kind of poison. Unlike Aristotle, who seems to view the ingestion of potentially harmful substances as sometimes salutary if it is done appropriately, and the excitation of emotions in order to balance emotions as psychically healthy, Plato seems to regard both of these as slipping into sickness. The classic expression of Plato's distrust of art occurs in book ten of the *Republic* where Plato describes what he calls the "ancient quarrel" between philosophy and poetry.[13] At the beginning of book ten Plato describes the way in which art is like a poison which needs an antidote of knowledge; "all such poetry is likely to damage the minds of the audience unless these have knowledge of its nature, as an antidote."[14] Derrida addresses this theme in Plato with a complex and fascinating treatment of the Greek concept of *pharmakon*, that is, a drug that either can be used to heal or to poison. Derrida examines two texts in detail, the *Phaedrus* and the *Timeaus*. In *Timeaus*, Plato seems to argue against using any drugs, except, perhaps, in the most extreme situations. After listing two salutary forms of motion (such as exercise and the surging motion of sailing), Plato identifies a third and unhealthy form of motion. Derrida gives the following quote from the Timeaus:

> the third sort of motion may be of use in a case of extreme necessity, but in any other will be adopted by no man of sense—I mean the purgative treatment (*tēs pharmakeutikes Katharseōs*) of physicians; for diseases unless they are very dangerous should not be irritated by medicines (*ouk erethisteon phaemakeiais*), since every form of disease is in a manner akin to the living being (*tēi tōn zōōn phusei*), whose complex frame (*sustasis*) has an appointed term of life. For not the whole race only, but each individual—barring inevitable accidents—comes into the world having a fixed span.... And this holds also of the constitution of diseases; if anyone regardless of the appointed time tries to subdue them by medicine (*pharmakeiais*), he only aggravates and multiplies them. Wherefore we ought always to manage them by regimen, as far as a man can spare the time, and not provide a disagreeable enemy by medicines (*pharmakeuonta*) (89a-d).[15]

The "disagreeable enemy" that Plato is referring to here would seem to be that which goes against our own natures, part of which seems to include for Plato disease. To rid ourselves of disease by this unnatural method, as opposed to the natural one of just exercise and proper eating, is to distort our essential natures, hence to give in to, even to celebrate, chaos, contingency, and chance.

Derrida's own pre-quote gloss on this passage is,

> Plato is following Greek tradition and, more precisely, the doctors of Cos. The *pharmakon* goes against natural life: not only

life unaffected by any illness, but even sick life, or rather the
life of the sickness. For Plato believes in the natural life and
normal development, so to speak, of disease. In the *Timeaus*,
natural disease...is compared to a living organism which must
be allowed to develop according to its own norms and forms,
its specific rhythms and articulations. In disturbing the normal
and natural progress of the illness, the *pharmakon* is thus the
enemy of the living in general, whether healthy or sick.[16]

In his discussion of the *Phaedrus*, Derrida explores the use of a text as a
pharmakon. That is, in the *Phaedrus* there is a text of a speech that
Phaedrus uses to seduce Socrates away from the city and out to the coun-
tryside. As Socrates says, "You seem to have discovered a drug for getting
me out."[17] Derrida makes explicit the suspicions he attributes to Plato
about this use of drugs or texts; "one and the same suspicion envelops in a
single embrace the book and the drug, writing and whatever works in an
occult, ambiguous manner open to empiricism and chance, governed by
the ways of magic and not the laws of necessity."[18] Derrida here taps into
the same explanation of Plato's motivations as Martha Nussbaum does in
her *The Fragility of Goodness*, namely, his response to, one might say fear
of, the contingency of the good in this radically contingent world.[19]

Drugs and art magnify this contingency rather than reduce it.
Reduction of the contingency is the function that reason can and ought to
serve. In Plato, however, there is an ambivalence that is recorded in the
Timeaus section quoted above, as well as in the *Phaedrus* with respect to
writing, as Derrida will point out; it is also in the passages in the *Republic*
that have to do with art in the ideal city. It is that some form of art may
always be necessary because not all of our experiences in the world will,
ultimately, be controllable by reason. Hence the reference to "very dangerous" diseases as the exception to the general rule against purgative medi-
cines, and the necessary conscription of the artists to the service of the
state in even the ideal city because not all people will be able to be guided
by their internal source of reason, and no people will be able to as children. This suggests a recognition even in Plato for the necessity of a
cathartic art as a corrective, at least in the complexly social polis he is
forced to construct after the abandonment by majority opinion of the
original simpler city.

So, one might say that Plato's official position is that both drugs and
poetry are pernicious and must be eliminated, say, purged, from the city;
but that he also has an informal, implicit position. This formulation of
Plato's position identifies a tension that is central to Plato's philosophy,
namely, that his opposition to art and emotion occurs within the contexts
of extremely dramatic, artistic, and emotion-laden dialogues. The man

protests too much. His protests themselves draw attention to, and perhaps obliquely acknowledge, the very contingency of life that his hyper-rationalism explicitly, if perhaps not entirely sincerely, denies. Plato himself even admits to a certain disingenuousness pervading his written philosophy in the generally credited second letter. There Plato writes, "... there is not and will not be any written work of Plato's own. What are called his are the works of a Socrates embellished and modernized."[20]

It is part of Derrida's point that the text, for Plato, is a *pharmakon*, hence is a drug that restores health. Drugs may be recommendable only in extreme circumstances, but all of this is leading to the conclusion that we all do live in extreme circumstances. We are all closer to Renton's position than we might want to acknowledge, and we are all involved in drug use in one form or another. The hyper-Apollonianism of the official Platonic position is as addictive as the Dionysian slide into heroin that Renton follows, and as tempting, and as destructive. It is destructive in its retentiveness, and because of the toxicity of what is retained.

Nussbaum talks about the "therapy of desire" and quotes Seneca on the idea of the appropriateness of different desires at different times in one's life: "Each period of life has its own constitution, one for the baby, and another for the boy, and another for the old man."[21] Desires themselves are neither good nor bad, but neither are they naturally moderate or self-patrolling, hence the need for therapy. Desires appropriate one day may no longer be appropriate on another day. We must determine for ourselves which desires and their modes of satisfaction are appropriate for us for a given time of our life. In judging our own, as well as those of others, full weight must be put of the demands of the contexts in which we find ourselves. Extreme contexts would seem to be more the norm than the exception today, and perhaps always.

With this notion of appropriate desires changing in response to changing contexts, and the necessity, therefore, for changing therapies, I would like to pick up on an idea by Bert Cardullo from his essay on *Trainspotting*, "Fiction into Film, or Bringing Welsh to Boyle." Cardullo compares the opening and final voice-over monologues by Renton in the movie. Cardullo persuasively argues that these monologues track the progress that Renton makes across the trajectory of the movie. His point is that the progress made between these, as he calls them, "framing soliloquies," is really not much. That is, the progress is really not much more than the substitution of one form of "mind-numbing, spirit-crushing philistinism" (in the form of the acceptance and determined pursuit of bourgeois diversions) for another (in the form of "soporific drug addiction").[22] I would like to look at these two monologues from a perspective slightly different from that of Cardullo, in order to come to a conclusion slightly different from his.

The opening monologue is a kind of *apologia* for Renton's use of heroin:

Choose life. Choose a job. Choose a career. Choose a family. Choose a fucking big television, choose washing machines, cars, compact disc players and electrical tin openers. Choose good health, low cholesterol and dental insurance. Choose fixed-interest mortgage repayments. Choose a starter home. Choose your friends. Choose leisurewear and matching luggage. Choose a three-piece suit on hire purchase in a range of fucking fabrics. Choose DIY and wondering who the fuck you are on a Sunday morning. Choose sitting on that couch watching mind-numbing, spirit-crushing game shows, stuffing fucking junk food into your mouth. Choose rotting away at the end of it all, pishing your last in a miserable home, nothing more than an embarrassment to the selfish, fucked-up brats you have spawned to replace yourself. Choose your future. Choose life. But why would I want to do a thing like that? I chose not to choose life. I chose somthin' else. And the reasons? There are no reasons. Who needs reasons when you've got heroin?[23]

This is a powerful existential lament, and not least because it strikes so close to home. What Renton has listed in this monologue is not just a version of the capitalist dream of total acquisition, but also the very kinds of concerns that I have tried to suggest Aristotle has partially in mind for the things about which we are retentive and so burdened by. If this soliloquy does not exactly make the alternative of heroin look attractive, it does make this particular alternative to heroin look pretty crazy. And pretty frightening.

In the concluding voice-over, after ripping off his friends, Renton has reached a very different conclusion:

So why did I do it? I could offer a million answers, all false. The truth is that I'm a bad person, but that's going to change, I'm going to change. This is the last of this sort of thing. I'm cleaning up and I'm moving on, going straight and choosing life. I'm looking forward to it already. I'm going to be just like you: the job, the family, the fucking big television, the washing machine, the car, the compact disc and electrical tin opener, good health, low cholesterol, dental insurance, mortgage, starter home, leisurewear, luggage, three-piece suite, DIY, games shows, junk food, children, walks in the park, nine to five, good at golf, washing the car, choice sweaters, family Christmas, indexed pension, tax exemption, clearing the gutters, getting by, looking ahead, to the day you die.[24]

This is quite a turn away from the opening monologue. If we take this literally, then I think Cardullo is absolutely right that not much progress has been made by Renton across the trajectory of the movie. Renton has simply exchanged an excessively Dionysian perspective for an excessively Apollonian one. Given all that we have come to know about Renton, however, his intelligence, his wit, his determination, not to mention his opening monologue, we might want to take this ironically. But to take it ironically is initially only to acknowledge that he does not mean exactly what he says. What he does mean remains unspecified, remains to be reconstructed. I have no definitive reconstruction to offer, but I do have some suggestions to make toward such a reconstruction.

If we accept Plato's prescription for the use of a *pharmakon*, that is, that while not the mode of preference, under severe conditions use of a *pharmakon* may be exactly what is required, then the adoption of bourgeois, capitalist dreams might be just the right *pharmakon* for a repeat heroin addict. If the accretion of this-worldly concerns signals the kind of retentiveness that defeats us (that will require a purging in order for us to remain healthy), then, perhaps, the very fact that Renton lists his new bourgeois, capitalist dreams ironically signals his intention to adopt them (use them as a *pharmakon*) only ironically, by which I understand to mean, provisionally, lightly, pragmatically, perhaps one might even say, aesthetically or artistically. The suggestion of his adoption of these dreams, but only ironically, seems to me to put Renton more or less in the company of Plato's own teacher on how to think about life, Socrates. That is, if Renton is adopting these bourgeois, capitalist dreams ironically, hence with the acknowledgment that they are only *pharmakon*s, and not the ultimate way to truth or happiness or the good life, then this will constitute definite progress over his angry, desperate, really unironic choice of heroin in the beginning of the movie. Then Renton, like Socrates (at least sort of), becomes one who is in search of the way to the good life, the way to happiness, and who is willing to use whatever tools, ideas, or stories that may present themselves to that end.

Trainspotting is as much a comedy as it is a tragedy. Nietzsche speaks explicitly of art as "a saving sorceress, expert in healing" and of the comic as "the artistic discharge of the nausea of absurdity."[25] Renton seems to be especially sensitive to the "nausea of absurdity," which is the source of most of his wit. In some sense, all of his choices can be seen in light of an attempt at this type of discharge, a discharge of the "nausea of absurdity." According to Aristotle, the original motivations for our retentiveness are the emotions of pity and fear. The cure will be their being purged. The aperient of choice is art, say, movies.

Trainspotting as a comedy and a tragedy picks up the suggestion that Socrates makes at the end of the *Symposium* that a tragedian ought to be able to write comedies as well; and perhaps he means, ideally, in the same work.[26] S. H. Butcher suggests that in a bourgeois, capitalistic society pure tragedies of the Aristotelian form are no longer possible because there are no longer clearly identifiable examples of people who are superior by birth, as the old aristocracy class system insisted.[27] Without the possibility of that sort of heroic failure, perhaps the best replacement form is a kind of tragic comedy, the tragic and comedic strivings of a common person in a difficult and hostile world. Such a tragic comedy would perforce include the tragic comedy of our biological natures; Renton in the dirtiest toilet in Scotland, us sitting in the dark staring open-mouthed and passive at a large screen, that is, at the movies. In these we see our own tragic comedies being played out and have added to our own anxieties the additional anxieties of the protagonists. Such an overload of anxiety over our daily vicissitudes undoes the seriousness with which we are wont to regard our own cases, and so purges us of them through a kind of tragic laughter. It is a *pharmakon* by means of which our extreme condition may be ameliorated, some sense of irony and perspective restored. We are refreshed, excited, calmed, and renewed. We are made aware of what we share with everyone else and in this feeling of unity we get about as much of beauty as Aristotle, or Nietzsche, or Socrates, allows there to be.[28]

7

Horror and Death at the Movies

Death plucks my ear and says, Live—I am coming.
—Virgil, *Minor Poems, Copa*

Introduction: The Seduction of Horror

There is a weird familiarity in the experience of watching a horror movie: as strange and awful as the things that are about to occur are, they are also somehow continuous with our ordinary lives in some deep way. It is that continuity that I would like to explore.[1]

In *The Night of the Living Dead*, for example, there is a liveliness to the walking dead that derives from the multiplicity of their ways of resonating. They resonate, for example, with the inhabitants of Dante's Hell. Dante regarded the scenes he witnessed in Hell, at least on one level, as simply the internal lives of his fellow Florentines externalized.[2] Presumably, for Dante, his journey through Hell was not unlike the strolls he once took through his native Florence, seeing on every hand the debilitating, dehumanizing, and, to some extent, self-imposed sufferings of his fellow citizens. It takes a certain moral sensitivity to see such extraordinary things amid ordinary situations, which is part of Dante's genius.

The zombies in *The Night of the Living Dead* also have a horrible familiarity about them, similar to the familiarity for Dante of the inhabitants of his Hell. This aspect of *The Night of the Living Dead* is picked up and maximally exploited in its sequel, *Dawn of the Dead*. There the vague familiarity one feels in the original is made comically explicit as zombies wander through a shopping mall, as interested in the dimly recalled habits of shopping as they are in eating flesh. Not only have I witnessed such scenes in real life, I have participated in them.

The pleasure of reading about such scenes, as in Dante's *Inferno*, or of watching them in *Dawn of the Dead*, would seem to involve a double recognition. First there is the recognition of the phenomenon itself. We

121

have seen people who look like they are zombies. This recognition rein-
forces our sense of our difference from them. There would then be the
recognition that we have been like zombies ourselves in a shopping mall.
This is a kind of double turn. The first turn is the recognition that people,
when looked at with a certain detachment, can look a lot like zombies. We
see the monotonous repetitiveness and thoughtlessness of their behavior.
The second turn is that we, too, when not taking this detached view, when
we are just doing our daily activities, must look like zombies as well. This
second turn can lead to a third, the turn toward a wisdom about how to
live a better life as a full human being, about how to avoid living as a
zombie. Certainly, it is the intent of Dante's *Inferno* to recount and to
effect this third turning. Our attraction to such scenes, then, may be com-
prised of both a kind of identification and a kind of instructive repulsion,
both of which fascinate us. They fascinate us with their weird familiarity
and with their cautionary directive of what to avoid.

A striking rumination on the closeness and the primitiveness of the
horrible in our everyday lives occurs in Don DeLillo's *Underworld*. Late in
the novel the character Bronzini is reflecting on the phenomenon of being
"it" in the game of tag:

> He was wondering about being *it*.... Another person tags you
> and you're it. What exactly does this mean? Beyond being
> neutered. You are a nameless and bedeviled. *It*. The evil one
> whose name is too potent to be spoken....
>
> A fearsome power in the term because it makes you sepa-
> rate from the others. You flee the tag, the telling touch. But
> once you're *it*, name-shorn, neither boy nor girl, you're the
> one who must be feared. You're the dark power in the street.
> And you feel a kind of demonry, chasing players, trying to
> put your skelly-bone hand on them, to spread your taint,
> your curse. Speak the syllable slowly if you can. A whisper of
> death perhaps.[3]

This wonderful description reveals in a children's game a kind of atavistic
re-enactment of some primitive horror scenario. Children love to play tag,
and the terror of being touched can be quite real in mid-game. There is a
deep familiarity we have with this phenomenon, and a deep attraction to
it. In choosing to play tag there is a kind of invocation of the sublime "it."
The game is a challenge to "it," a declaration of one's determination and
ability to avoid "it," but it is also an invitation, a summoning. There is
something in the experience of being in the presence of "it," in the frisson
of its nearness, that we welcome.

The walking dead are themselves strangely attractive. Not only is
there a certain erotic allure to the inevitable young and naked zombies,

but there is also the singularity of their desire that gives them a kind of unconflicted, unreflective, group cohesion that is also attractive. Their sheer numbers, the relentlessness of their appetite and their approach, and the fragility of the living make resistance seem futile. And, in the end, why resist? Why not just give in to this relentless desire and join them? Why not give up the struggle? Why not go to them willingly? Although it is difficult to answer these questions, the imperative not to give up is quite powerful.

In *Night of the Living Dead*, a brother and sister are visiting the cemetery where the body of their father was buried long ago. They make the visit every year; they feel compelled to do so, but do not seem to fully understand why. One might say that they are drawn to, but also repulsed by, this place of the dead. The sister kneels at the gravestone of their father and prays, while the brother makes derogatory remarks about such prayer and says that prayers are for church, a place he no longer goes. The brother recounts the story of when they were once there at that cemetery as children and he hid, then leaped out to frighten his sister. It is then, almost as though summoned by the impiety of the brother in this place of the dead, or maybe just as an illustration of his story, that a man is seen in the background, stumbling awkwardly toward the brother and sister. The brother pretends that the man is a zombie, "They're coming for you Barbara. Look! There comes one of them now!" The sister calls him "ignorant" and seems irrationally terrified. Not so irrationally, as it turns out, since the man *is* a zombie and he *is* coming to eat them.

Horror and Death

> "...You must travel down
> to the House of Death...."
> —Circe to Odysseus, Book 10, *The Odyssey*

One of the first extant horror narratives, a narrative that has many of the themes and characteristics that we associate with horror movies today, occurs in book eleven of Homer's *The Odyssey*. Book eleven involves a narrative that is known as the katabasis, literally, the descent.[4] It is when Odysseus must descend into Hades, the realm of the dead, in order to put a question to Tiresias, the blind seer. It is only by hearing Tiresias's answer that Odysseus can continue his return to his home, the island of Ithaca.

The story is quite complex, both in terms of its structure and in terms of its content, and I will only be able to indicate a few of the complexities and ambiguities of the story here. First of all, the story does not occur in real time but is a story within a story. It is a story that Odysseus is telling some considerable time after the fact, to his hosts, the

Phaeacians, themselves a people in a place invented by Homer. It is difficult to find the relevant beginning of the story of the katabasis because it seems to draw the whole of the narrative of *The Odyssey* into it. To begin somewhat arbitrarily and unsatisfactorily, Odysseus has been roused from his life of physical comfort and pleasure with Circe by his men, who want to get moving on after a year stuck on that mythical isle. Odysseus petitions Circe for permission to leave. She grants him his wish to leave but tells him that first, before heading for home, it is necessary that he descend "to the House of Death" to consult Tiresias. He is distraught by such grim news, weeps, then recovers and is ready for the journey. Circe gives him very specific instructions about how to get there and what to do once he arrives.

Circe tells Odysseus that when they arrive at the place of the dead he must make offerings, first of milk, honey, wine, water, and barley. He must promise future offerings, to be made upon his return to Ithaca. Finally, he must fill a small trench with the blood of a ram and a black ewe. The dead will come, drawn by the sacrificial blood. Odysseus must keep them away from the blood until Tiresias arrives. Tiresias must be the first to drink for Odysseus to hear his words.

What follows will be in many ways quite familiar to an appreciator of contemporary horror films. The dead begin to approach. Odysseus is at first interested, amazed, curious about the appearance of the many dead, but then as they get closer his interest turns to horror:

> I took the victims, over the trench I cut their throats
> and the dark blood flowed in—and up out of Erebus they came,
> brides and unwed youths and old men who had suffered much
> and girls with their tender hearts freshly scarred by sorrow
> and great armies of battle dead, stabbed by bronze spears,
> men of war still wrapped in bloody armor—thousands
> swarming around the trench from every side—
> unearthly cries—blanching terror gripped me![5]

The turn in this passage is beautifully represented (by the translator) with a dash. Odysseus begins by regarding the dead with great sympathy and compassion. He, no doubt, identifies with the suffering of the old men, and recognizes the tender hearts of the dead young women. But then something begins to happen. Odysseus begins to feel overwhelmed by the shear number of dead, especially the less individually distinguishable dead fallen in battle. His interest and sympathy suddenly turn to terror.

This, it seems to me, is a basic pattern of horror. There is an initial fascination, a fascination with death and with the dead, a fascination that in one way or another works to summon some manifestation of the dead. Once the dead begin to arrive, however, once the reality of death becomes evident, there is a turn. The fascination becomes horror. There is very likely something universal in this pattern, as universal as death itself. The fascination with death seems to begin just about when a person begins to be aware of the reality of death, which I take to be in about one's teenage years. There is a trajectory here; one can successfully negotiate it, or one can fail to negotiate it. The trajectory itself is engaged by, and is a kind of working through of, a deep ambivalence about death and the dead.

The first of the dead that Odysseus encounters in Hades is his own recently dead comrade Elpenor. Elpenor died the night before they left Circe's island for Hades. It was not a noble death. He got drunk and fell off a roof, and so beats Odysseus to Hades. Odysseus's first response to Elpenor is tinged with guilt. In their hurry to leave Circe's island and to make their way to Hades, they left Elpenor's body behind, "unwept, unburied." This, as it turns out, is what Elpenor has come to ask of Odysseus, that Odysseus return to Circe's island to give his body proper funeral rites. He asks Odysseus to burn him in his armor by the sea "so even men to come will learn my story."[6] Odysseus promises him what he asks.

In *Looking Awry*, Slavoj Žižek identifies the "fundamental fantasy of contemporary mass culture" as being the "fantasy of the return of the living dead." Žižek goes on to ask and then answer the question, "why do the dead return? The answer offered by Lacan is the same found in popular culture: *because they were not properly buried.*" The dead return, as Žižek says, because of "a disturbance in the symbolic rite," because of "some unpaid symbolic debt."[7] The move to recognize the dead as a *problem* is a move that is the result of reflection. It is a move in the direction of philosophy.

This move is what I understand Wittgenstein to be referring to when he speaks of "the raw materials of philosophy" (*Investigations*, §254). A moment of reflection gives rise to the awareness of a problem to which our first response is to be tempted to an evasion. The dead pop up, we want to run away. We will need a little more philosophy in order to help us to negotiate this apparent threat successfully.

To recognize a symbolic debt to the dead is to have achieved a certain level of detachment from oneself and even from this world, and in such detachment begins philosophy. To worry about what is owed to the dead is to think from the perspective of the dead. We do this, presumably, by thinking from the perspective of ourselves as if we were dead. It is to ask oneself what we will want of the living (what we are now) once we are dead (which we will be). These feelings, no doubt, are engaged by a sense of guilt, a guilt we may feel toward the dead. The dead live and haunt us because we do not know how to make them rest easy, which is just a way of saying that we do not know how to feel easy about their death. This seems to be an especially pressing problem today

when so much emphasis is put on being young, and so little done to prepare anyone for age and death.

What do the dead want? Well, if Elpenor speaking from among the
dead can be taken as representative, they want a proper burial "so even
men to come will learn...[their] story." The proper burial, seems to be
more a means than an end. The goal is to be remembered. This is really
what we the living need. We need a way of remembering the dead so that
we can continue to live with them. If we do not have a way of remembering them so that they continue to live with us, if they disappear into an
abyss of death, the abyss of the unremembered, which is correlated with
the abyss of our unconscious, they will return for our blood, to eat our
brains, to stalk us with the necessity of their recognition.

I read Odysseus's katabasis as a symbolic analogue for a philosophical
adventure. He has departed Troy and left many dead friends and com-
rades behind. His return has itself been fraught with tribulations, leaving
little time for reflection. He has had some time, on the island with Circe,
and his mind has been freed to pursue more reflective pathways. It is a
thing to deal with, the dead. It is a thing for him to deal with, he with so
many dead. When Circe tells him that he must go to the House of the
Dead he does not ask why. He fears the journey, but also seems to accept
its necessity. When he descends into Hades, among the many famous
shades female and male that he will see and talk to, the most significant
will be *his* dead that he will see and talk to: Elpenor, his mother,
Agammenon, and Achilles.

It is a grim scene, the match of any horror movie, when Odysseus
talks with his mother. After he speaks with Tiresias, Odysseus holds off
the swarming shades waiting for the reappearance of his mother. "I kept
watch there, steadfast till my mother/approached and drank the dark,
clouding blood."[8] Yikes! Similar scenes occur in *Night of the Living Dead*
and countless other horror movies, where a family member or loved one
has died and turned into one who thirsts for the blood of the living. In this
case it is a sacrificial lamb's blood, but still, to see one's mother slurping
up "dark, clouding blood" has to disturb. The dead—at least the
unmourned and insufficiently remembered—have an insatiable appetite
for living flesh. The somewhat ironic wisdom seems to be that the dead
will only leave us alone when we sufficiently pay attention to them.

The katabasis adventure ends with a repetition of the initial trajectory.
Odysseus is longing to see the shades of still more ancient heroes, to continue this confrontation with the dead, but then,

>   ...the dead came surging around me,
>   hordes of them, thousands raising unearthly cries,
>   and blanching terror gripped me....[9]

Repetition characterizes neuroses, it characterizes what the repressed does (it returns), and it certainly characterizes what happens in horror movies. One way of reading horror movies is as katabasis, as a kind of descent out of the ordinary, everyday world to a place where one must confront the reality of death.

Martin Winkler says, "katabasis seems inevitably to entail at some level a search for identity. The journey is in some central, irreducible way a journey of self-discovery, a quest for a lost self."[10] This seems right to me, but to need some clarification. That is, one may be searching for one's lost pre-anxiety-in-the-face-of-death self, but that cannot be what one discovers. What one needs to discover is one's post-anxiety-in-the-face-of-death self. What we must discover is a way to think about death that tempers the horror of death for us.

Paradoxically, it will be the direct confrontation with death that will purge us of some of our fear of death. Horkheimer and Adorno in the *Dialectic of Enlightenment* describe a trajectory of laughter that strikes me as working as well for the horror of death. Their discussion of laughter comes in as part of their discussion of Odysseus's katabasis, his descent into Hades. They describe a dialectic of laughter, a trajectory that starts off in one direction only to make a turn in the opposite direction:

> Even though laughter is a sign of force, of the breaking out of blind obdurate nature, it also contains the opposite element—the fact that through laughter blind nature becomes aware of itself as it is, and thereby surrenders itself to the power of destruction.... Laughter is marked by the guilt of subjectivity, but in the suspension of law which it indicates it also points beyond thralldom. It is a promise of the way home. It is homesickness that gives rise to the adventures through which subjectivity (whose fundamental history is presented in the Odyssey) escapes from the prehistoric world.[11]

This description, if we replace the experience of horror with that of laughter, strikes me as a rather precise summary of the psychological components involved in Odysseus's katabasis, as well as of the dynamics of horror in general.

To fully confront the eruption of our horror at the reality of death actually works to de-horrify it. The guilt of our horror, like the guilt of our laughter, is a guilt of subjectivity, the guilt of being an independent and living subject. This is a suspension of the law because it is a manifestation of ourselves as an independent consciousness, not bound to a universal conformity. The suspension of the law shows us the limits of a universal conformity and a way beyond that universal conformity. It promises a way to return to ourselves (a way home) that we had lost because of a preoccupation that we could not confront. The confrontation with death, like laughter, is a confrontation with the "beyond the law" and so helps us to recognize a way back to our authentic selves. We escape from the hauntings of our unconscious to reemerge into the bright lights of a conscious world in which we are more fully ourselves. We are more fully ourselves because we have purged ourselves of the hauntings of the dead. They are purged not by total elimination but by acknowledgment.

Horror movies seem to hold a special fascination for teenagers. That may be a function, in part, of that being a time when one first has to deal with one's own dead, with friends who have died in car accidents and grandparents who have died of illness or age. It may also be a function of an emerging subjectivity. The development of the body in adolescence, especially the immense increase in the sexual imperative of the body, forces a kind of alienation from the body, a sense of "the witness of the body," hence an increase in the acuity with which one feels one's own subjectivity. Just as Odysseus must leave the comforts of the island of Circe, we all must leave the relative physical comfort of our child bodies. From this guilt and confusion are bound to reign. Teenage fascination with horror may be less about dealing with the symbolic burial of the dead and more about just dealing with the ambivalent love-hate relationship we have at that time with our bodies. The threat of extreme violence done to our bodies is both the most horrific thing that can be imagined and a secret fantasy of justice demanded by our subjectivity.

Odysseus is well past this Scylla and Charybdis. His guilt is different. But there is something similar to the pattern of the successful trajectory that needs to be achieved. Odysseus, like the heroine of a teenage slasher movie, must confront his worst fears about the dead and death and survive this confrontation. Something is learned in this confrontation that is fortifying, but is also difficult. This wisdom will also carry a certain responsibility. The heroine who outwits and evades the slasher's attacks knows something that her peers do not know, cannot know, and this knowledge will set her apart. It will be a burden, but also a source of strength. Odysseus, too, will have to learn a similar thing before he is prepared to return to his home.

When Odysseus encounters Achilles in Hades and speaks of his, Achilles', great blessings for having died so heroically, Achilles replies,

> No winning words about death to me, shining Odysseus!
> By god, I'd rather slave on earth for another man—
> some dirt-poor tenant farmer who scrapes to keep alive—
> than rule down here over all the breathless dead.[12]

What Odysseus and the heroine will learn is something about the reality of death, its banality, its real horror; death is not something to romanticize or wish for before its time. This, ironically enough, is the lesson that gets one past the horror of death. If this lesson is not learned, the horror is repeated over and over again, as it is in so many horror movies. This exemplifies the failure to complete the trajectory. The heroine is the one who can make it stop because she is the one who can learn something from it. Both Odysseus and the heroine will learn something not just about death, but also about life. They will learn that no matter how difficult it can be, death, by comparison, is a dim shadow of life. They will understand that death is coming, but not yet. Right now it is time to live.

Movies and Death

> Death is a rendez-vous...
> —Baudrillard, *Seduction*

Going to the movies has something of the katabasis about it. It is a kind of descent from out of our ordinary world into a dark cave in which we confront the specters of people, bodiless, but not soulless. In one sense, only some of the specters are actually dead (like Cary Grant and Humphrey Bogart), but in another sense, they are all from out of the past, selves that no longer belong to the living. Not all movies are horror movies, but it may be that all movies are a *Nekyia*, an underworld journey, and have something to do with death.[13]

There are some characters in specific movies like *The Sixth Sense* or *Leaving Las Vegas* about whom one could say (as the character Cheyenne says about Harmonica in Sergio Leone's great *Once Upon a Time in the West*): "People like that have something inside them, something to do with death." I would add, following Freud's identification of thanatos as an instinctual drive, that we all do. How does death connect with popular movies in a more general way?

There is an interpretation of popular movies as quite dangerous, and not just dangerous, but evil, deceptive, nefarious. I have in mind, for example, the Horkheimer and Adorno critique in their essay, "The Culture Industry: Enlightenment as Mass Deception" from *The Dialectic of Enlightenment*. Horkheimer and Adorno argue that the adversary of the individual is "the absolute power of capitalism" and that forms of popular culture, like Hollywood movies (as opposed to fine arts), are just forms of manipulation and dominance. They describe popular film, for example, as "the triumph of invested capital...; it is the meaningful content of every film, whatever plot the production team may have selected."[14] Their basic argument is that the culture industry creates the values that serve its own purposes, namely, to do business more profitably, and that these values are inauthentic and alienating to the mass of people who are compelled to adopt them. It induces a kind of passiveness and bland receptivity in individuals that is the very opposite of the point of real art. Horkheimer and Adorno say, somewhat cryptically, that *real* art portrays "the necessary failure of the passionate striving for identity."[15] While there is certainly something paradoxical in that description, the idea is that the striving for one's individual identity, whether successful or not, is in itself a good, and one that is lost in the identical-making forces of popular culture's faux art forms.

Alexander Nehamas finds a similar objection to mass media in Plato. What Nehamas takes Plato to be really objecting to in the *Republic* is not art or poetry per se, or even imitation, but rather what Nehamas calls "imitativeness." The real problem Plato had, according to Nehamas, was the "transparency" of popular art forms like comedy and tragedy. That is, they appear to the audience as more or less literal representations of what really happens (Nehamas refers to an account of women so frightened by Aeschylus's *Eumenindes* that they miscarried) so that our experience becomes one of reacting directingly to the popular art form as though it were reality; this differs from the more removed and active response we now associate with the encounter with fine art. The result, would be lives that become imitative of (which I take to mean, having their expectations formed by) what is experienced at, say, the movies. This would make those peoples' lives inauthentic and derivative. They would be lives lived in (as Nehamas puts it) a "perverted, and dismal reality."[16]

Objections of this form certainly seem relevant and pressing. Something does seem to be lost in the experience of mass-produced art forms like the movies. Walter Benjamin describes the loss of an "aura," the glow, presence, and "uniqueness" of a non-mass-produced work of art,[17] that occurs in the degraded experience of mass-produced works like movies. I do not want to resist this idea of a loss at the movies, nor do I want to deny a certain danger in viewing movies, but this is only to admit that going to the movies is a powerful psychological experience, and so will necessarily have its dangers. However, powerful experiences that are potentially dangerous can also be powerfully positive. I want to argue that there are great positive powers at work at the movies and that these forces are connected to our relationship with death.

Death is a theme that has been quietly persistent in the history of philosophy and Western culture. From Anaximander's very early and rather piquant description that, "...things that are perish into the things out of which they come to be, according to necessity, for they pay penalty and retribution to each other for their injustice in accordance with the ordering of time...."[18] to Plato's claim that the aim of philosophy is "to practice for death and dying,"[19] in Christianity's "dust to dust" and the preoccupation with a man dying on a cross, and Schopenhauer's dark wisdom about the futility of all of our striving, through to Heidegger's treatment of the delimiting function of death in our lives, the question of death quietly abides. I say "quietly" because, overall, there is not much philosophical and cultural discussion of death and what there is strikes me as generally evasive.

The primary evasion takes the form of a promise that death is not what it pretty clearly seems to be, a finitude confirmed by the dissolution of our organic selves into inorganic matter. Plato's idea of philosophy as a preparation for death ends up at the end of the *Phaedo* as a story about a kind of life after death. After Plato has Socrates confess his "low opinion of human weakness"[20] Socrates admits to telling "a tale."[21] His tale of life after death is not without its anxieties, but the promise is that if one lives one's life philosophically, one's death will be a great pleasure. That would seem to be a tale that tells a greater truth. The truth is, or seems to be, that death is most fearful to those who live poorly, and is not something that is feared by those who have lived well. Socrates, of course, is the most singular example of that idea.

Literally, death is not an actual part of our lives. As Epicurus says, "while we exist death is not present, and whenever death is present, we do not exist."[22] It may be, therefore, that Plato's strategy is necessary; one must speak, not so much elliptically, but simply narratively and fictitiously about death, in order to speak of it at all. Is there, however, a more primal way of understanding the nature of death, a way through experience, that philosophy can draw attention to, if not articulate clearly in argument form? I find suggestions to this effect in the great psychologists of the modern era, Nietzsche and Freud.

The question of death is most radically wrestled with in the unequivocally pessimistic philosophy of Schopenhauer. Nietzsche picks up some of the major themes in Schopenhauer's philosophy, but he attempts to transform the pessimism into optimism, to see what good can be made out of the tragedy so clearly articulated by Schopenhauer. For Schopenhauer, life is ceaseless struggle and stress, with only momentary respites. As individual entities we are defined by our willing and, as Schopenhauer says, "All *willing* arises from lack, from deficiency, and thus from suffering."[23] That is basically our life, for Schopenhauer; suffering. That is our life except for art (and philosophy). In art we can momentarily transcend our constant desiring, and so we can transcend the constancy of our suffering. It is, however, only a temporary solution, and our suffering soon returns. Art also plays a very important role for Nietzsche. In *The Birth of Tragedy*, Nietzsche describes the oppositional forces in art and in us of the Apollonian and the Dionysian, which are a kind of reinvention of Schopenhauer's idea of the world as will and representation. As I suggested earlier (in chapter 6), what characterizes the experience of the

Dionysian is specifically the loss of what Nietzsche refers to as, using a phrase of Schopenhauer's, the *principium individuationis*. The *principium individuationis* is the principle of one's individuation, one's sense of one's own essential integrity. To give that up is to be subsumed by a larger unity in which one's own unity is lost. This experience was ritualized in ancient Greece in Dionysian festivals that included theater productions, drinking, and sometimes sparagmos, the ritual and literal tearing apart of a living beast, an experience to which the bacchantes themselves aspired in their desire to become one with Dionysus.[24] The Dionysian is a kind of intoxication in which we are freed from the sense of necessity of maintaining our individual integrity; this freedom yields a feeling of joy, a feeling of ecstasy, of being beside oneself. As Nietzsche describes it, "under the influence of the narcotic draught, of which the songs of all primitive men and peoples speak... these Dionysian emotions awake, and as they grow in intensity everything subjective vanishes into complete self-forgetfulness."[25] I take modern movies to be a kind of cultural corollary to the primitive songs that Nietzsche refers to here.

The Apollonian energies are those that work toward maintaining our individuality. The Apollonian is about tightness and coherency of form, the fierce resistance to the breakdown of form; it is the force underlying social pressures to maintain our integrity and to conform. Nietzsche's physicianly diagnosis of the illness of modernity was a hyper-Apollonianism. Too much anal retentiveness and not enough joyful and terrifying giving-in to the loss of control, to a release of the fierce hold on our sense of our own integrity. What he calls for is more play and more willingness to engage the seductive states in which control is given up, in which we forfeit our control in order to experience being in the grip of forces larger and differently directed from own small agendas.

Nietzsche does not suggest that we should (or even could) live in a purely Dionysian manner. There must be a balance between Apollonian control and commitment to our personal integrity, and Dionysian surrender of control, which releases us from our preoccupation with ourselves. This Dionysian release is also a kind of giving-in to larger forces, forces of nature, forces that emerge within us over which we, as individuals, have little control. The relation between these two forces would seem to be, ideally, a harmony, but a harmony that can only be achieved through some kind of cyclical shift in emphasis on one or the other of the two forces. The goal is neither simply control or loss of control, but rather an increase in power and energy, in the intensity of one's life.

Appropriating the terminology of Gilles Deleuze, the Nietzschean ideal can be described in terms of active and reactive forces.[26] What we want to maximize is our own activity. The alternative is being reactive, which is sometimes necessary, but which diminishes the overall power and the intensity of our lives. To be either hyper-Apollonian or too deeply Dionysian is to slip into reactive modes. The ideal is Dionysian energies tempered by Apollonian forms that yield an individual self of maximum energy, creativity, and vitality.

Freud gives a somewhat less mythic analysis of this dynamic, but preserves the essential dualism suggested by Nietzsche. Psychological health, for Freud, is characterized by a healthy ego. The ego must negotiate between internal drives and external forces that impinge upon the person from the environment. The ego is largely identified with our conscious self, who we think we are, and has various mechanisms and strategies for maintaining its (which is to say, our) health. One mechanism or strategy is repression. Libidinal forces endanger the ego. They come from within us, but are, as it were, stupid, animalistic, and untamed; they do not know what is appropriate. Through repression the ego suppresses and re-channels some of those libidinal energies so that our behavior is socially acceptable, which will, at least ideally, maximize our ultimate satisfaction.[27]

Another strategy of the ego is regression. In regression, the ego finds itself having to negotiate a situation in which its powers seem to it insufficient. That is, it is overwhelmed by the stress of a specific situation and so, as it were, it retreats. The ego regresses, that is, attempts to return to an earlier condition in which it was not threatened by this new and stressful context.[28] Both repression and regression, then, are, according to Freud, mechanisms or strategies employed by the ego to achieve or maintain a kind of health, and health here seems to be characterized by a homeostasis, balance, or harmony. The harmony occurs when internal forces are balanced against external circumstances in a way in which stress is minimized for the individual and gratification is maximized. All of these dynamics can be explained in terms of what Freud calls "the pleasure principle." Even neuroses are just examples of the pleasure principle gone awry, situations in which the ego's strategies and mechanisms have proven inadequate or have been misapplied to a situation.

In *Beyond the Pleasure Principle*, however, Freud grapples with an apparently contradictory impulse that is clearly manifested in both children and adults, and yet does not seem to be explainable in terms of the pleasure principle, namely, compulsions to repeat an apparently unpleasurable situation (Freud first notices the phenomenon in the *fort-da* game of a young boy which Freud reads as a repetition in play of the disappearance of the child's mother[29]). Furthermore, certain forms of the compulsion to repeat seem to derive from deeper parts of us; they seem to be more than merely ego strategies. As Freud says, "The manifestations of a compulsion to repeat...exhibit to a high degree an instinctual character and, when they act in opposition to the pleasure principle, give the appearance of some 'daemonic' force at work." The problem of what this "daemonic force" might be is what *Beyond the Pleasure Principle* is about. Freud says, "we cannot escape a suspicion that we may have come upon the track of a universal attribute of instincts and perhaps of organic life in general which has not hitherto been clearly recognized or at least not explicitly stressed. It seems, then, that an instinct is an urge inherent in organic life to restore an earlier state of things which the living entity has been obliged to abandon under pressure of external disturbing forces...."[30]

As Freud speculates about the very origins of life, life itself is something of an aberration. He refers to life, especially in its initial form in the primordial soup, as a "tension," which initially was no more than a momentary tension, and which, by some accident of external forces, came to an inorganic entity. The first "instinct," then, the first "drive," was simply to return to the inorganic condition, which those initial organic entities presumably did fairly immediately. Complications, however, developed, and this tension persisted for longer and longer durations, one might say both because of and in spite of external forces. The goal, however, of the initially inorganic substance to which this tension had come (if one can speak meaningfully of a goal at all here, say, the drive, the natural propensity of the thing), was to return to its initial inorganic condition. Freud draws the following conclusion: "If we are to take it as a truth that knows no exceptions that everything living dies for internal reasons—becomes inorganic again—then we shall be compelled to say that 'the aim of all life is death' and, looking backwards, that 'inanimate things existed before living ones'."[31]

The primary instinct or drive, then, would be not libido but thanatos. What we really want to do is, as the Sibyl says, "To die."[32] Of the instincts toward self-preservation Freud says, "They are component instincts whose function it is to assure that the organism shall follow its own path to death, and to ward off any possible ways of returning to inorganic existence other than those which are immanent in the organism itself."[33] The ultimate point of life, then, is to die, but to die our own death, and all of the struggles, the anxieties, and machinations of the ego are primarily attempts to ward off the competitors that would kill us before we can die our own self-determined deaths.

Regression would seem to be more than just a defensive strategy of the ego. By this interpretation, it ties in with the very point of life, the ego's ultimate goal. Going to the movies is certainly a regressive activity. What the critiques of mass media of Adorno/Horkheimer and Plato/Nehamas are attacking is just this regressive aspect of popular art forms. What is shared between these two critiques is the accusation that mass media compels groups of people to experience the same thing in the same ways and that it induces a passivity that does violence to the individual. For both Adorno/Horkheimer and Plato/Nehamas the critique comes down to an objection to mass media's subverting the power of individuals to determine their own lives. The accusation is that mass media is enslaving, and the accusation is leveled in order to liberate us, or, at least, some of us, from this enslavement. Aristotle, of course, saw the matter differently. For Aristotle, popular art forms are cathartic; they provide a release from dammed up pressures that is cleansing and restorative, as well as educational. For Aristotle, the enslavement would be to have to live without these popular art forms.

I see a third possibility that acknowledges both of these analyses, but which incorporates the insights of Nietzsche and Freud. That is, it may be true that going to the movies is a regressive activity, and one that does induce a certain level of passivity in the audience. If, however, there are dual forces that are deep, instinctual forces in us, whether called Apollonian/Dionysian or Eros/Thanatos, and both forces are essential but also conflicting, and, furthermore, one of these forces is better served by our conscious reason, while the other remains largely "mute"[34] (to use Freud's phrase to describe thanatos) and so is suppressed, then it may very well be that a certain state of passivity is required. That is, to use Freudian terminology, in order to have access to the energies in our conscious lives of the otherwise suppressed force which is thanatos, the overanxious superego may need to be stilled. Aristotle is right that there is a purgation—and the purging of our hyper-Apollonian, repressive super-ego preoccupations, allows access to the muted energies that are the most creative. These energies, because they transcend the goal-specific forces of the libido and of the individual ego, encompass a more generalized response to life and the world.

Adorno/Horkheimer and Plato/Nehamas identify legitimate issues with respect to mass media and film, but I think that they fail to see the potential good in the very passivity that so frightens them about our experience of mass media and especially film. There is a regression that provides access to forces that are otherwise largely unconscious and successfully repressed. There is a loss of the presence of the real, an escape from the tensions of preserving one's life in the face of the pressures that would unravel it. This is in favor of a return to a more passive state in which one's consciousness loses its individual direction and autonomous integrity and merges with other consciousnesses to be directed in a larger, unifying order, a larger, unifying narrative which is experientially death-like. According to this reading, and contrary to Adorno and Horkheimer, movies largely contribute to the point of life. In going to the movies I both lose the sense of impinging reality and feel completely satisfied with the (frankly, rather minimal) activity in which I am engaged. I emerge from the movies refreshed and with a renewed sense of resolve, replete with new strategies for arranging more perfectly my own and ultimate death.

The dangers are still present. One can slip into iterative regressive patterns which Freud calls neuroses. One can be neurotic about movies as well as anything else. The solution is to maintain some measure of Apollonian control and distance. A primary indication of health, then, would be the willingness, the eagerness to talk about what one has just experienced, treating movies not as transparent, but as Dionysian vehicles. As Nietzsche suggests, one must transcend simply reactive responses and actively engage with the movie for one's own empowerment, to increase one's intensity and one's vitality in life.

Freud freely admits to the speculativeness of his theory of thanatos, but appeals to its explanatory force as its justification. As he says, "We have no longer to reckon with the organisms puzzling determination (so hard to fit into any context) to maintain its own existence in the face of any obstacles. What we are left with is the fact that the organism wishes to die in its own fashion...."[35] Movies, then, that not only include the death of characters but also seem to reflect on the nature of death, would be doubly self-reflexive. This would account for the surprising popularity of movies about the dead and dying, like The *Sixth Sense* or *Leaving Las Vegas*. The popularity would, in part, be attributable to the audience's recognition that these movies are articulating some of the deepest themes in their own lives. Along similar lines, and as an explanation of the relevance of the wish fulfillment involved in going to the movies, is it any wonder that so many popular movies are about protagonists who are very skilled at evading an arbitrary and externally imposed death?

Death and Delusion

> The lighthouse invites the storm...
> —Malcolm Lowery, "The Lighthouse Invites the Storm"

There seems to be a peculiar dynamic that is characteristic of our strongest desires, a contradictory dynamic. That is, that which we most long for seems also to be that which we least wish to have. Philosophic analysis of this peculiar dynamic begins with Aristotle's attempt to explain the pleasures and terrors of tragedy. In the *Poetics* Aristotle identifies two inherently pleasurable activities that account for the pleasurable appreciation of any poem or play, even a tragic one. He says that we instinctually love imitation and that we love to learn, to infer. There is an elegant simplicity to this account. It is elegant because it captures so much in so little. It is simple because its force derives from its naturalism. I read Aristotle to be saying that we have a natural desire to participate in what is unknown to us and that we have a desire, an instinctual compulsion, to know. Both of these parts of our nature may invoke the contradictory dynamic of our desiring what we least want to have. That is, what is other from us may in fact be harmful to us, and what we may find out in our pursuit of knowledge may be some knowledge that we in fact cannot bear to have.

The uncanny invokes just the sort of experience I have described, a kind of awful attraction. Freud attributed the sense of the uncanny to what he referred to as "the return of the repressed."[36] That is, as Noël Carroll glosses Freud, "To experience the uncanny...is to experience something that is known, but something the knowledge of which has been hidden or repressed."[37] We hide or repress that which is too terrible or difficult for us to bear, especially things about our self. (Of course, for Freud, the repressed is largely sexual or violent in nature.) There is, then, something circular in the experience of the uncanny; what we discover is something that we already know. What makes this circle possible is that we do not know that we know what we know. It is a kind of delusion. Interestingly, "delusion" has as its root the Latin *ludere*, to play. This would suggest that our delusions are, or were once thought to be, the result of some kind of play, presumably the nefarious play of one who would delude us. In the case of the uncanny, however, or of repression in general, the deluder and the deluded are one and the same person. Self-delusion would seem to be a kind of game that we play with ourselves, albeit for mortal stakes. If Aristotle is right, then, given these suggestions of some kind of pattern, we will want to know about this game, what its rules are, and what it might have to do with a simultaneous attraction and repulsion, with death and horror.

In *The Art of the Ridiculous Sublime: On David Lynch's* Lost Highway, Slavoj Žižek identifies a dynamic that he calls (following Lacan) "inherent transgression."[38] He begins his discussion of inherent transgression by analyzing a scene from *Casablanca,* responding to the interpretation of the scene by Richard Maltby. The scene in question is the ellipsis between when Rick takes Ilsa into his arms after she says how much she still loves him, and when the camera returns to Rick's office sometime later, with Rick standing by the window smoking a cigarette and Ilsa sitting rather comfortably on the couch. The ellipsis itself is marked by a low angle shot looking up at a great tower with a rotating searchlight on top of it. Maltby's interpretation is that there are two possible, and even necessary, consistent interpretations of this scene: that Rick and Ilsa had sex during the ellipsis and that they did not. Žižek takes Maltby's analysis to be exemplifying the dynamic of inherent transgression and describes this dynamic psychoanalytically in terms of an opposition. He says, "this opposition is...the opposition between symbolic Law (Ego-Ideal), and obscene superego: at the level of the symbolic Law, nothing happens, the text is clean, while, at another level, it bombards the spectator with the superego injunction, 'Enjoy!'—give way to your dirty imagination."[39]

That is, I take the dynamic of inherent transgression to be a kind of game that a certain narrative structure will allow us to play with ourselves. The game is something like "I can enjoy watching this transgressive scene because I know that I disapprove of it just like I am supposed to." We get to transgress and enjoy what we ostensibly object to, but secretly desire, because we are ballasted by our self-delusion that our real commitment is to our objection, and not to our enjoyment.

In *The Art of the Ridiculous Sublime* Žižek is doing a kind of Hegelian reading of David Lynch's *Lost Highway*. That is, he is treating *Lost Highway* as a kind of apotheosis of the noir and horror genres. He is claiming that *Lost Highway* is explicitly about what noir and horror have always been implicitly about. Žižek's reading of the film subsumes it under the category of the sublime, actually, under what he calls the "ridiculous sublime," but he also identifies some specific moments of horror in the movie, and it is to his remarks on horror that I would like to turn.

In preparation for describing the plot of *Lost Highway* Žižek identifies "the opposition of two horrors: the fantasmatic horror of the nightmarish noir universe of perverse sex, betrayal and murder, and the (perhaps much more unsettling) despair of our drab, 'alienated' daily life of impotence and distrust." He goes on to say,

> It is as if the unity of our experience of reality sustained by fantasy disintegrates and decomposes into its two components: on the one side, the 'desublimated' aseptic drabness of daily reality; on the other side, its fantasmatic support, not in its sublime version, but staged directly and brutally, in all its obscene cruelty. It is as if Lynch is telling us this is what your life is effectively about; if you traverse the fantasmatic screen that confers a fake aura on it, the choice is between bad and worse, between the aseptic impotent drabness of social reality and the fantasmatic Real of self-destructive violence.[40]

Another form of horror that Žižek identifies is "the ultimate horror of the Other who has direct access to our (the subject's) fundamental fantasy." The idea of the "fundamental fantasy" is a Lacanian idea that Žižek describes as "the subject's innermost kernel, as the ultimate, proto-transcendental framework of my desiring which, precisely as such, remains inaccessible to my subjective grasp." Žižek identifies a paradox in association with the fundamental fantasy. Not only is what is most me inaccessible to me, but "the moment I approach it much, my subjectivity, my self-experience, loses its consistency and disintegrates."[41] That is, what I would most want to know about myself I cannot (and *must* not) know about myself because to know it is to lose all sense of myself, since my sense of myself depends on, and originates in, my fundamental fantasy. To identify with the Other that would know this in me is to will by own dissolution, which is terrifying.

If what Aristotle says about us is true, however, then we will both want to identify and to know this Other. This dynamic is clearest in Aristotle's analysis of the plot of tragedies and of the character of the tragic hero. Aristotle says that the plot of a tragedy should be marvelous or amazing, inspiring fear and pity. The plot will involve a discovery and a reversal.[42] The hero will be superior to us in birth and nobility, but otherwise, like us and so easy to identify with. That is, a tragedy will present us, the audience, with various tantalizing conundrums. They are tantalizing because so nearly familiar to our own lives, conundrums because they remain strange and amazing to us. I take the dynamic of inherent transgression to be a similar kind of game that allows just those things to happen, so that we can identify and know what we cannot identify or know. This dynamic is further complicated by the fact that, in some sense and in some cases, I may already know that which I feel I want to know, and already know that I cannot afford to know it. The horrors that Žižek has described seem to me to be the very horrors that we generally are suspicious that we do know and that we cannot afford to know, but, of course, on the Aristotle principle, still desire to know, it is the horror of the absolute fantasmatic (whatever *that* means) nature of our fundamental fantasy, and the alternative horror of the absolute drabness of our lives, sans that fundamental fantasy.

This opposition seems to be completely hopeless. The imperative to know makes the fundamental fantasy unsustainable. A complete capitulation to drabness in our lives is insupportable. Treating Žižek's own theoretical discussion elliptically, I want to go to a surprising conclusion that he draws. Žižek describes the problem and its paradoxical solution as follows:

> One is ineluctably enticed in conflicting directions; we, the interactors, just have to accept that we are lost in the inconsistent complexity of multiple referrals and connections. The paradox is that this ultimately helpless confusion, this lack of a final point of closure serves as a kind of denial which protects us from confronting the trauma of finitude, of the fact that our story has to end at some point. There is no ultimate, irreversible point, since, in this multiple universe, there are always other paths to explore, alternate realities in which one can take refuge when one seems to reach deadlock.[43]

I read Žižek to be suggesting that the apparent conflict between our fundamental fantasy and drabness is only an opposition if it must be one or the other, *tertium non datur*. There is, however, the alternative that they can both be simultaneously true of our experience, or constituent of our experience, in which case the opposition (and hence the insupportability of the opposition itself) dissolves. Rather than our dissolution at the approach to the fundamental fantasy, we discover a multiplicity of fundamental fantasies in which we can take refuge. Žižek says, "The final conclusion to be drawn is that 'reality,' and the experience of its density, is sustained not simply by A/ONE fantasy, but by an INCONSISTENT MULTITUDE of fantasies; this multitude generates the effect of the impenetrable density that we experience as 'reality'... the fantasmatic support of reality is in itself necessarily multiple and inconsistent."[44]

When in the beginning of *The Night of the Living Dead* the brother tells his sister about when they were children and he leapt out at her at this very same spot and pretended to eat her, we see, off in the distance, a stumbling man who looks like he is sleepwalking; he will turn out to be a flesh-eating ghoul. When he jumps out and tries to eat her, it would certainly seem to be, on some level, a return of the repressed. The implicit message seems to be that she, on some level, wants this to happen, even as she is horrified by it. But what exactly is the "this" that she wants? Does she want her brother to do this to her? Is it an expression of her desire to be eaten by the dead? Is it that she wants to return to her childhood condition? Is it that she wants to become dead herself, and so she aspires to the condition of the ghoul, free of this ordinary world's concerns and with only the reduced concern of finding flesh to eat? Is it a kind of return of a suppressed suspicion that that *is* her life, that she is a kind of sleepwalking ghoul already? Is this regression, repression, discovery, transgression, expression of thanatos and libido, thanatos or libido, fantasy, sublime, ridiculous, uncanny, or what? Why not any or all of these things, individually or simultaneously? Is not that exactly the "impenetrable density that we experience as 'reality'"? Is that not what we already know about reality, but repress—because it is so much to know and so difficult to know, and so difficult to sustain—yet exactly what we want to know and must keep searching for so that we can know it? Isn't this the storm that the lighthouse invites? Isn't that what the Mystery Man is there to tell us in *Lost Highway*, that in this baffling multiplicity of our experiences, this tangled matrix of our desires, drives, expectations, assumptions, and the world, lies the impenetrable density that is our life.

Conclusion

The Dialectics of Interpretation

Wittgenstein's Fly-Bottle and Zimzum Moments in The Matrix

In section 309 of *Philosophical Investigations* Wittgenstein has his imaginary interlocutor ask him the question, "What is your aim in philosophy?" Wittgenstein's not unambiguous answer is, "To shew the fly the way out of the fly-bottle." What is the problem for the fly in the fly-bottle? The problem is that the fly is trapped by what it cannot perceive. To the fly, the impediment of the glass of the fly-bottle is a conundrum, an invisible barrier the contours of which it cannot make out. Interestingly, what must appear to the fly as invisible yet uninterrupted impenetrable surface is, in fact, interrupted and penetrable. There is a way out; the mouth of the fly-bottle remains open. The great agitation of the fly could be calmed immediately if the fly could find its way to the mouth of the fly-bottle. It is what the fly does not know, what it cannot *see*, about fly-bottles that traps it, that imprisons it. Wittgenstein is speaking allegorically here and he is suggesting that many of us are like the fly, trapped by what we cannot see, imprisoned by what we do not conceptually understand, and that his purpose in his philosophy is to help us see, to show us how to understand, so that we may be freed.

Wittgenstein's idea of the fly-bottle has considerable similarities with Plato's allegory of the cave in book seven of the *Republic*. There Plato describes a cave in which people are chained and watching simulacra of reality, mere shadows of real things, that they do not know are simulacra. Both the people in Plato's cave and Wittgenstein's fly are imprisoned in a prison that they do not understand, in a prison they cannot see and do not know that they are in. Both Plato and Wittgenstein are invested in showing the way out of the prison. Both Plato and Wittgenstein, however, are invested in showing the way out of the prison primarily, perhaps exclusively, to philosophers. This is true of Plato because for Plato only philosophers can attain or handle the truth that is outside the cave, and for Wittgenstein because only philosophers get caught in the fly-bottle in the first place.

A further complication of appealing to Plato as a way to understand popular movies is the fact that Plato's cave, that which is false and should be escaped, is an almost exact representation of a movie theater: a dark space in which everyone is facing in one direction, gazing at images projected from an anterior light source. Wittgenstein's philosophy, too, would seem to be somewhat unsympathetic to popular movies insofar as what he seems to regard as outside the fly-bottle is just the ordinary ways of living in the real world that most people (i.e., not philosophers) inhabit and live in easily and (more or less) happily.

What makes Plato and Wittgenstein so indispensable is their idea of our imprisonment, an imprisonment of which we remain mostly unaware. What makes them indispensable is their suggestion that there is a way out, a way out that is simply there, available to any and all who can manage to locate it. Both suggest that the way out is best found through a new kind of philosophy. I want to pick up Richard Shusterman's call in *Practicing Philosophy* for a new, "democratized" view of the philosophical life.[1] On this view, the philosophical life is not just for the elite or hypereducated, but for everyone. After the movie, everyone gets to leave one kind of cave. The questions that remain, however, are: How many caves or prisons are there in which we are trapped? What are the caves or prisons that trap us? What is the way out? Is the way out a way that will be accessible to all?

Wittgenstein's philosopher fly is buzzing to get out, but does not understand the nature of the confinement that constrains it. Plato's cave prisoners are more passively constrained. They are chained to their spots, but there does not seem to be much struggle against these chains. The cave dwellers do not struggle because they are unaware of certain kinds of possibilities of human experience. They do not struggle for freedom because they do not know that there is a kind of freedom that they have not dreamt of. For all that, one supposes that there is a sense of emptiness, a suspicion that there may be more to life than their portion of it as they have it. My sense is that a sense of emptiness and the suspicion that what we know may not be all there is to know are fairly pervasive impressions that people have about their lives, at least, or especially, in this hypercapitalized United States. Is there an imaginative paradigm, on the model of Plato's allegory of the cave, that might help us to get a clearer sense of this scenario?

In *The Matrix*, by the Wachowski brothers, a realm not unlike Plato's cave is portrayed.[2] Peoples' bodies are enchained in biological-life-sustaining pods, while their minds are entertained with visions of simulacra. (Interestingly, Jean Beaudrillard's book *Simulacra and Simulation* makes an appearance in the movie.) The plot of the movie is about how Neo escapes from this imprisonment (with the help of Morpheus and his crew) and finds his way out of the cave. By the end of the movie Neo seems to present, bodily represent, the possibility of a mass liberation of the people still imprisoned in the pods, a liberation that, at the end of the movie, remains to possibly take place in the future.

I read Plato's allegory of the cave, and Wittgenstein's story of the fly in the fly-bottle, as symbolically true stories. That is, if one really understands what Plato and Wittgenstein are talking about, what they have to say really does shed light on our condition. I think it is true that we, many of us, perhaps all of us some of the time, are confined in prisons that we can neither see nor understand, but which substantially constrain our powers, impede our freedom, inhibit the possibility of a more complete satisfaction and happiness. Since *The Matrix* seems to be a relatively faithful updating of Plato's story, are there truths to unravel in that story as well? Does it have something to add to Plato's story that is more peculiarly suited to the twenty-first century A.D. as opposed to the fifth century B.C.E.?

At the beginning of *The Matrix*, the character Neo has had the suspicion for some time that there is something peculiar about the reality he inhabits, a suspicion that there is more going on than what appears to be going on. There are certain signs, certain indications of inconsistencies that arouse his suspicion. He wants to know what is going on, which is to say, he feels the call of philosophy. With help, he begins to understand the nature of the cave in which he is confined. He cannot escape the cave by himself. He needs help (as do we all) and he gets it from Morpheus, who will lead him out of the cave (flush him, really), blinking and weak, into the sharpness of a new reality.

Neo chooses to leave the cave. He chooses philosophy. He takes the red pill. It is not a fully informed choice; how many choices ever are? To survive outside the cave requires skills and strengths that have remained dormant or undeveloped in him while he was in the cave. A period of intense training is required. When his strength and certain skills have been developed, he is taken to see an oracle who offers him elliptical, oracular, information about who he is and what there is for him to do. Neo leaves. He seems to misinterpret the message from the oracle, but in the end discovers powers within himself that he did not know he had. With the discovery of these powers he also discovers a purpose for his life, a responsibility that he has because he has these powers.

An unseen prison or a confinement with which we may be unknowingly complicit, could take the form of something like a false responsibility. In the essay "Wittgenstein's Later Work in Relation to Conservatism," J. C. Nyíri refers to a speech given at the University of Munich in 1927 by the Austrian poet Hugo von Hofmannsthal in which Hofmannsthal says, "life becomes livable only through a system of genuine obligations."[3] Nyíri precedes this reference with a discussion of an essay by Paul Ernst called "What Now?" in which Ernst is contrasting "an organic mode of life" with "an inorganic one." An inorganic form of life Ernst associates with bourgeois forms of life. Nyíri quotes Ernst: "All those forms of life are bourgeois which imbue not the whole man [*sic*] but merely some part of him, and it is within those forms that terms such as profession and status, work and personality, have acquired their contemporary meaning. Here the life of the individual is no longer settled in a natural way. . . ."[4]

The possibility that is being raised here is the idea of a life that is constrained by obligations that one does not feel are really one's own; of a mode of life that is not confluent with one's own nature, so that one always feels out of step, off balance, a nagging dissatisfaction. I would substitute for Ernst's reference to "bourgeois," a "capitalist" form of life. Capitalism, the assessment of all things in terms of a price, in terms of the inorganic standard of money, is, it seems to me, the primary threat to the finding of our genuine obligations and the founding of an organic, holistic form of life. Which is not to say that capitalism is the enemy or is evil. Capitalism is what it is, and what it is is a very powerful political, economic, and social force. Capitalism does not strike me as inherently bad—if anything, the possibility of democracy seems to be connected with some form of capitalist economy—but there are tremendous forces that are contained in capitalism that can make it dangerous to us as individual human beings. It is dangerous to us especially if we do not know what those forces are, do not see how they work on and in our lives. Insofar as we do not see them our lives are unwittingly controlled and constrained by them. To become aware of them, and of how they work on us, is to begin to work our way out of the cave.

One essay in Jean Beaudrillard's *Simulacra and Simulation* is entitled "Hypermarket and Hypercommodity." I understand "hypermarket" to be a reference to a shopping mall, or, even more dramatically, to the cybermalls of the Internet. These are places where, for Beaudrillard, a certain kind of postmodern, capitalist work gets done. Beaudrillard says,

> At the deepest level, another kind of work is at issue here, the work of acculturation, of confrontation, of examination, of the social code, and of the verdict: people go there to find and to select objects-responses to all the questions they may ask themselves; or, rather, they *themselves* come *in response* to the functional and directed question that the objects constitute. The objects are no longer commodities: they are no longer even signs whose meaning and message one could decipher and appropriate for oneself, they are *tests*, they are the ones that interrogate us, and we are summoned to answer them, and the answer is included in the question.[5]

I take Beaudrillard to be saying here that in a hypermarket the principles of exchange have been transformed from those of traditional markets. In the original form of the marketplace, a farmer would come to the village or city bringing his or her produce. The produce would be sold in the marketplace to people who needed the produce to eat and live.

In the hypermarket, no one (i.e., corporations) sells nothing (i.e., what is sold is more about an idea of need, a dream of satisfaction—a hypercommodity—rather than a specific needed object, like some produce) to nobody (i.e., we who go to the hypermarket do not understand ourselves or, most poignantly, we do not understand our own needs and desires, and so, in effect, "we" are not really there as we do our shopping). Our felt need, which is a need to feel some kind of satisfaction (which is really a need to feel the satisfaction that is organically ours, which, in part, is to satisfy the call to our genuine responsibilities) gets transformed in the hypermarket (to which we are drawn by our need) into a redefinition of our need in terms of the hypercommodities on the shelves at the mall. Since we have lost touch with our own real needs, we look to the hypercommodities to help us define what our needs might be. The hypercommodities, then, become a kind of test, a test of our responsiveness to their promise of satisfaction.

It is a test that we are constantly failing because the hypercommodities never address our real need, so we never feel satisfied. Then we try harder to buy more so that we can live up to the expectations and promises of the hypermarket that we will be fully and completely satisfied. This process, then, is a process of acculturation, an acculturation that serves to define our needs in terms of the hypercommodities upon the shelves of our malls and in the infinity of images accessible on our computer screen. This, of course, is very good for the capitalist economy, as well as for our individual financial economy (if not for our personal psychological economy), and so the whole of the process is self-reinforcing.

This process is good for the capitalist economy, and I am myself in favor of a healthy capitalist economy, but it can be quite anxiety provoking for the individual members of the capitalist society. As Beaudrillard says in an earlier essay in *Simulacra and Simulation*:

> Whence the characteristic hysteria of our times: that of the production and reproduction of the real. The other production, that of values and commodities, that of the belle epoque of political economy, has for a long time had no specific meaning. What every society looks for in continuing to produce, and to over-produce, is to restore the real that escapes it. That is why today this "material" production is that of the hyperreal itself. ...Thus everywhere the hyperrealism of simulation is translated by the hallucinatory resemblance of the real to itself.[6]

The hysteria that Beaudrillard refers to here I take to be a largely repressed hysteria, not unlike the "quiet desperation" that Thoreau refers to. It is the hysteria that possesses Neo at the beginning of *The Matrix*, which drives him to try to make sense of his suspicion that there is something wrong with or missing from the world he seems to inhabit.

One interpretation of what the missing "real" is is that it is the sense of our own genuine responsibilities and a connection with our own genuine organic needs. From our vantage point within the prison of the hypermarket all we see are the parade of hypercommodities, like the shadows of real objects that are projected onto the wall of Plato's cave. The hypermarket seems to offer us a profusion of choices, and we feel as if, amidst this plenty, we can have no reason to complain; yet as excited as we are by the plethora of choices available, we also have a deep suspicion about their shadowy and hypercommodity nature. In fact, very few are choices that connect with the deepest needs of our organic natures or with the demands of our genuine responsibilities. There may be produce to be found, real apples and oranges (although even that is unlikely), but perhaps it is not simply produce that we require. We need produce, but perhaps we have a need as well for something like digging and planting and waiting and hoping and planning and celebrating the harvest with our neighbors when the squash comes in and the grapes are ready for pressing. I am not making some kind of Luddite call for a return to primitive living, but I am suggesting that there may be more to our organic needs and genuine responsibilities than, for all its promise, a mall can deliver.

Beaudrillard's point, however, is that when all we are able to see is our choices among the hypercommodities, our failure to be satisfied by them would seem to be simply our own personal failure. That is what I understand by his saying that *they* test *us*. What I see Plato and Wittgenstein and even Beaudrillard and the Wachowski brothers to be saying, however, is that these are not the only choices that are out there. In fact, these are not even the real choices, these are just apparent choices, simulacra of choices. To be able to understand what the real choices are, however, we must first be able to see the falseness of the choices between which we have been trying to decide. This will take some training, some help, some, I want to say, philosophy.

Clearly, the invocations of Plato, Thoreau, and even of Wittgenstein suggest that this is not just a late twentieth-century, early twenty-first-century, phenomenon or problem. We are born into a world that we did not create, full of values we sometimes can barely understand. The problem of finding oneself among choices that do not seem to one genuine, but without obvious genuine alternative ones available, is not an exclusively contemporary problem. On the other hand, the particular permutations of the problem for us who live today may be new. The basic form of the cave or the fly-bottle may remain the same, but the interior design, the forms of the particular shadows are very different. We constantly need new descriptions of the cave in order to be able to perceive its interior landscape so that we can better negotiate that landscape and perhaps escape its confining walls. Wittgenstein says in his preface to *Philosophical Investigations*, "The philosophical remarks in this book are, as it were, a number of sketches of landscapes...."[7] We need these sketches because, even though we may live in communities that are in some ways familiar to us, or seem familiar to us, we often feel, for all the apparent familiarity, like strangers in a strange land without maps or markers to help us to distinguish the right way. We often do not know the way to the satisfaction of our genuine organic needs and the recognition of our genuine responsibilities.

There is another important way to speak of the cave or fly-bottle that can imprison us. So far I have emphasized a sort of haplessness about our imprisonment, as though our being in prison had nothing to do with us, with what we do, and that escape is only possible with outside help. In fact, however, I think that as ready as the social world is to imprison us according to its own logic and needs, we are also responsible for our own imprisonment. In a chapter of a work that remained unpublished in his lifetime, a chapter entitled "Philosophy," Wittgenstein wrote, "...the very things that are most obvious can become the most difficult to understand. What has to be overcome is not a difficulty of the intellect, but of the will." In the next paragraph Wittgenstein goes on to say, "Work on philosophy is... actually more of a // a kind of // work on oneself. On one's own conception. On the way one sees things. (And what one demands of them.)"[8] This idea of the impediment that can be presented by our own will, and by what we may, inappropriately, demand of things, is a very interesting element of Wittgenstein's later philosophy. It is helpfully discussed by Stanley Cavell in his *This New Yet Unapproachable America: Lectures after Emerson after Wittgenstein*.

In his "Introductory Report" Cavell identifies the virtue that Wittgenstein admits to of his own philosophical method of writing. Wittgenstein writes in series of remarks that seem to begin and end rather spontaneously. Cavell cites Wittgenstein saying that he does not "force them [the remarks] in any single direction against their natural inclination."[9] That is, the virtue to which Wittgenstein is trying to be responsible is that of being responsive to the logic of our ordinary language practices, instead of trying to manipulate concepts into a form that would satisfy some personal need of his own. For philosophers in general, and Wittgenstein is especially attuned to his inner philosopher (which could be said to be responsible for the *Tractatus Logico-Philosophicus*), the primary personal need seems to be to reduce the ambiguity and indeterminacy of our everyday experiences to definitive universal facts. Of course, this struggle to defeat ambiguity and indeterminacy is not peculiar to philosophers; only their manner of attempting to do so is. Part of the discovery that marks Wittgenstein's later philosophy, the philosophy found especially in *Philosophical Investigations*, is the recognition that the best way to come to terms with the apparent ambiguity of the ordinary is not to try to force it into some preconceived template, but to try to understand it by being responsive to it in its nuances and subtleties. As Cavell says, "The power of this recognition of the ordinary for philosophy is bound up with the recognition that refusing or forcing the order of the ordinary is a cause of philosophical emptiness (say avoidance) and violence."[10] The issue here is one of apparent power or control. That is, philosophical avoidance is about wanting to avoid the relative indeterminacy of the ordinary.

The contexts of our ordinary lives, the language of our ordinary encounters with other people, are riven with ambiguity and indeterminacy. Both ordinary reality and other people are in some sense fundamentally underdetermined for us. As much as we might understand, there will always be some remainder that we do not, whether it is the subjectivity of the other person or the limitless extendedness of the web of significance of all things in every context with all things in all contexts. Ambiguity and indeterminacy are frightening to us, but, somewhat ironically, the way to maximum connection, the way to maximum understanding, is not by reducing the ambiguity by denial of the ambiguity, by reductive interpretation of the indeterminacy; it is by acknowledgment and responsiveness to the ambiguity and indeterminacy.

Cavell reads Wittgenstein's remark at *Philosophical Investigation* §124 "[Philosophy] leaves everything as it is" as a call for forbearance and later says, "Philosophy's virtue is responsiveness."[11] In the essay, "Finding as Founding: Taking Steps in Emerson's 'Experience'," Cavell refers to the opposite of this idea of forbearance as "clutching." Cavell explains this idea of clutching as "when we conceive thinking, say the application of concepts in judgments, as grasping something, say synthesizing." This idea of clutching, for Cavell, is an expression of denial on our part: "we seek to deny the standoffishness of objects by clutching at them." Cavell describes the opposite of clutching in terms of "being drawn to things."[12] I take this idea of being drawn to things as being a description of Plato's conception of the philosopher as lover. This suggests an erotics of understanding the world, which Plato offers explicitly in the *Symposium*. The erotics of "being drawn to things" opposes the autocratics of clutching, controlling, and reductive interpreting. From this perspective, the escape from the cave is as much about love as it is about liberation.

Simone de Beauvoir, in *The Ethics of Ambiguity*, speaks of a similar phenomenon in terms of "disclosure."[13] I understand this to mean allowing things, people, contexts to disclose themselves to us. The contrast, then, would be between going to an encounter with the intent to impose your own interpretation on whatever you find there, versus withholding your interpretation in order to allow what is encountered to reveal itself to you, in all of its complexity, ambiguity, and indeterminacy. Of course, the former will *seem* more powerful, there will be less sense of doubt or confusion or uncertainty. The latter will *seem* less powerful, producing as it inevitably will, uncertainty, confusion, and the fear of our own incommensurateness to the demands of the situation.

What *seems* more and less powerful, however, is misleading. Insofar as we are reduced to encountering the world only on our own terms we become more and more solipsistic. We end up not really encountering things in the world but only visions and revisions of our own selves, and, as Beauvoir says, this leads to meaninglessness and emptiness: "If I were really everything there would be nothing beside me; the world would be empty."[14] Real power comes from real interactions with things as they authentically are, or as near to that as we can get. That kind of closeness can only be achieved through a kind of receptive, alert, informed but not autocratic passiveness.

Harold Bloom describes what I take to be the same phenomenon with a term from the Kabbalah called *zimzum*. Bloom describes *zimzum* as a "dearth-in-meaning" or "limitation that compels subsequent substitution."[15] *Zimzum*, or *tsimtsum*, is a word from the Kabbalah of Isaac Luria (1534–1572). The *tsimtsum*, in the Lurianic myth, is the contraction of God to make space for His creation, or, as Gershom Scholem explains it:

> The *tsimtsum* ushers in the cosmic drama. But this drama is no longer, as in older systems, an emanation or projection, in which God steps out of Himself, communicates or reveals Himself. On the contrary, it is a withdrawal into Himself. Instead of turning outward, He contracts His essence, which becomes more and more hidden. Without the *tsimtsum* there would be no cosmic process, for it is God's withdrawal into Himself that first creates a pneumatic, primordial space...and makes possible the existence of something other than God and His pure essence.[16]

I understand a *zimzum* moment to be a moment in which one finds oneself in a situation that is underdetermined, in which there has been, as it were, a withdrawal of meaning. That is, there simply is not enough information in the context of the situation to supply a clear judgment about the situation, and yet a judgment is called for, it is demanded by the situation. A poem invites but defies interpretation, and yet we must interpret it. In some sense, as Bloom insists, our interpretation will necessarily be a misinterpretation. At some point, we must stop trying to impose an interpretation, and allow an interpretation to emerge.

The real power of this kind of contraction emerges of itself, automatically, which is to say, naturally, in the *zimzum* moment. In the act of restraining oneself from forcing an interpretation, one reenacts the original act of the Lurianic God. Our retreat creates the space into which genuine new meaning (as opposed to the imposition of what we already know) can emerge. I see this emergence of meaning as a version of the Deweyan idea (from *A Common Faith*) of "adjustment."[17] It is the result of a combination of our responsiveness to the situation and the situation's responsiveness to us. As Michael Eldridge puts it, the "adjusting attitude" is a "harmonizing of the self with the world in terms of both passive and active changes."[18] Such harmonizing is only possible after the fact of our withdrawal because until our withdrawal there is nothing in the space but us, or our version of (our vision of) every object, its place, and its relationship to other objects, which, of course, includes other people. In some sense, we can never fully remove ourselves, nor is the meaning and understanding that emerges completely separate from what we already know, any more than God's creation would be completely distinct from His existence, but much more of what is other and new become accessible through our withdrawal.

For Simone de Beauvoir in *The Ethics of Ambiguity*, the enemy of this type of attitude, the opposite of this willingness to withdraw, this *active* passiveness, is "the serious man" whom she also refers to as "the subman."[19] The "serious man" accepts ready-made values without question or examination, and imposes them on himself (or herself) and others. The "serious man" is in denial with respect to ambiguity and indeterminacy out of fear. What appears as a kind of active control and authority is, in fact, the real form of inactive passiveness. As Beauvoir explains:

> They have eyes and ears, but from their childhood on they make themselves blind and deaf, without love and without desire. This apathy manifests a fundamental fear in the face of existence, in the face of the risks and tensions which it implies. The sub-man rejects this "passion" which is his human condition, the laceration and failure of that drive toward being which always misses its goal, but which thereby is the very existence which he rejects.[20]

In his (or her) refusal to allow disclosure, the sub-man neither sees nor hears, and so does not know his (or her) own passion, does not know what he (or she) might be passionate about. He (she) will know neither his (her) own real organic needs, nor his (her) genuine obligations. Without this kind of receptivity to the risks and tensions of existence, that is, without allowing them to disclose themselves to us, we will not know the risks we run, nor be able to run them effectively. What is ultimately disclosed in passive receptivity is not so much something about the world as it is something about us. We learn what we really care about in the confrontation with what is really at stake. To feel a passionate commitment to something, to feel like one has real choices to make, is to be genuinely empowered.

There is a *zimzum* moment in *The Matrix*. In *The Matrix* this moment is also a moment of reversal (*peripeteia*, to use Aristotle's language) that will lead to a change from ignorance to knowledge (*anagnorisis*). Neo (Keanu Reeves) has been told by the Oracle (Gloria Foster) that he is not the "one," the savior who will lead the human race from out of the bondage to the machines—or, at least, that is what Neo has heard the Oracle say. Morpheus (Laurence Fishburne), the leader of the group of rebels and the one who has helped Neo to escape from the bondage, has willingly offered his own life to save Neo's. Morpheus does not die, but is held captive by "agents," the computer program pseudo-people within the Matrix that act to protect the Matrix from the rebel insurgents. Morpheus has knowledge that if acquired by the agents would doom all hope of any successful insurgency by the rebel human beings and so condemn humanity to endless slavery to the machines. Several of the rebel insurgents, one of whom is Neo, are confronted with a classic tragic choice, that is, one with no apparent good or happy solution: unplug Morpheus from the Matrix program, which would keep him from divulging what he knows and save the hope for a future successful insurgency but would kill him; or let Morpheus live and almost certainly doom the insurgency, and so condemn the future of humanity to slavery. There is another possibility which would seem to be so impossible as not to be a real possibility at all; to return to the Matrix and attempt to rescue Morpheus. The agents appear to be indestructible—no human has ever defeated an agent in combat—so this possibility of rescue seems not to be a possibility at all. The situation is dire and ambiguous. It is radically underdetermined in the sense that there appears to be no right answer, and yet something must be done and done immediately.

Neo believes that the Oracle has predicted that he will be given a choice between saving Morpheus's life or his own. He has also been told by the Oracle that without Morpheus the insurgents would be lost. He also believes that he is not the "one," so he believes that he cannot return to the Matrix, defeat the agents, and save Morpheus. The "right" response is relatively clear and is pronounced by Tank (Marcus Chong), one of the other insurgents. They must unplug Morpheus to save Zion, the city outside the Matrix where the free human beings live. Neo resists that obvious conclusion. This confrontation with ambiguity and indeterminacy reveals to Neo something about himself: He is himself willing to die for Morpheus and for the sake of Zion and the future of humanity. The *zimzum* moment makes possible a kind of self-knowledge that would not otherwise be available to Neo. In fact, as it turns out, Neo *is* the "one," a fact that Neo would not have discovered if he had not discovered first his passionate commitment to something other than himself. That passion was only revealed to him in a moment so underdetermined that there appeared to be no right way to understand it, no right thing to do.

Most dramatically it is Neo's discovery of his willingness to die for the sake of Morpheus and the cause of Zion that is the result of the *zimzum* moment. Less dramatically, but more accessibly, the *zimzum* moment, the moment of the withdrawal of meaning that makes the discovery of meaning possible, yields the discovery of another and rather closer-to-home pleasure and responsibility: Trinity (Carrie-Anne Moss). That is, in the high-drama of the movie, the plot stakes the hope of the future on the discovery of the protagonist's commitment to that future. This is rendered symbolically in the opposition of a person, Neo, against the computer program of the Matrix. Less symbolically rendered, however, are the more literal stakes of our discovery of our commitment to (our ability to commit to) a whole that is larger than ourselves, i.e., the ability to recognize and respond to the offer or possibility of love. For Trinity herself, it is only when she sees Neo falter, when Neo loses confidence in his own powers to act autonomously in the Matrix, that she will give to him the kiss that will revive him. Her response, too, is a response to a *zimzum* moment. Neo's apparent death is a withdrawal of meaning that she responds to in an irrational, inexplicable, yet unhesitating way. Without the kiss, the pointlessness of the world of the Matrix becomes universal. With the kiss, the moment of potential absolute vacuum of meaning is filled in with an in-rush of rich meaning. Not only is the hope for a future for humanity established, but that hope itself follows the establishment of the possibility of the very ad hoc, personal possibility of love between two people. In that way the movie, it seems to me, literally describes, in its allegorical story, the condition of human beings in society.

My own sense is that there are many *zimzum* moments for all of us. We are all, and frequently, confronted with situations and contexts that are underdetermined, yet demand a response from us. There is great power in the receptivity that comes with our contraction, with the *zimzum*, but there is also an epistemological problem. That is, what we fear is what we do not know. The most important thing that we do not know about is whether we have sufficient power and resources to handle the ambiguity and indeterminacy with which we may be confronted. The denial of ambiguity may lead to an empty world, but it has its securities. To be willing to handle the unknown in the ambiguous requires a certain amout of faith—faith in oneself, faith that one's own powers will be commensurate with the demands that the ambiguous may make on us. Our faith is certainly reinforced through experience. The more experiences that we have in which we move from a relatively passive, observant receptivity to confrontation with the ambiguous and the indeterminate to successful connection with others and with our own genuine needs and obligations, the more confidence we will have in our own abilities. Yet our future ability to be able to respond successfully to the challenges the world will present us with will still be a matter of faith. There may arise a situation to which our powers are not commensurate and we are undone. But, presumably, we would be undone by that situation anyway, and probably we would have been undone much earlier, never having known what powers were really ours to access, never having accessed them because of our denial of what we were really being confronted with.

The Matrix, then, can be read as a narrative of a person learning that he possesses powers that he was unaware that he possessed because he trusts himself to make a choice that is not obviously or conventionally the right choice. Further, I read in the invitation that the movie offers us to identify with the character of Neo to be a suggestion that this is a narrative that applies to all of our lives. It seems clear to me that that is what the movie, at least on one level, is about, but it takes a reading of the movie to make that explicit. A movie itself can represent a *zimzum* moment. If anything, the difficulty of popular movies, like the difficulty presented by people whom we know or whom we encounter in familiar situations (which is also the difficulty of familiar situations in general), is the difficulty of our own receptivity to it, of recognizing, which is really acknowledging, that there are ambiguities there, no matter how familiar the movie genre or situation or person we are encountering may be to us. That is, the challenge with popular movies is to regard them not as simply overdetermined, as obvious, but rather to trust that there may be more going on in them than may at first be obvious.

I see this as a problem that occurs not just at the movies. We are all, or at least most of us (perhaps most Americans especially), susceptible to autocratic encounters with other people and situations. Which is to say that great mysteries, great opportunities for learning, the possibilities for intense experiences, exist all around us, but we miss them because of our lack of receptivity to them. Learning about this receptive attentiveness at the movies may be a step in learning the power of attentive receptivity in the world at large, and especially, in developing faith in our own powers to be responsive, to see and hear and successfully respond to what we really encounter. Of course, this receptiveness is just a first step. Receptivity must be followed at some point by active engagement, which will include judgments, interpretations, assessments. One form this stage might take is talk. It might take the form, that is, of a conversation after a movie. And, of course, as in a good conversation, even the judgments, assessments, interpretations that we have made should be held lightly, which is to say, passionately but open to revision; that is, we should never be far from the attitude of receptivity.

Certainly, *The Matrix* is a somewhat ambiguous example as a positive philosophical text. If part of what haunts Neo is the thinness of the world of hypermarkets, that message is complicated by the glamour of life for the heroes within the Matrix as compared with life outside the Matrix. The movie cannot be about how superficial cool clothes are because cool clothes are so clearly glamorized in the movie. Although the movie contains some powerful scenes suggestive of deep philosophical issues, the overall plot of the movie reverts to pretty conventional Hollywood style elements that undo much of the movie's philosophical import. My sense, however, is that what made the movie so hugely powerful, what separated it from the hundreds of other sci-fi, futuristic adventure movies, were the *zimzum* moments. These are moments of maximum growth, maximum creativity, and maximum intensity. They are moments of radical interpretation based on radical discoveries that result from a kind of heightened sensitivity and receptivity. Our best moments are *zimzum* moments, and we can sometimes find them at the movies.

Every Story Is True: On the Question of Interpretation

What can the status be of an interpretation of a scene in a cyber-space/virtual-reality movie like *The Matrix* that is based on an idea from a relatively obscure sixteenth-century theological text, the Kabbalah? What is the point of an interpretation, anyway, and can an interpretation go too far? I want to say that every story, and every interpretation of a story, is true. This is not an ontological or an epistemological claim so much as it describes an attitudinal stance. That is, when I say that every story, every interpretation, is true, I am speaking pragmatically about the most useful and productive attitude to take toward stories and interpretations.

In an interview for CTHEORY, Slavoj Žižek, speaking of what can be found in popular commercial films, says, "You can detect what goes on at the profoundest, most radical level of our symbolic identities and how we experience ourselves."[21] This remark by Žižek raises for me the possibility that if a story or interpretation seems false to me it may be because I have not understood its truth or application at a deep enough level. What may strike me as patently false may in fact be patently false at the level at which I am considering it, but I may be missing the truth of the story, or of a given interpretation, that exists on a deeper level of our symbolic identities. That is, I see the challenge of stories and of interpretations as, in some sense, to see, to find, the truth that is in them. This, in some sense, may be hardest to do in stories that are the most familiar or accessible to us. I say "in some sense" because of course complex foreign films or art films will be difficult to understand or to make sense of sometimes, but at least we recognize this difficulty and the requirement of our active attempt to interpret the film. With popular films, however, the difficulties may not be so apparent.

The difficulties that are not apparent, of course, are not just the difficulties of familiar popular films. There are also the difficulties that are not apparent in our familiar regular lives. The philosophical impulse begins with the impulse to be amazed at what is familiar, ordinary, close to home. Stanley Cavell, in describing what he sees as what makes philosophy philosophy says, "I understand it as a willingness to think not about something other than what ordinary human beings think about, but rather to learn to think undistractedly about things that ordinary human beings cannot help thinking about."[22] What makes popular films popular will necessarily be the fact that they are responsive and satisfying to needs that many people have. The limits to our responsiveness to popular films, like the limits to our responsiveness to our own lives, will be the distractions that keep us from being alert to the truths and, one might say, the poetry that occur there.

Cavell identifies a certain kind of knowledge that he refers to as "the poetry of the ordinary." He says that all of the arts will be drawn to this knowledge, but that film "democratizes the knowledge."[23] I take this reference to a knowledge of the "poetry of the ordinary" to be describing something like a sensitivity to the sublime and mysterious that is immanent in the ordinary. Our potential responsiveness to the "poetry of the ordinary" I take to be a naturalistic fact about us, but the experience of it is more often absent than present in our lives. I see a merging of purpose in Cavell's identification of film as a place where a particular kind of knowledge is democratized, and in Shusterman's call for a democratization of philosophy. That is, I see in popular film, as I see in our everyday lives in the world, the potential for intense and revelatory experiences that are frequently overlooked. What is required is that we learn to look at them, in Cavell's phrase, undistractedly, which, I would say, is to learn to interpret them.

I see learning to interpret as, as much as anything, a learning how to come at things, how to regard things, which, ironically, may be learning how to be regarded by things. Cavell, in the chapter "The Politics of Interpretation," suggests the paradoxical formula of "turning the picture of interpreting a text into one of being interpreted by it."[24] I see in this reconception of the idea of interpretation an invocation of what I have been referring to as a *zimzum* moment. That is, the way to best gain access to a text is to avoid the temptation of projecting onto it what you already know. Instead, one must try to open oneself up to, make space in one's thinking for, the text, which means being responsive to its permutations as they manifest themselves. This is a kind of being interpreted by the text in the sense that the place where the value is presumed to reside is expressed through the text, and it is our responsibility to seek it out and be responsive to it. We are the ones being interpreted insofar as it is our ability to determine the presence of the value that is being tested.

The goal here however, is, as Cavell says, "freedom."[25] We learn from the text in order to be empowered to move on from the text. The first step toward this freedom, toward this power, ironically, is to allow oneself to be seduced by or captured by the text. The nature of the *zimzum* experience is the discovery of unexpected powers. What looks like submission gets transformed into liberation, but then, all genuine learning has that trajectory. The great danger is the sense that we have no more to learn, or no more to learn from, say, these common, everyday experiences or from these popular movies. Opening oneself up to learning from a movie will begin with asking questions like; Why am I so fascinated by this story?, Why am I moved by that particular scene?, What is really going on here?

This notion of interpretation is, paradoxically, the inverse of Baudrillard's analysis of what goes on in the hypermarket. That is, although Baudrillard describes a scenario that sounds similar, in which the products of the hypermarket test us, so that we, as he says, are the ones who are interpreted by the commodities, in fact the dynamic is quite the opposite. The issue comes down to the point of who is in control of the ultimate evaluation of value. There is submission that is enforced externally and there is submission that is undergone voluntarily, internally, intentionally, in the service of some greater good. Without interpretation (that is, an *intentional* willingness to be interpreted), without the *zimzum* act of intentional contraction, we really are more or less pawns to the will of the controllers of the hypermarket. As Hamlet says, "The readiness is all" (Act 5, Scene 2), and the readiness, in this case, means an attitudinal stance towards texts, and towards the world in general, that presumes that there is something to learn, and expects that the learning will require an act of interpretation.

To say that every interpretation is true would seem to miss a deep intuition that some interpretations are simply false. As Umberto Eco says in *Interpretation and Overinterpretation*, "To say that a text has potentially no end does not mean that every act of interpretation can have a happy end."[26] Eco argues that there is an "intention of the text" to which any interpretation must be true in order for it to be a valid interpretation. Richard Rorty, in a response to Eco's claims, disagrees. Rorty contrasts the model of the "code-cracker" with that of the pragmatist, and in his essay entitled "The Pragmatist's Progress" says that "all anybody does with anything is use it." Rorty goes on to say, "Interpreting something, knowing it, penetrating to its essence, and so on are all just various ways of describing some process of putting it to work."[27]

The code-cracker model of interpretation favored by Eco (although this is Rorty's gloss on Eco's position) assumes that there is something *in* the text (an "intention") that the interpretation has to be right about in order to be valid. The pragmatic understanding of what an interpretation is is that it is just one more way that people try to get on in the world, and the better interpretation will just be that one that helps us more in our getting on in the world. For Rorty, there is a valid question of evaluating interpretations, but it has nothing to do with what is "in" the text. As he says, "all descriptions...are evaluated according to their efficacy as instruments for purposes, rather than their fidelity to the object described."[28] Of course, the best use will result from a proper assessment of the properties of the thing we want to use, and this is what I have in mind when I speak of receptivity to the text. The value of the interpretation, however, will have nothing to do with what is "in" the text, but how useful the interpretation is to us in our lives at large. Every interpretation is true in the sense that any interpretation a person offers will be of some use, even if only as an initial foray into the process of interpretation itself.

If every interpretation, and every story, is true, what then is the truth of Eco's interpretation of interpretation and what even further advantage does Rorty's interpretation yield? What strikes me as certainly true in Eco's suggestion of an "intention of the text" to which an interpretation must be responsive to be valid, is just the idea that we should come to a text with the attitude that we might learn something from the text. That is, the best use we can make of a text is to allow the text to change us. To be willing to be changed by a text requires that we give something up. We must give up some of our sense of our own rightness, say, our arrogance with respect to texts. We must give up our desire to interpret simply in terms of what we already know, which is really just a form of projection, a projection of our established views onto the text, that makes us invulnerable to being changed by the text.

On the other hand, there is something true in Rorty's description of Eco's conception of an "intention of the text" as a code-breaker model of interpretation. A third interpretation, not of interpretation but of a feature prevalent in certain popular movies today, by Žižek, may help to shed some light on the limitations of this code-breaker model. Žižek identifies an often repeated scene in contemporary movies in which a protagonist is faced with the necessity of breaking a code, usually on a computer, in a very limited amout of time. Virtually all of Žižek's interpretations emerge from a Lacanian, psychoanalytic perspective, which is itself a slightly odd form of interpretation, but which frequently breaks open strikingly new ways of looking at something. In this case, Žižek sees the fascination we feel in watching these code-breaking scenes as the result of "the retreat of the Big Other." The "Big Other" is the Lacanian term for "the symbolic order or code of accepted fictions."[29] The retreat of the Big Other, then, seems to refer to a vacuum that has developed in the social authority structure. This vacuum may have many sources, from, say, the death of God, to the loss of faith in our elected politicians, to a loss of conviction about the foundations of our moral principles, or to doubts about the direction in which our country is moving. Žižek goes on to say, "Believing there is a code to be cracked is of course much the same as believing in the existence of some Big Other: in every case what is wanted is an agent who will give structure to our chaotic social lives."

In a typical Žižekian irony, scenes of attempts to crack an esoteric code are symbolically not about the defeat of some central authority (as they are often portrayed) but are rather the expression of a desire for just such an authority to make its authority manifest. This strikes me as a brilliant interpretation that also sheds light on Eco's code-breaker interpretation of interpretation. Eco's insistence that there is "an intention of the text" which any valid interpretation must discover and be true to seems to reflect a real felt need, but one that will lead to projection and the limitation of our powers rather than to learning and an increase of our powers. That is, while the sense that there is a code to be cracked, something "in" the text to be discovered, may be a good and natural response, the *insistence* that there is some real, one thing "in" there is to insist too much. What will be lost will be a responsiveness to a variety of readings of the text, an openness and playfulness that is able to recognize and so make use of any interesting interpretation. This openness opposes the constraint imposed by the fear of being duped by some "false" interpretation. The goal, as Cavell has suggested, is freedom. Rorty's conception of interpretation ultimately seems more freeing, and so more empowering, than Eco's.

Let us consider a specific interpretation of a specific scene in a film. The film is Alfred Hitchcock's *North by Northwest* and the interpretation is by Stanley Cavell in his chapter on *North by Northwest* in *Themes Out of School*. Cavell makes a series of more or less outrageous interpretive claims about the movie. Early in the essay he starts making some fairly large claims, specifically that the movie is alluding to other movies that seem quite different from *North by Northwest*, for example, *Bringing Up Baby* and *The Philadelphia Story*, and that *North by Northwest* is not just alluding to, but really extending the story of these other films. Cavell says that he will not ask us "out of the blue" to accept these claims but, in fact, he will never explicitly justify most of the claims he makes. By the end of his essay, his claims will become, in their number and limited plausibility, genuinely outrageous if not vertiginously overwhelming. After the initial salvo of somewhat wild claims he proposes beginning "as uncontroversially as we can."[30]

Among his "uncontroversial" claims are that Cary Grant in *North by Northwest* is being made to atone for some of the guilt that he acquired in roles in other movies such as *Notorious* and *Suspicion*. He claims that the movie's title is a reference to Shakespeare's *Hamlet* and, further, that the movie itself is a kind of rewriting of *Hamlet*. He claims that the movie is about redemption and the redemption of marriage. These are big claims for a popular Hollywood adventure movie, and those are just his "uncontroversial" claims. About half way through the essay Cavell says, "I must now put the uncontroversial aside and put forward a bunch of assertions."[31] Cavell goes on to make, among other claims, claims about the landscape in the famous crossroads/crop-dusting scene being Eve's (the female protagonist of the movie) body; that the attack of the plane is a reenactment of the sexual encounter between Eve and Roger Thornhill (the male protagonist) from the night before (which is paradoxical because if the landscape is Eve, then the airplane would logically be Roger Thornhill, but the airplane is shooting at Roger Thornhill); that "the Mount Rushmore Memorial is a crazy American literalization of [the] ambition of reciprocity with the world"[32] (a claim made after invoking Thoreau's *Walden*); and, culminating for me in outrageousness, the near final claim in the final paragraph of his essay that the microfilm that tumbles out of the broken statuette near the end of *North by Northwest* is the film *North by Northwest*.

For all of their apparent outrageousness, however, these claims do make some sense, if not individually, then in the sheer weight of their accumulating evidence that Hitchcock was indeed up to something, and that that something is large, political, and, ultimately, philosophical. Cavell reads the film *North by Northwest* as being an example of the "comedies of remarriage," a genre he has himself identified (invented, one might say). What *North by Northwest* is really about, on Cavell's reading, is how a marriage gets ratified, and the political significance for all of us of marriages that are ratified. Cavell reads the film allegorically and symbolically, as though it were a canto of Dante's *Divine Comedy*. From this perspective, what looks like the protagonist running away from a plane that is shooting bullets at him is really about a man running away in terror from the possibility of a kind of intimacy and a kind of self-knowledge for which he feels emotionally unprepared. Dante intended his poetic masterpiece to be read on several different levels, its literal level and then on three other allegorical levels, as he makes clear in his letter to Can

Grande. Hitchcock explicitly denies that there is anything symbolic in *North by Northwest*.[33] How are we to think about Cavell's claims about symbolic meanings, especially in light of Hitchcock's explicit, if certainly playful, denial that there are any symbolic meanings? Is there any justification for treating Hitchcock's popular Hollywood movie like Dante's *Divine Comedy*, and if so, what will count as an adequate justification? Is Cavell right that the film that falls out of the statuette at the end of *North by Northwest* is the film *North by Northwest*?

In *Art as Experience* Dewey refers to the "unifying phase" of criticism, which he describes as "a function of the creative response of the individual who judges."[34] Dewey goes on to say, "It is at this point that criticism becomes an art." Dewey sees a moral dimension to art, and criticism is connected with that moral dimension. As Dewey says, "The moral function of art itself is to remove prejudice, do away with scales that keep the eye from seeing, tear away the veils due to wont and custom, perfect the power to perceive. The critic's office is to further this work, performed by the object of art." I read Dewey as saying here that the moral function of art is to foster what I have been referring to in terms of passive receptivity. That is, what art can do for us is to surprise us into receptivity; it can attract us or draw us in, and in so doing overcome our autocratic tendencies to categorize things in terms of our wont and custom. One might say that art arouses us, seduces us from our quotidian pathways of thinking and being, suggests to us possibilities of things we have not encountered or experienced before. Ideally, we will get the sense that there is something more there, something more going on that we, as yet, do not understand but want to understand. That, it seems to me, is the essence of the original philosophical impulse, of philosophy's beginning, as Plato and Aristotle agree, in wonder.

To be receptive to the new and different is to be prepared to incorporate it into one's own being. It is to be open to the possibility of growth, of increased complexity, and for Dewey, increased complexity is the ultimate good: "As an organism increases in complexity, the rhythms of struggle and consummation in its relation to its environment are varied and prolonged, and they come to include within themselves an endless variety of sub-rhythms. The designs of living are widened and enriched. Fulfillment is more massive and more subtly shaded."[35] It is hard to imagine what we are searching for if it is not fulfillment that is more massive and more subtly shaded. Criticism, like art, can contribute to our more massive and more subtly shaded fulfillment by creatively demanding of us more, in some sense, than we have to give. The best criticism, like the best art, will require of us that we extend ourselves beyond our established parameters, beyond our up-to-this-point habitual ways of being and seeing and experiencing the world.

Is Cavell right about the film in the belly of the statuette? I think he absolutely is right. He is right in the pluralist, meliorist, and pragmatic sense that the film in the belly of the statuette being the film *North by Northwest* makes the film *North by Northwest* a better, more complicated, and more interesting film. That is reason enough to say that Cavell is right about that. My own experience with Cavell's interpretation of *North by Northwest*, and especially of the film in the belly of the statuette, was to laugh out loud at the wildness of his claims. Slowly, however, it began to dawn on me (the dawning of an aspect is a major concern of Wittgenstein's in *Philosophical Investigations* part 2, xi) that, of course, the movie must be about something like what it is like for two adults to really authentically get to know one another, and how it might come to be that an authentic marriage might get ratified. It is about the only explanation that makes sense of the shear bizarreness of the movie itself. Once that initial step is made to acknowledge that there may be more going on in the movie than the obvious literal story, then all sorts of possibilities begin to open up. Of course, that opening step, which is a *zimzum* step (a step that is an intentional contraction of oneself), is the step in which one recognizes the potential limitations of one's own established categories for making judgments about things. The consequence of taking that step is to see the need for a kind of heightened alertness to see how one might need to revise those categories.

Once one takes the step of accepting that *North by Northwest* is about how one, or rather two, put together an authentic marriage, the fact that such a topic would have political as well as philosophical ramifications is hard to dismiss. Whatever else it will take to authenticate a marriage, it will certainly take a degree of self-knowledge on the part of both people involved, which, itself, will require a certain amount of reflection, say, self-reflection. If *North by Northwest* is about that, that is to say, about the self-knowledge that comes from reflection, a reflection on oneself that comes through interaction with another, then it is no longer so implausible that it might know that about itself, and that it would want to convey that self-knowledge to us, to, as it were, exemplify the wisdom it is advocating. At this point I find it difficult to see any alternative reading to Cavell's. The film in the belly of the statuette must be *North by Northwest* if the film *North by Northwest* is about anything at all.

Could Cavell have been wrong? I find this a more troubling question, but I think so. Perhaps "wrong" is not the right word, but, just as there are great artworks, and artworks that are really not that good, there will be great, creative, masterpiece-making criticism, and criticism that leaves a thing less interesting than it might have even been without the criticism. The ideal of criticism (and I take "ideal" here in Dewey's sense of ideals; "Ideals are like stars; we steer by them, not towards them"[36]) is to make works of art, in which I include popular movies, more interesting, more exciting, and more complex, so that we become more complex and hence, more excited, more interested, and probably, more exciting and more interesting as well.

Notes

Preface

1. Ludwig Wittgenstein, *On Certainty*, ed. G. E. M. Anscombe and G. H. von Wright, trans. D. Paul and G. E. Anscombe (New York: Harper & Row, Publishers, 1972), §467.

2. Norman Malcolm, *Ludwig Wittgenstein: A Memoir* (New York: Oxford University Press, 1962), 100.

3. Stanley Cavell, *Contesting Tears: The Hollywood Melodrama of the Unknown Woman* (Chicago: University of Chicago Press, 1996), xii.

Introduction

1. Malcolm, *Ludwig Wittgenstein: A Memoir*, 27–28.

2. Ludwig Wittgenstein, *Philosophical Investigations*, 3rd ed., trans. G. E. M. Anscombe (New York: Macmillan Publishing Co., Inc., 1969), §133.

3. See Ray Monk's excellent biography of Wittgenstein, *The Duty of Genius* (New York: Free Press, 1990), especially the first chapter, 3–137.

4. Constance Penley, *The Future of an Illusion: Film, Feminism, and Psychoanalysis* (Minneapolis: University of Minnesota Press, 1990), 61.

5. I am regarding the movies that I refer to as primary texts and so all quoted dialogue is, unless otherwise noted, taken directly from the movies themselves.

6. Stanley Cavell, *Must We Mean What We Say?: A Book of Essays* (New York: Cambridge University Press, 1976), 196.

7. Stanley Cavell, *Contesting Tears: The Hollywood Melodrama of the Unknown Woman* (Chicago: University of Chicago Press, 1996), xii.

8. John Dewey, *Art as Experience* (New York: Perigee Books, 1980), 35–37.

9. Ibid., 15.

10. Ibid., 35.

11. Ibid., 53.

12. Ibid., 44.

13. Ibid., 38.

14. Ibid., 14.

15. Noël Carroll, "The Power of Movies," *Daedelus* 114, no. 4 (1985).

16. Dewey, *Art as Experience*, 45.

17. Richard Rorty, *Contingency, Irony, and Solidarity* (New York: Cambridge University Press, 1989), 28.

18. Charles Sanders Peirce, *Chance, Love, and Logic: Philosophical Essays,* ed. Morris Cohen (Lincoln: University of Nebraska Press, 1998), 10–11.

19. Ibid., 16.

20. Susan Sontag, "Against Interpretation," in *Film and/as Literature,* ed. John Harrington (Englewood Cliffs, NJ: Prentice-Hall, Inc., 1977), 364.

1. John Ford's *The Searchers* as an Allegory of the Philosophical Search

1. Wittgenstein, *Philosophical Investigations*, ixe. All further references to the *Investigations* will be made by noting the section number after the quotation, e.g., (§109).

2. Stanley Cavell, *Pursuits of Happiness: The Hollywood Comedy of Remarriage* (Cambridge, MA: Harvard University Press, 1981), 7.

3. Jean-Louis Comolli, "Notes on the New Spectator," trans. Diana Matias, in *Cahiers du Cinéma: 1960-1968: New Wave, New Cinema, Reevaluating Hollywood*, ed. Jim Hillier (Cambridge, MA: Harvard University Press, 1986), 210–15. In this essay Comolli explicitly exempts Ford from his condemnation of the bourgeois, hence essentially mindless seductions of darkness and the dreaminess of movie theaters and Hollywood movies. In spite of this exemption, I find Ford to be doing more or less what Comolli seems to condemn: capitalizing on the darkness and invoking dreaminess in the spectator—although to an end, if not by a means, that Comolli would no doubt endorse.

4. Ibid., 213. Comolli says, among other things:

This is no doubt why the *auteur* cinema is only just tolerated by the spectator, and even then with bad grace. There is a wide gap between the state of the spectator in a darkened cinema and the state of receptivity or lucid participation demanded by any film not made simply for the consumer. Why? Either the film is a natural extension of the dark, an ante-chamber of dreams, so that the spectator, having left the world behind, denies himself and others, and himself as another. Alone, he follows the sweet, simple thread of a dream which envelopes him like a cocoon; the world unfolds its shapes before his eyes with dreamlike ease. There is hypnotic sympathy at work which any encroachment on anticipated forms and expected themes would shatter painfully. Or the film, despite and beyond the darkened cinema, aims to be an extension of and comment on the outside world. If that is the case the spectator is lost.

I see Ford, with his technique in *The Searchers*, as denying this dichotomy and using the dark and dreamlike quality of movies to the very end of helping us to become more adept in "the outside world," just as paying attention to one's dreams might.

5. Ludwig Wittgenstein, *Culture and Value*, trans. Peter Winch, ed. G. H. von Wright (Chicago: University of Chicago Press, 1980), 65e.

6. Wittgenstein, *On Certainty*, §467.

7. Friedrich Nietzsche, *Human, All Too Human: A Book for Free Spirits*, trans. Marion Faber and Stephen Lehmann (Lincoln: University of Nebraska, 1984), §§5 and 9.

8. Erwin Panofsky, "Style and Medium in the Motion Pictures," in *Film Theory and Criticism: Introductory Readings*, 2nd ed., ed. Gerald Mast and Marshall Cohen (New York: Oxford University Press, 1979), 246.

9. For example, see James Monaco, *How to Read a Film: The Art, Technology, Language, History and Theory of Film and Media* (New York: Oxford University Press, 1977), 253; and Andrew Sarris, *The John Ford Movie Mystery* (Bloomington: Indiana University Press, 1975), 174.

10. Even Ford didn't seem to know how to completely account for Ethan's past. In an interview with Peter Bogdanovich he says of Ethan, "It's the tragedy of a loner. He's the man who came back from the Civil War, probably went over into Mexico, became a bandit, probably fought for Juarez or Maximilian—probably Maximilian, because of the medal. He was just a plain loner—could never really be part of the family." In Peter Bogdanovich's *John Ford* (Berkeley: University of California Press, 1970), 92-93.

11. *Pursuits*, 8–9. Cavell says, "I wish to take the opportunity to acknowledge that philosophy, as I understand it, is indeed outrageous, inherently so. It seeks to disquiet the foundations of our lives and to offer us in recompense nothing better than itself—and this on the basis of no expert knowledge, of nothing closed to the ordinary human being, once, that is to say, that being lets himself or herself be informed by the process and the ambition of philosophy."

12. For an account of *The Searchers* as a kind of classical Greek tragedy in the Aristotelian mode, see Martin M. Winkler, "Tragic Features in John Ford's *The Searchers*," in *Bucknell Review: Classics and Cinema*, ed. Martin M. Winkler (Lewisburg: Bucknell University Press, 1991), 185–208.

13. I am indebted here, and in general, to Tag Gallagher's excellent discussion of *The Searchers* in his very fine *John Ford: The Man and His Films* (Berkeley: University of California Press, 1986), 328.

14. For more along this line see Joseph McBride and Michael Wilmington, *John Ford* (New York: Da Capo Press, 1975), 152.

15. Friedrich Nietzsche, *On the Genealogy of Morals*, trans. Walter Kaufman and R. J. Hollingdale (New York: Vintage Books, 1989), 127.

16. Ibid., 71.

17. These themes are pervasive in the work of Nietzsche and I will not offer lengthy argument or textual support in defense of this claim. I will mention the importance of solitude, and of confronting the forbidden that appear, for example, in Nietzsche's preface to *Human, All Too Human*. Wittgenstein says, "The philosopher is not a citizen of any community of ideas" (*Zettel* [Berkeley: University of California Press, 1970], §455) and I understand his point to be roughly Nietzsche's; that clarity in thinking demands a certain amount of independence from conventional ways of thinking.

18. Aristotle, *Nichomachean Ethics*, trans. Martin Ostwald (Indianapolis: Bobbs-Merrill Educational Publishing, 1981), book 9, ch. 9. See also John Cooper, "Aristotle on Friendship," in *Essays on Aristotle's Ethics*, ed. Amelie Oksenberg Rorty (Berkeley: University of California Press, 1980), 301–40.

19. This idea is suggested by J. A. Place in *The Western Films of John Ford* (Secaucus: Citadel Press, 1974), 169–70.

20. I am not entirely satisfied with this interpretation of the scalping scene, which, in conjunction with his embrace of Debbie, strikes me as making sense, but beyond consistent literal interpretation. An alternate, nonliteral, and equally unsatisfying interpretation is to say that, as a kind of dream interpretation, Ethan's good side (represented by Marty) killed his bad side (represented by Scar) which then makes possible his eventual merciful embrace of Debbie.

21. I want to thank Kendall D'Andrade and an anonymous reviewer for comments on earlier version of this chapter.

2. A *The Usual Suspects* Moment in *Vertigo*

1. A similar phenomenon occurs in *The Crying Game*. In that movie there is a dynamic where the audience is led to identify with a character who seems to be slipping into a complicated, but heterosexual (so not *that* complicated) relation-

ship. All of the tension for the audience surrounding the developing relationship derives from who this woman is, and not from whether she is a woman or not. When the character is revealed to be not a woman but a man, suddenly the protagonist (and we, the audience) is completely taken aback. The more significant, and more devastating recognition is not that this person is really a man, but how much of a difference that makes to the protagonist and to us, how that changes the complexion of all of one's previous experiences with this character. The real, and really devastating, shock is not the Otherness of Gil, but one's own otherness to one's image of oneself.

2. Aristotle, *Poetics*, trans. with notes by Richard Janko (Indianapolis: Hackett Publishing Company, 1987), 7 (49b25–30).

3. François Truffaut, *Hitchcock*, with the collaboration of Helen G. Scott (New York: Simon and Schuster, Inc., 1985), 243–48.

4. Ibid., 243.

5. Ibid., 244.

6. Tania Modleski, *The Women Who Knew Too Much: Hitchcock and Feminist Theory* (New York: Routledge, 1989), 87.

7. For an interesting analysis of Scottie's "rationality" see Dan Flory, "Hitchcock and Deductive Reasoning: Moving Step by Step in *Vertigo*," in *Film and Philosophy*, vol. 3, 1996, 38–52.

8. Ironically, one can say that Madeleine, too, is a criminal of whom Scottie is in pursuit (although he does not realize that at the time) when he experiences his debilitating vertigo.

9. An amusing but not inappropriate Freudian reading that suggests these conclusions is Robin Wood's, who suggests the interpretation that the three men running across the rooftops in the opening shot represent Scottie's id (the fleeing criminal), his ego (Scottie), and his superego (the policeman). This reading suggests that subconsciously Scottie wants his id to escape to freedom and his superego to be done away with. See Robin Wood, *Hitchcock's Films Revisited* (New York: Columbia University Press, 1989), 380.

10. Ibid.

11. Max Horkheimer and Theodor W. Adorno, *Dialectic of Enlightenment* trans. John Cumming (New York: Continuum Publishing Company, 1997) 120–25.

12. Marian Keane, "A Closer Look at Scopophilia: Mulvey, Hitchcock, and *Vertigo*," in *A Hitchcock Reader*, ed. Marshall Deutelbaum and Leland Poague (Ames: Iowa State University Press, 1986), 233.

13. Slavoj Žižek, *The Sublime Object of Ideology* (New York: Verso Press, 1989), 104.

14. Ibid., 104.

15. Ibid., 106.

16. Ibid.

17. Ibid., 114-15.

18. Michel Chion, *The Voice in Cinema*, trans. Claudia Gorbman (New York: Columbia University Press, 1999), 18–21.

19. Ibid., 156.

20. Keane, "A Closer Look at Scopophilia," 245.

21. Modleski, *Women Who Knew Too Much*, 90. Although I am critical of Modleski's reading right here, I am in fact deeply indebted to her reading of *Vertigo* in her essay in this volume entitled, "Feminity by Design: *Vertigo*."

22. Slavoj Žižek, *The Metastases of Enjoyment: Six Essays on Woman and Causality* (New York: Verso Press, 1994), 103–4.

3. The American Sublime in *Fargo*

1. Rob Wilson, *American Sublime: The Genealogy of a Poetic Genre* (Madison: University of Wisconsin Press, 1991), 11.

2. Immanuel Kant, *The Critique of Judgment*, trans. J. H. Bernard (New York: Macmillan Publishing Co., Inc. 1951), 104.

3. Ibid., 83.

4. Aristotle, *Poetics*, 21 (52a 30).

5. Harold Bloom, *Poetry and Repression: Revisionism from Blake to Stevens* (New Haven: Yale University Press, 1976), 255.

6. Ralph Waldo Emerson, "The American Scholar," in *The Portable Emerson*, ed. Carl Bode (New York: Penguin Books, 1981), 53.

7. Ethan Coen and Joel Coen, *Fargo* (Boston: Faber and Faber, 1996), 6.

8. Ibid.

9. Ibid., 3.

10. See Stanley Cavell's remarkable discussion of Emerson's use of the idea of pregnancy in "Experience" in Stanley Cavell, *This New Yet Unapproachable America: Lectures after Emerson after Wittgenstein* (Albuquerque: Living Batch Press, 1989), 100ff.

11. Simone de Beauvoir, *The Ethics of Ambiguity*, trans. Bernard Frechtman (Secaucus, NJ: Carol Publishing Group, 1997), 35–45.

12. Jean-François Lyotard, "The Sublime and the Avant-Garde," in *The Lyotard Reader,* ed. Andrew Benjamin (Cambridge, MA: Basil Blackwell, 1989), 209. This essay was originally published in *Art Forum* 22, part 8 (April 1984); 36–43, in a translation by Lisa Liebman.

13. Slavoj Žižek, *Looking Awry: An Introduction to Jacques Lacan through Popular Culture* (Cambridge, MA: MIT Press, 1997), 157.

14. Emerson, "Experience," *Portable Emerson,* 282.

15. John Dewey, *Experience and Nature,* in *The Later Works of John Dewey, 1925–53, vol. 1, 1925,* ed. Jo Ann Boydston (Carbondale: Southern University Press, 1988), 43–44.

16. Ibid., 105, 101.

17. Ibid., 105.

18. Coen and Coen, *Fargo,* 11.

19. Ibid., 45.

20. "Compensation," *Portable Emerson,* 181.

21. "Nature," *Portable Emerson,* 27.

22. "Napoleon; or, the Man of the World," *Portable Emerson,* 345.

23. *Experience and Nature,* 305.

24. Ibid., 307.

25. Ibid., 305.

26. Ibid., 280–81.

27. Ibid., 281.

28. Cavell, *This New Yet Unapproachable America,* 57.

29. Kant, *Critique of Judgment,* §27.

4. Visions of Meaning

1. Plato, *Five Dialogues,* trans. G. M. A. Grube (Indianapolis: Hackett Publishing Company, 1981), 33a.

2. Arthur Danto, *The Transfiguration of the Commonplace: A Philosophy of Art* (Cambridge: Harvard University Press, 1981), 164.

3. Emphasizing the importance of seeing as a metaphor in *Crimes and Misdemeanors* is certainly not original to me. All three essays on *Crimes and Misdemeanors* in *Film/Literature Quarterly* 19, no. 2 (1991), with a special section on the films of Woody Allen, make some reference to this idea. All three

essays are quite good. See Peter Minowitz's "Crimes and Controversies: Nihilism from Machiavelli to Woody Allen"; Edward Quattrochi's "Allen's Literary Antecedents in *Crimes and Misdemeanors*"; and Dianne Vipond's "*Crimes and Misdemeanors*: A Retake on the Eyes of Dr. Eckleburg."

4. Plato, *The Republic of Plato*, trans. Allan Bloom (New York: Basic Books, 1968), 359d.

5. Sander Lee argues for the philosophical seriousness of Allen's work in his essay "Sartrean Themes in Woody Allen's *Husbands and Wives*" in *Film and Philosophy*, vol. 1, 1994, 55–61.

6. Friedrich Nietzsche, *The Birth of Tragedy,* trans. Walter Kaufman (New York: Vintage Books, 1967), 34.

7. Ibid., 50–52.

8. Vipond, "*Crimes and Misdemeanors*: A Retake," 99, 102.

9. 9Dewey, *Art as Experience*, 60 (see introduction, n. 7).

10. Ibid., 22.

11. Vipond, "*Crimes and Misdemeanors*: A Retake," 103.

12. Danto, *Transfiguration*, 173.

13. *Art as Experience*, 23.

14. Plato, *Republic*, 612b.

15. Sander Lee, *Woody Allen's* Angst: *Philosophical Commentaries on His Serious Films* (Jefferson, North Carolina: McFarland and Company, Inc., 1997). Not only is Lee's essay clearly written and provocative, but it is especially good in discussing traditional Jewish ceremonies and some of the philosophical ramifications of those ceremonies as presented in Allen's film.

16. Quoted in *Woody Allen's* Angst, 286–87.

17. *Woody Allen's* Angst, 287.

18. In an appendix to *Woody Allen's* Angst, Lee includes some questions that he wrote to Allen and to which Allen responded. *Woody Allen's* Angst, 288.

19. *Woody Allen's* Angst, 289.

20. Walter Benjamin, *Illuminations: Essays and Reflections*, ed. Hannah Arendt (New York: Schocken Books, 1969), 96.

21. Ibid., 88-89.

22. Ibid., 96.

23. Ibid., 90.

5. Oedipus Techs

1. Constance Penley, somewhat indirectly, suggests this comparison when she describes *The Terminator* as a popularized version of Chris Marker's *La Jetée*, of which *12 Monkeys* is a remake, in her excellent article, "Time Travel, Primal Scene, and the Critical Dystopia," in *Close Encounters: Film, Feminism, and Science Fiction*, ed. Constance Penley, Elizabeth Lynn Spigel, and Janet Bergstrom eds. (Minneapolis: University of Minnesota, 1991), 76.

2. Jean-François Lyotard, *The Postmodern Condition: A Report on Knowledge*, trans. Geoff Bennington and Brian Massumi (Minneapolis: University of Minnesota Press, 1984), xxiv.

3. Ibid., 63–64.

4. Martin Heidegger, *Being and Time*, trans. John Macquarrie and Edward Robinson (New York: Harper and Row, 1962), 126–27. (The pagination refers to "the later German editions as indicated in [the] margins" of this edition of *Being and Time*.)

5. Hubert L. Dreyfus, *Being-in-the-World: A Commentary on Heidegger's Being and Time, Division I* (Cambridge: MIT Press, 1991), 152–53.

6. Of course, an exception to this account would be those who are in, for example, research and development parts of corporations who are, within very specific constraints, expected to think differently.

7. François Jacob, *The Possible and the Actual* (Seattle: University of Washington Press, 1982), 7–8. Jacob describes sex as "a diversity-generating device."

8. *Being and Time*, 184.

9. *Being and Time*, 187.

10. Piotr Hoffman, "Death, Time, History: Division II of *Being and Time*," in *The Cambridge Companion to Heidegger*, ed. Charles B. Guignon (New York: Cambridge University Press, 1993), 198.

11. Dreyfus, *Being-in-the-World*, 313.

12. *Being and Time*, 188.

13. Ibid., 189, 185.

14. Ibid., 385.

15. Ibid., 391.

16. Dreyfus, *Being-in-the-World*, 26–27.

17. This idea is discussed in several of Nietzsche's works. See for example, Friedrich Nietzsche, *Ecce Homo*, trans. R. J. Hollingdale (New York: Penguin

Books, 1979), especially the chapter "Why I Am So Clever," 51–68; and *Thus Spoke Zarathustra*, trans. R. J. Hollingdale (New York: Penguin Books, 1969), part 3, "The Convalescent."

18. Alexander Nehamas, *Nietzsche: Life as Literature* (Cambridge: Harvard University Press, 1985), 150.

19. Ibid., 155.

20. Harold Bloom, *Poetry and Repression*, 232 (see chap. 3, n. 5). See also his *The Anxiety of Influence: A Theory of Poetry* (New York: Oxford University Press, 1973).

21. *Poetry and Repression*, 236.

22. Ibid., 237.

23. Ibid., 240.

24. Ibid., 244.

25. Wittgenstein, *Philosophical Investigations*, §108 (see introduction, n. 2).

26. Rorty, *Contingency, Irony, and Solidarity*, 75 (see introduction, n. 17).

27. Dreyfus, *Being-in-the-World*, 321.

28. Interestingly, in the original Chris Marker film *La Jetée*, the only movement in the whole film is the blink of the eyes of the woman.

29. Sophocles, *The Oedipus Cycle*, trans. Robert Fitzgerald (New York: Harcourt Brace, 1949), 161–62.

30. An earlier version of this chapter was read at the 1998 meetings of the SPSCVA that were held in conjunction with the central meetings of the APA in Chicago. Dan Flory was the respondent and I would like to express my gratitude for his comments, which I have tried to respond to in this chapter.

6. Into the Toilet

1. Aristotle, *Parts of Animals*, trans. William Ogle, in *Aristotle: On Man in the Universe* (Roslyn, NY: Walter J. Black, Inc., 1943), 46 (640b 17–20).

2. Aristotle, *Parts of Animals*, 49 (645a 15–25).

3. George Lakoff and Mark Johnson, *Philosophy in the Flesh: The Embodied Mind and Its Challenge to Western Thought* (New York: Basic Books, 1999), 3.

4. James Joyce, *Ulysses* (New York: Modern Library, 1992), 69.

5. Jacob Bernays, "Aristotle on the Effect of Tragedy," in *Articles on Aristotle, vol. 4*, trans. Jonathon Barnes and Jennifer Barnes, ed. J. Barnes, M.

Schofield, and R. Sorabji (London, 1979). For further discussion of this controversial subject see, Jonathon Lear's "Katharis," as well as Martha Nussbaum's, "Tragedy and Self-Sufficiency: Plato and Aristotle on Fear and Pity" and Richard Janko's, "From Catharsis to the Aristotelian Mean," all in *Essays on Aristotle's Poetics*, ed. Amelie Oksenberg Rorty (Princeton: Princeton University Press, 1992).

6. Aristotle, *On Poetry and Style*, trans. G. M. A. Grube (Indianapolis: Hackett Publishing Company, 1989), 12.

7. Nietzsche, *The Birth of Tragedy*. See especially sections 1, 3, 5, and 7 (see chap. 4, n. 6).

8. Camille Paglia, *Sexual Personae: Art and Decadence from Nefertiti to Emily Dickinson* (New York: Vintage Books, 1991), 91.

9. Nietzsche, *Birth of Tragedy*, 35.

10. Ibid., 40.

11. Ibid., 43.

12. Ibid. 37, 36.

13. Plato, *Plato's Republic*, trans. G. M. A. Grube (Indianapolis: Hackett Publishing Company, 1974), 251 (607b5).

14. Ibid., 595b.

15. Jacques Derrida, *Dissemination*, trans. Barbara Johnson (Chicago: University of Chicago Press, 1981), 101.

16. Ibid., 100.

17. Ibid., 70–71.

18. Ibid., 72–73.

19. Martha C. Nussbaum, *The Fragility of Goodness: Luck and Ethics in Greek Tragedy and Philosophy* (New York: Cambridge University Press, 1989). See especially chapter 5.

20. Plato, *The Collected Dialogues of Plato: Including the Letters*, ed. Edith Hamilton and Huntington Cairns (Princeton: Princeton University Press, 1980), 1567 (314b–c).

21. Martha C. Nussbaum, *The Therapy of Desire: Theory and Practice in Hellenistic Ethics* (Princeton: Princeton University Press, 1994), 333.

22. Bert Cardullo, "Fiction into Film, or Bringing Welsh to Boyle," in *Literature/Film Quarterly*, 25, no 3 (1997): 158–62.

23. Ibid., 160. Quoted in the Cardullo essay from John Hodge, *Trainspotting: The Screenplay* (New York: Hyperion, 1996). Speaking of popular culture phenomena, it is interesting that there is a recently produced DJ mix CD called "Ultra-Mix 98," produced, mixed, and mastered by Chris Cox that includes

a track of this "choose life" soliloquy, featuring the voice of Ewan McGregor, it is called "Choose Life." (Manufactured by Priority Records, 1998.)

24. Cardullo, "Fiction into Film," 159.

25. *Birth of Tragedy*, 60.

26. *Symposium*, 574 (223d). In Plato, *Collected Dialogues*.

27. S. H. Butcher, "The Function of Tragedy," in *The Proper Study: Essays on Western Classics*, ed. Quentin Anderson and Joseph A. Mazzeo (New York: St. Martin's Press, 1962), 190.

28. An earlier version of this chapter was presented at the meetings of the SPSCVA that were associated with the 20th World Congress of Philosophy in Boston, MA, August, 1998. I would like to thank Kendall D'Andrade for comments and suggestions that he made on an earlier draft of this paper, and especially for steering me toward the Bert Cardullo article.

7. Horror and Death at the Movies

1. In addition to my own interest in the genre of horror, I was drawn to this subject by Noël Carroll's *The Philosophy of Horror or Paradoxes of the Heart* (New York: Routledge, 1990). In that work Carroll identifies two paradoxes of horror: "1) how can anyone be frightened by what they know does not exist, and 2) why would anyone ever be interested in horror, since being horrified is so unpleasant?" (p. 8). I, too, will be addressing these issues, although I will be concerned primarily with the latter.

2. See Dante's description of the polysemous dimension of his *Comedy* in his letter to Can Grande, published in Robert S. Haller's *Literary Criticism of Dante Alighieri* (Lincoln: University of Nebraska Press, 1973), 98–100. As Dante says of the first two, of four, levels of meaning, "The subject of the whole work, then, taken literally, is the state of the soul after death, understood in a simple sense; for the whole movement of the work turns upon this and about this. If on the other hand the work is taken allegorically, the subject is man, in the exercise of his free will, earning or becoming liable to the rewards or punishments of justice" (99).

3. Don DeLillo, *Underworld* (New York: Scribner Paperback Fiction, 1997), 677.

4. The katabasis theme recurs in some of the greatest literature of Western civilization. It occurs not only in Homer's *Odyssey*, but also in book six of the *Aenid*, Dante's *Inferno*, James Joyce's *Ulysses*, and, if understood even more symbolically, it can be seen in Augustine's *Confessions*, Shakespeare's *Hamlet*, and many contemporary films.

5. Homer, *The Odyssey*, trans. Robert Fagles (New York: Viking Penquin, 1996), book 11, lines 40–48.

6. Ibid., line 85.

7. Žižek, *Looking Awry*, 22–23.

8. Homer, *Odyssey*, book 11, lines 173–74.

9. Ibid., lines 720–25.

10. Martin M. Winkler, "The Katabasis Theme in Modern Cinema," in *Classical Myth and Culture in the Cinema*, ed. Martin M. Winkler (New York: Oxford University Press, 2001), 26.

11. Max Horkheimer and Theodor W. Adorno, "Odysseus or Myth and Enlightenment," in *The Dialectic of Enlightenment*, 77–8 (see chap. 2, n. 11).

12. *Odyssey*, book 11, lines 555–58.

13. Charles Segal, *Singers, Heroes, and Gods in the* Odyssey (Ithaca: Cornell University Press, 1994), 41.

14. Max Horkheimer and Theodor W. Adorno, "The Culture Industry: Enlightenment as Mass Deception," in *Dialectic of Enlightenment*, 124.

15. Ibid., 131.

16. Alexander Nehamas, "Plato and the Mass Media," in *The Monist* 71, no. 2 (April 1988); 214–25.

17. Walter Benjamin, "The Work of Art in the Age of Mechanical Reproduction," in *Illuminations*, 223 (see chap. 4, n. 24).

18. *A Presocratics Reader: Selected Fragments and Testimonia*, ed. Patricia Curd, trans. Richard D. McKirahan, Jr. (Indianapolis: Hackett Publishing Company, Inc., 1996), 12.

19. Plato, *Phaedo*, in *Five Dialogues*, 67e (see chap. 4, n. 1).

20. Ibid., 107a.

21. Ibid., 110b.

22. Epicurus, *The Essential Epicurus: Letters, Principle Doctrines, Vatican Sayings, and Fragments*, trans. Eugene O'Connor (Buffalo: Prometheus Books, 1993), 63.

23. Arthur Schopenhauer, *The World as Will and Representation*, trans. E. F. J. Payne, vol. 1 (New York: Dover Publications, Inc., 1969), §38, 196.

24. E. R. Dodds, *The Greeks and the Irrational* (Berkeley: University of California Press, 1956), 277–78.

25. Friedrich Nietzsche, *Birth of Tragedy*, §1 (see chap. 4, n. 6).

26. Gilles Deleuze, *Nietzsche and Philosophy*, trans. Hugh Tomlinson (New York: Columbia University Press, 1983), 39–72.

27. Sigmund Freud, *The Ego and the Id*, trans. Joan Riviere, rev. and ed. James Strachey (New York: W. W. Norton and Company, 1960), 8.

28. Sigmund Freud, "Types of Neurotic Nosogenesis," in *A General Selection from the Works of Sigmund Freud,* ed. John Rickman (New York: Doubleday Books, 1957), 64.

29. Sigmund Freud, *Beyond the Pleasure Principle*, in *The Complete Psychological Works of Sigmund Freud*, vol. 18, trans. and ed. James Strachey and Anna Freud (London: Hogarth Press, 1973), 14–17.

30. Ibid., 35–36.

31. Ibid., 38.

32. T. S. Eliot refers to the Sibyl of Cumae from Petronius' *Satyricon* in the epigraph to *The Waste Land.*

33. *Beyond the Pleasure Principle*, 39.

34. Freud, *Ego and the Id*, 46.

35. *Beyond the Pleasure Principle*, 39.

36. Freud, "The 'Uncanny'," in *Complete Psychological Works*, vol. 17, 249.

37. Carroll, *Philosophy of Horror*, 175.

38. Slavoj Žižek, *The Art of the Ridiculous Sublime: On David Lynch's Lost Highway* (Seattle: University of Washington Press, 2000), 5.

39. Ibid.

40. Ibid., 13.

41. Ibid., 20.

42. Aristotle, *Poetics*, 13 (52a 2–10), 14 (52a 23–5264) (see chap. 2, n. 2).

43. Žižek, *Ridiculous Sublime*, 37.

44. Ibid., 41.

Conclusion

1. Richard Shusterman, *Practicing Philosophy: Pragmatism and the Philosophical Life* (New York: Routledge, 1997), 50.

2. This connection between the movie *The Matrix* and Plato's allegory of the cave is not a particularly original one. There are several references in several different essays in *The Matrix and Philosophy: Welcome to the Desert of the Real* (ed. William Irwin [Chicago: Open Court, 2002]) that make this connection. None, however, will pursue the particular line of thought that I am proposing in this chapter.

3. J. C. Nyíri, "Wittgenstein's Later Work in Relation to Conservatism," in *Wittgenstein and His Times*, ed. Brian McGuinness (Chicago: University of Chicago Press, 1982), 54.

4. Ibid., 53.

5. Jean Beaudrillard, *Simulacra and Simulation*, trans. Sheila Faria Glaser (Ann Arbor: University of Michigan Press, 1994), 75.

6. Ibid., 23.

7. Wittgenstein, *Philosophical Investigations*, ixe.

8. Ludwig Wittgenstein, *Philosophical Occasions 1912–1951* ed. James Klagge and Alfred Nordman (the English translation of "Philosophie" was done by C. G. Luckhardt and M. A. E. Aue) (Indianapolis: Hackett Publishing Co. 1993), 161–63.

9. Cavell, *This New Yet Unapproachable America*, 17 (see chap. 3, n. 10). Cavell is quoting here from the Wittgenstein's preface to *Philosophical Investigations*.

10. Ibid., 33.

11. Ibid., 45, 74.

12. Ibid., 86–87.

13. De Beauvoir, *Ethics of Ambiguity*, 12 (see chap. 3, n. 11).

14. Ibid., 71.

15. Bloom, *Poetry and Repression*, 140 (see chap. 3, n. 5).

16. Gershom Scholem, *On the Kabbalah and Its Symbolism*, trans. Ralph Manheim (New York: Schoked Books, 1969), 110–11.

17. John Dewey, *A Common Faith* (New Haven: Yale University Press, 1968), 15–16.

18. Michael Eldridge, *Transforming Experience: John Dewey's Cultural Instrumentalism* (Nashville: Vanderbilt University Press, 1998), 150.

19. *Ethics of Ambiguity*, 42ff.

20. Ibid., 42.

21. Žižek, "Civil Society, Fanaticism, and Digital Reality: A Conversation with Slavoj Žižek," in *CTHEORY*, February 21, 1996. *CTHEORY* is an electronic journal that can be found at http.//ctheory.com/article/a037.html.

22. Stanley Cavell, *Themes Out of School: Effects and Causes* (San Francisco: North Point Press, 1984), 9.

23. Ibid., 14.

24. Ibid., 52.

25. Ibid., 53.

26. Umberto Eco, with Richard Rorty, Jonathan Culler, and Christine Brooke-Rose, *Interpretation and Overinterpretation*, ed. Stefan Collini (New York: Cambridge University Press, 1992), 24.

27. Ibid., 93.

28. Ibid., 92.

29. Slavoj Žižek, " 'You May!,' " in *The London Review of Books* 21, no. 6, (March 18, 1999).

30. Cavell, *Themes Out of School*, 154.

31. Ibid., 162.

32. Ibid., 167.

33. Hitchcock actually says, "There are no symbols in *North by Northwest*. Oh yes! One. The last shot, the train entering the tunnel after the love-scene between Cary Grant and Eva-Marie Saint. It's a phallic symbol. But don't tell anyone." (From *Cahier du Cinéma*, no. 102. Cited in Wood, *Hitchcock's Films Revisited*, 131 [see chap. 2, n. 9].)

34. *Art as Experience*, 313 (see introduction, n. 7)..

35. Ibid., 23.

36. John Dewey, *The Early Works of John Dewey*, ed. Jo Ann Boydston, vol. 4, *The Study of Ethics: A Syllabus* (Carbondale: Southern Illinois University Press, 1971), 262.

Index

absurdity, 118
abyss, 40, 43, 47, 51, 53, 54, 60, 62, 72, 76, 78, 79
acknowledgment, 6, 25, 27, 29, 31, 32, 55–56, 65, 101, 128, 161
acousmatic (*acousmêtre*), 48, 49, 50
Aeschylus, 130
aesthetics, 2, 7, 10, 59, 66, 73, 75, 84, 118
alienation, 26, 46, 48, 53, 129, 138
allegory, 21, 101, 141
Allen, Woody, 85, 87, 88, 90–93
ambiguity, 62–63, 65, 148, 149, 150–51, 153
America, American, x, 8, 10, 12, 44, 55, 57, 59–61, 62, 64, 65, 73, 76, 96, 105, 153
American sublime, 12, 57–62, 66, 72, 73, 75, 104, 105, 107
anagnorisis, 59, 151
Anaximander, 130
anxiety, 12, 16, 36, 60, 95, 97, 99, 100, 101, 103, 105–107, 111, 119, 127
Apollo, Apollonian, 112–13, 118, 131–36
Aristotle, ix, 4, 6, 16, 25, 30, 36, 59, 60, 81, 82, 91, 109, 110, 111, 113, 117, 118, 119, 135–37, 139, 151
art, 8, 13, 75, 82, 85, 88, 89, 91, 104, 112–15, 118, 130, 131, 162
artist, 82, 84, 85, 88, 91, 92
aura, 130

authenticity, 97, 99, 100, 101, 103, 106–107, 108, 128

beauty, beautiful, 10, 56, 78–79, 112
Beaudrillard, Jean, 129, 144–46, 156
Beauvior, Simone de, 62–64, 148–49, 150–51
Bel Geddes, Barbara, 41
Benjamin, Walter, 92, 130
Bernays, Jacob, 110
Bible, viii
Biehn, Michael, 99
big Other, 44, 45–48, 53, 55, 56, 158
Blake, William, 58
Bloom, Harold, 60, 104–05, 149–50
Bloom, Leopold, 63
Bogart, Humphrey, 129
Boileau and Narcejac, 38
bourgeois, 116, 118–19, 144, 164 n. 3
Boyle, Danny, 109
Brahms, Johannes, 2
Bringing Up Baby (1938), 158
Burwell, Carter, 58
Buscemi, Steve, 61
Butcher, S. H., 119
Byrne, Gabriel, 35

Cameron, James, 9
capitalism, 96, 98, 117–19, 129, 144–45
Cardullo, Bert, 116, 118
Carroll, John, 76
Carroll, Noëll, 8, 137, 174 n. 1
Casablanca (1942), 137